VIOLENCE PREDICTION

ABOUT THE AUTHORS

Ronald S. Ebert, Ph.D. is the co-Director of Psychological Services, Inc. (PSI) in Braintree, Massachusetts, and the Senior Forensic Psychologist at the McLean Hospital, in Belmont, Massachusetts, where he conducts independent forensic examinations of dangerousness, competency, and criminal responsibility. He has testified hundreds of times in state and federal courts as well as before the U.S. House of Representatives Committee on Armed Services. He consults to industry concerning potentially violent employees and offers training to mental health professionals on matters of dangerousness to clinicians and the assessment and management of violent individuals. He is a Diplomate of the American Board of Professional Psychology in Forensic Psychology and is a Designated Forensic Supervisor in Massachusetts.

Harold V. Hall, Ph.D., the senior author, is the Director of Psychological Consultants, Inc., and is the President of the Pacific Institute for The Study of Conflict and Aggression in Kamuela, Hawaii. He is a consultant for the criminal justice system agencies and the Federal Bureau of Investigation, the U.S. Secret Service, and the Federal Bureau of Prisons. He has testified more than 100 times as an expert witness in murder and manslaughter trials. He is a Diplomate in both Forensic Psychology and Clinical Psychology of the American Board of Professional Psychology and is a Fellow of the American Psychological Association. He has written or edited seven books and numerous articles on forensic-clinical issues.

Extracts of the following articles by the senior author were first published in the *American Journal of Forensic Psychology*, a publication of the American College of Forensic Psychology, 26701 Quail Creek, Laguna Hills, California, 92656. "Predicting Dangerousness for the Courts" (1984, 2, 5–25); "Dangerousness Myths About Predicting Dangerousness" (1984, 2, 173–193, with E. Catlin, A. Boissevain, and J. Westgate); and "The Forensic Distortion Analysis: A Proposed Decision Tree" (1986, 4, 31–59). The American Psychological Association (APA) has allowed the authors to reproduce sections of the APA Continuing Education forms that are helpful in setting up violence prediction training workshops as well as sections of The Ethical Principles of Psychology and Code of Conduct (1992). The case described in Chapter 1 is a version of one originally published in *The Psychiatric Times* (1987, 12, 4–30). A section of Chapter 7 stems directly from the U.S. Department of Justice National Survey of Crime Severity (NCJ-96017, June (1985), and is so indicated. Sections of Chapter 10 are taken from *A Legal Update on Forensic Psychology* (1995) published by The Council for the National Register of Health Service Providers in Psychology, 1120 G Street N.W., Suite 330, Washington, DC 20005, and are so indicated.

Second Edition

VIOLENCE PREDICTION

Guidelines for the Forensic Practitioner

By

HAROLD V. HALL, Ph.D.

and

RONALD S. EBERT, Ph.D.

Charles C Thomas
PUBLISHER · LTD.
SPRINGFIELD · ILLINOIS · U.S.A.

Published and Distributed Throughout the World by

CHARLES C THOMAS • PUBLISHER, LTD.
2600 South First Street
Springfield, Illinois 62704

© 2002 by CHARLES C THOMAS • PUBLISHER, LTD.

ISBN 0-398-07241-8 (cloth)
ISBN 0-398-07242-6 (paper)

Library of Congress Catalog Card Number: 2001037863

Printed in the United States of America
MM-R-3

Library of Congress Cataloging-in-Publication Data

Hall, Harold V.
    Violence prediction : guidelines for the forensic practitioner. -- 2nd ed. / by
Harold V. Hall and Ronald S. Ebert.
        p. cm.
    Includes bibliographical references and index.
    ISBN 0-398-07241-8 (cloth) -- ISBN 0-398-07242-6 (paper)
    1. Criminal behavior, Prediction of. 2. Violence--Forecasting. 3. Criminal behavior,
Prediction of--United States. 4. Violence--United States--Forecasting. I. Bert, Ronald S.
II. Title.

HV6241 .H35 2001
364.3--dc21   2001037863

To the Medina Family
Vali, Mario, Christopher, and Taylor
H.V.H.

To my wife
Susan S. Ebert, Ph.D.

FOREWORD

Our society is becoming more violent. Dangerousness is a matter of public concern especially since schools, the workplace, the post office, the hospital and even once calm rural communities have become increasingly more frequent sites of assault, shootings, threats and killings! Television announcers regularly report such events in graphic detail repeatedly. Citizen's report anxieties and fears and even panic about personal safety. Reports of the rapid escalation of the population of local, State and Federal lockups, jail and prisons enhance the fear environment. In the United States the increasing frequency of alcohol and drug violations and the widespread usage of dis-inhibiting substances creates anxiety and fear in citizens. This panoply of emergency emotions leads to increasing police and security operations. This leads to lawyers and prosecutors and defense personal requiring more frequent and accurate evaluations of dangerousness in persons before such events transpire.

In the two decades most recently passed, the accuracy and evaluation of accuracy of predictions have been increasing. Short-term predictions have proven more accurate than long term predictions. More important, the prediction capacity and accuracy have gradually become more than clinical hunches or historical recurrences-both of which are helpful, but not sufficient of themselves. Careful statistics and testable hypotheses including more specific clinical judgements have been generated in this extraordinarily complex venture. This seminal treatise includes the specifics of the notable progress that has been made in a readable and understandable for practical insight in such detail and how to manage language that psychologists, psychiatrists, forensic specialists, lawyers and defense and prosecutional professionals and judicial and sentencing and correctional personnel will be able to master and assimilate in rapid fashion.

Such a major step forward will surely be catalytic to greater and more inclusive insights into this aspect of human behavior.

The reader will find himself or herself intellectually stimulated and eager to pursue the process and will appreciate this major contribution of these outstandingly competent forensic professionals and researchers.

SHERVERT H. FRAZIER, M.D.
PSYCHIASTRIST IN CHIEF, EMERITUS
MCLEAN HOSPITAL, BELMONT, MA

PREFACE

Since the mid-1980s, when the major mental-health organizations were issuing statements against the practice of prognosticating dangerousness, opining that mental health professionals could not, and did not, reliably and validly predict the phenomenon, violence risk analysis has made quantum leaps in methodology and accuracy. Forensic practitioners were timid and hesitant in this critical area.

Today, we possess empirically based methods that predict anywhere from three months (e.g., based on "HOT" factors of History, Opportunity, and Triggers) to ten years (the VRAG and SORAG). This book reviews, for example, more than 15 quantitatively based methods and factors derived from meta-analysis involving more than 100,000 persons and dozens of peer-reviewed investigations. Forensic practitioners have rightly become less tentative and more confident of their databases, thus increasing their usefulness to the criminal courts and other sources of referral where violence is an issue.

The purpose of this book is to empower the forensic practitioner in violence risk analysis, as well as to present the evolving literature on this fascinating area. This second edition is largely the child of Dr. Ronald Ebert, who devoted endless hours to the task, building on the first edition, with my contribution primarily in data-based systems and methods of violence prediction.

H.V.H.

ix

PREFACE TO FIRST EDITION

M OST VIOLENT ACT: "The most violent act I ever committed was beating up a prostitute in a hotel in Atlanta. After I paid her the money we talked about her service and she pulled a switchblade and demanded my wallet. I was able to grab the lamp from the nightstand and strike her in the head before she could get any momentum in swinging the knife. I must have hit her pretty hard because a pool of blood was already forming on the carpet. The thing that got me about the incident was that it made me feel good. I left and never looked back."

The above true account comes from a research project by the author called "1,000 Violent Americans." Here, adult, employed men and women of all walks of life in this country were asked to write down their most violent act, their "almost" most dangerous deed in order to assess inhibitions to aggress, a faked account of violence, and to fill out several detection measures to gauge response set. The results of this research effort, combined with findings from several other violence-related investigations since 1969, were aimed at developing violence prediction systems that explicitly represent the decision path and utilized content of the predictor. Overall, progress toward these goals can be characterized as promising and increasing in momentum. A more rigorous evaluation would point out that violence prediction analysis has now progressed beyond the nominal into the ordinal stage of classification. Much work is still qualitative. Some subareas such as plotting severity of violence over time, based on a 60,000-respondent survey by the National Institute of Justice, are purely quantitative in application.

This book is designed for the forensic professional who is involved with the assessment, research, or training of individual violence prediction. Many different methods are presented in this book so long as violence prediction accuracy, decision-analysis, or impact can be positively affected as a result.

By the end of the book, you should be able to compare and contrast true and false positives and negatives, cite development experiences associated with later violence, point out opportunity factors to violence, isolate triggering stimuli, and be cognizant of various inhibitions to aggress. You will become aware of the approximately 25 forensic deception styles used by examinees in presenting previous violence along with a number of techniques to determine he existence, direction, and magnitude of client misrepresentation and distortion. You will become acquainted with why dangerousness is nearly impossible to predict from psychiatric diagnosis and why it is hazardous to do so. Most importantly, you will be able to proceed through your own violence-prediction decision path and yield reasonable, testable, and circumscribed conclusions is regard to human predatory violence, and in doing so, clearly communicate to your referral source the basis for preoffered conclusions.

Several caveats are in order: (1) All cases in this book are true but disguised to protect the identification of both victim and perpetrator. Follow-up data to assess prediction accuracy is available in each case; (2) This book is atheoretical and geared towards practice; the behavioral science literature is discussed when appropriate but is not the predominant concern; (3) The state of the art in dangerousness prediction is nominal/ordinal rather than having desired interval/ratio properties. Continuing research will greatly expand the basic concepts of this book, with a breakthrough probably represented by a composite battery of psychometric devices measuring the different and overlapping areas of predictee violence, much as in neuropsychology and some other psychological subfields; (4) Overlearning is necessary to ingrain application of dangerousness prediction methods and to prevent predictor regression to baseline levels of decision analysis and accuracy. In this sense, this book is deliberately designed for redundancy; (5) This book requires participants to examine their own decision paths. Yet, many predictors are reluctant to change their biases and values in regard to violence, especially when loss of self-esteem or prestige is equated with giving up cherished beliefs about dangerous behavior; (6) A common complaint is that proper dangerousness prediction requires much time and effort, adding to an already overloaded work schedule. This is true, but the author has no sympathy for this problem. Tough! The issues raised in dangerousness prediction are of high importance for both society and the individual. Much time can be saved by use of the recommended procedures and formats. Obsessive-compulsiveness and a strong spirit of the hunt for the truth and impact are very helpful.

Many thanks are owed to the late Dr. Evan Wolfe, consultant to the State of Hawaii Adult Probation Division, who initially inspired much of the early interest in violence prediction. Dr. John (Joe) Blaylock, as the writer's previous supervisor at the State of Hawaii Courts and Corrections Branch, allowed for the opportunity to explore violence to others from a research and training context. Dr. Udo Undeutsch of the University of Cologne, Federal Republic of Germany, probably the finest forensic psychologist in Europe, clearly showed how much we Americans can learn from our international contemporaries in terms of distortion and deception analysis. Dr. John Monahan of the University of Virginia School of Law was very helpful in discussing the corrective factor question for unreported violence. The trek through Markov chains and other group prediction schemes was assisted by Dr. Terrill Holland of the California State Department of Corrections at Chino. Other individuals, too numerous to name, are owed thanks for the development of this book and for this, the author is deeply grateful.

H.V.H.

CONTENTS

TABLES

FIGURES

VIOLENCE PREDICTION

Chapter 1

DANGEROUSNESS PREDICTION

Process and Content

D AMN INSURANCE FORMS. Joe White (all names used in this and other cases are fictitious, although each case is based upon actual events), a third-year psychiatry resident, was working on the pile of papers in the nursing station. He had just started leafing through his worn copy of DSM-III when he felt the unexpected chill of December air suddenly blowing through the open door. Looking up, he was startled to see Bill Green entering the unit. Bill had escaped only two days earlier, declaring that he needed to leave the hospital to get a gun with which to kill himself.

That brief hospitalization, like so many others for Bill, began when he self-admitted because of delusional thoughts that others could read his mind and that he needed to kill himself because of their sexualized thoughts about him. It ended, as had the others, when he impulsively fled treatment, ultimately discontinued his medication and sank into his paranoid psychosis.

The significant difference between Bill's latest admission and all the others was his statement about wanting to buy a gun to kill himself. This outburst resulted in an evaluation by a forensic psychiatrist who concluded her report: "staff was notified that this man was both homicidal and suicidal, and he was started on anti-psychotic medications."

It had been four days since that chilling assessment had been made and only two days since his escape. Why was he back?

Bill stormed up to the psychiatric resident, demanding to talk. The young psychiatrist made the mental note that Bill was angry, agitated, and had a press of speech. Probably psychotic, Joe guessed. He led Bill to the small interviewing room down the corridor and had barely closed the door when Bill pulled a pistol from inside his pants. Waving it wildly, he yelled that he needed to kill the young physician "because you're reading my mind . . . controlling me . . . playing games with my mind . . . messing up my mind with drugs . . . and it's time for a revolution!"

For the next ten minutes, Dr. White tried his best to calm Bill, trying to persuade him to give up the gun in return for treatment. Both men were sweating, tense, and frightened. When the sound of voices in the corridor convinced Dr. White that help was on its way, he lunged for the gun, grabbing Bill's right wrist. It was over in a matter of seconds and the stronger, frantic patient overpowered the young doctor, who now slumped back in his chair. Bill was much angrier now. He was ranting "I should die! I should end it all right now!" Suddenly and without warning, Bill pointed the gun and fired. The bullet smashed into the tiled wall to the right of the physician's head. The small room echoed with the shot. Thick smoke filled the air, and tile fragments scattered everywhere. There was a moment of stunned silence and before bullet flew, this time on the other side of the resident's head. Once again the wall exploded with shards of tile. When questioned later, Dr. White was able to recall that Bill had seemed to take "dead aim" at his head, but appeared to swerve his hand at the last minute to avoid hurting him. Dr. White felt that, despite Bill's terrifying threats, his psychotic ambivalence had prevented him from carrying out the threatened violence.

Now the ward had been alerted because of the noise of the shots. Raised voices and running feet could be heard through the closed door. Bill still sat, looking stunned and staring at the weapon in his hand, saying nothing. The room was filled with acrid smoke and neither man spoke, but a sharp knock at the door snapped them to attention. Dr. Black, the senior psychiatrist on the ward, slowly opened the door and peered in. Quickly assessing the crisis, he began to speak to Bill from the doorway, trying to engage him, as Dr. White had done a few minutes earlier. He asked and then received permission to enter the room and to sit in the remaining empty chair.

Now both physicians began to try to reason with Bill, and the debate picked up where it had left off: threats to kill, complaints about people reading his mind and "messing up" his brain, and "time for a revolution." Although the strain was evident in their faces, both psychiatrists worked to reason with the confused and agitated man. Unlike the intense young resident, Dr. Black conveyed a sense of resigned expectations—as if he was thinking "I've been through worse before, just calm down and we'll get on with our work."

Unexpectedly, Dr. Black's arm brushed a piece of paper from the desk onto the floor. The discussion ended in midsentence as the three men watched it float gently down. It lay on the floor no more than a few seconds when Dr. Black shifted in his seat and bent to pick it up. As he straightened up that the gun shot broke the silence. In the noise and smoke, Dr. Black slumped in the chair, blood flowing from a wound to his head.

Once again Bill looked stunned, and this time softly said "please go" to

Dr. White, without shifting his gaze from his wounded victim. The shaken resident slowly left the room, leaving the door ajar. The ward was evacuated and police were called. Bill allowed them to remove Dr. Black and in the silence that followed, the ambulance could be heard speeding from the hospital. A four-hour siege ended with Bill's ultimate surrender and arrest.

Dr. Black died of severe brain trauma two days later, never regaining consciousness. Bill was charged with murder and sent for forensic assessment to the state's maximum-security hospital. After two years of treatment, he was finally deemed competent to proceed with the trial, and two-and-a-half years after the murder, was found not guilty by reason of insanity.

He remained at the maximum security hospital for eight more years, and at his family's request, was transferred to a maximum-security hospital in their home state, some 600 miles away. He was discharged to his family's care six months later, judged no longer dangerous to himself or to others (adapted from Ebert, 1987).

What can we learn from tragedies such as this? Could it have been prevented if the clinicians involved had been trained in violence prediction? Could anyone be expected to predict the behavior of a psychotic, agitated patient? Certainly the clinicians in this case knew Bill, knew his diagnosis of paranoid schizophrenia, and his history of suicide attempts. They also knew that he had been recently assessed by a forensic clinician who said he was both suicidal and homicidal. In addition to these facts, they were aware that he had left the hospital with the stated intent of buying a gun, albeit to kill himself. Was this information sufficient to predict his dangerousness?

Take a moment to put down this book and consider your current criteria for a dangerousness assessment in this case. Draft a list of those factors you consider of highest priority. Put the list aside and be prepared to consult it and to modify it as your reading proceeds.

How much information is enough information if the goal is to try to prevent such terrible events? How much do you need to know about the patient sitting in front of you? Do you need a full and complete history, dating back to early childhood, or is it sufficient to have a current mental status that delves into the individual's thoughts and fantasies? Would it have helped the clinicians to know that Bill's agitation was based in part on his recent discovery that his mother planned to marry a man whom Bill despised? Could the clinicians have known that Bill had spent the morning drinking in order to build up the courage to kill himself, and by the time he entered the ward, he was intoxicated? How much is enough? How much data is too much, a flooding of information? Is there ever enough?

The purpose of this book is to try to prevent violence by learning enough about those salient factors that enable us to anticipate when it will (or might) occur. If, as a result of understanding contemporary thinking about violence prediction, one further violent act is prevented, the work that went into this volume will have been completely worthwhile. Predicting violence or predicting any human behavior is a complex enterprise. In the years since publication of the first edition of this book, much has been written about and much has been discovered in the field of violence prediction. The authors will attempt to provide the reader with an up-to-date survey of the literature and a clear understanding of violence prediction. The focus of this book is pragmatic, with the anticipation that the reader will follow the suggested exercises, practicing and honing skills as he or she proceeds. Appendices offer sample reports, instruments, and teaching tools to further the process.

Magnitude of the Problem: Some Epidemiological and Qualitative Data

It is not surprising that members of certain professions encounter more violence than does the general public. Inpatient mental health professionals, as described earlier in this chapter, often work with people in agitated and aggressive states. In most jurisdictions, commitment laws require that in addition to being diagnosed as mentally ill, a person must also be found "dangerous" by a Court if they are to be hospitalized involuntarily.

Clinicians are not the only ones who need to worry about risk. Violence in the workplace is a significant concern; more than two million United States residents were victims of violent crimes while at work or on duty between 1992 and 1996, according to the National Crime Victimization Surveys for 1992–96 developed by the U.S. Department of Labor Bureau of Justice Statistics (BJS). Of these two million violent incidents, more than one thousand a year are homicides. A growing concern in the workplace is the extension of domestic violence into that setting. Occupational security forces are well aware of the need to protect female employees from angry husbands or boyfriends who lurk in parking lots after hours or show up unexpectedly at the front desk. Coworkers are even more aware of the threatening phone calls, occasional black eyes, or the employee who comes in early and stays late to avoid going home.

Even schools, once thought to be safe and secure institutions, are now frequently the scene of violence, mirroring behaviors and events of society at large. Inner-city schools have long been affected by the intrusions of local gang warfare, drugs, and street violence. Children in these settings have often been preyed upon going to and from school and have occasionally needed protection while there. Now, the danger of the inner-cities has spread democratically across this great country to small rural villages and hamlets. A series of well-publicized shootings in rural and suburban schools in 1998, which continued through this writing, resulted in a flurry of activity to develop special programs to predict and prevent violent behavior among school-children. As is often the case, crises generate public awareness, and this in turn results in political response, often with short-term solutions that fade away with public memory of the event. It will remain to be seen if newly instituted antiviolence programs will gain hold in schools and will become part of the infrastructure, much as metal detectors have become ubiquitous in the nation's airports.

Of course the therapist, the office worker, or the student may not be much safer returning home, for domestic violence has become a focus of concern in recent years as well. Laws against stalking, increased use of restraining or stay-away orders, and subsequently increased use of courts to protect partners from each other are features of daily life. Probation officers and Court personnel now provide at least as many services to troubled marital partners as do family therapists or other counselors.

Our contemporary society sees violence at every turn and danger lurking around every corner. Is this an accurate reflection of our world or is it a distorted response to violence-filled television and movies, and a growing awareness of our vulnerability in the face of increasingly complicated technological advances?

Until 1994, violence in America appeared to be a growth industry. The National Crime Victimization Survey (NCVS) (Bureau of Justice Statistics, 1997) provided dramatic data that explained why more and more people were double locking their doors; moving to gated, secured communities; and monitoring their children's whereabouts at all hours. In 1994, U.S. residents over the age of 12 had a 1-in-20 chance of being violently victimized and a 1-in-3 chance of having their household or possessions violated. While property crime was then on the decline, the crime rate had been unchanged for some years. Those most vulnerable to violent crime were males, the young, and blacks. Thus, the likelihood of experiencing violent crime in 1994 was 1 in 17 for males (compared to 1 in 24 for females), 1 in 16 for blacks (compared to 1 in 20 for whites), and an astonishing 1 in 9 for persons age 12 to 15 (compared to 1 in 196 for those older than age 65).

Most striking were those statistics that described the likelihood of victimization for individuals in poverty as opposed to those living in more comfortable circumstances. Compared to people with annual incomes of $15,000 or more, those with lesser incomes were three times more likely to be raped or sexually assaulted, twice as likely to be the victim of robbery, and one-and-a-half times more likely to be the victim of an aggravated assault.

As has always been the case, it is likely that the crime statistics were an underestimate, because the Bureau of Justice Statistics noted, for example, that almost two thirds of the victims of completed rapes did not report the crime to the police. Perhaps this is explained in part because two thirds of

Violence Prediction

TABLE I
RATES OF VIOLENT VICTIMIZATIONS BY AGE OF VICTIM, 1992–94

Type of crime by age of victim	Victimization rates per 1,000			Percent distribution		
	1992	1993	1994	1992	1993	1994
All violent crime	49	51	51	100%	100%	100%
12 to 15	114	121	115	15	17	16
16 to 19	107	117	122	15	15	16
20 to 24	98	94	99	18	16	17
25 to 34	58	59	61	24	23	23
35 to 49	39	43	40	21	23	22
50 to 64	13	17	15	4	5	5
65 or older	5	6	5	2	2	1
Robbery	6	6	6	100%	100%	100%
12 to 15	13	14	12	15	16	14
16 to 19	11	12	12	12	12	13
20 to 24	14	11	11	21	15	16
25 to 34	8	7	8	27	24	24
35 to 49	4	5	5	16	22	23
50 to 64	2	3	2	6	8	6
65 or older	2	1	1	5	3	3
Aggravated assault	11	12	12	100%	100%	100%
12 to 15	20	23	22	13	14	14
16 to 19	27	30	34	16	16	19
20 to 24	23	27	27	19	20	20
25 to 34	13	15	14	23	24	23
35 to 49	10	9	8	23	20	18
50 to 64	3	4	3	4	5	5
65 or older	1	1	1	2	1	1

the victims of rape or sexual assault knew their assailants. As could best be determined, 42 percent of the violent crimes that were committed in 1994 were reported to the police. A higher rate of robberies, aggravated assaults, and simple assaults were reported (55, 52, and 36 percent respectively) than of sexual assaults (36 percent of rapes, 20 percent of attempted rapes, and 41 percent of sexual assaults). Table I shows the victimization rates for persons age 12 and over in 1994.

The Bureau of Justice has collected this sort of data since 1973, and charted trends in violent crime rates over the quarter century. They note a variable trend with rates dropping by almost 20 percent from 1981 to 1986 followed by a 15 percent rise from 1986 to 1991. Overall rates appeared stable until 1994, when a dramatic decline began to emerge, continuing to recent days. The 1997 National Crime and Victimization Survey of the Bureau of Justice Statistics indicates that property and violent crime rates are currently the lowest recorded since the survey's inception. In 1997, for example, violent crime rates were 21 percent lower than in 1993 and property crimes rates 22 percent below 1993 rates. Newspaper headlines screamed the good news: "U.S. crime rate dips to 25-year low" (*Boston Globe,* December 28, 1998), or the *New York Times* (November 23, 1998) rather more subdued headline, "Crime Drops in 97; Murders are at 30-Year Low."

After 20 years of collecting crime statistics, The Bureau of Justice Statistics confirmed that a number of optimistic long-term trends had been identified (BJS, 1993). Perhaps most importantly, the number of criminal victimizations had dropped 6 percent since the survey began in 1973, with the steepest declines in household burglary and theft.

Yet, despite these recent overall declines in the violent crime rate, blacks continued to be substantially more likely to become victims than whites, and young minority males in central cities were found to be victimized at the highest rates ever recorded. An important cautionary note was highlighted in 1993 by Lawrence Greenfield, the BJS director: "In 1973, about 15 percent of all crimes were violent compared to 20 percent in 1992. Moreover, about a third of all victims of violence reported injury." (BJS, 1993) Thus, what was initially identified as good news, seemed good only for those in the right place and the right community. Black male teenagers between 12 and 19 are more likely to become crime victims than any other group. Their rate of victimization is 113 per 1,000 or almost 1 in 9. White male teenagers were only slightly less likely to be victimized: 90 per 1,000 or 1 in 11. Looking at these figures, it becomes clear that despite a reduction in the rate of criminal behavior, the quality of that behavior has changed: criminal behavior is more violent and destructive than in the past.

The trend of race, age, and sex appears consistent over time in predicting victimization. Adult black males (35 to 64 years) were victimized at a rate of 35 per 1,000, while adult white males were at risk at the rate of 18 per 1,000, adult white females 15 per 1,000, and adult black females 13 per 1,000. Black males ages 65 and over were at risk at the rate of 12 per 1,000; black females within the same age were at risk at the rate of 10 per 1,000, white males 6 per 1,000, and white females 3 per 1,000.

A meta-analysis shows variable decline in some communities, continuing high rates in most southern states and in some age groups. As reported in the Juvenile Justice Bulletin (U.S. Department of Justice, December 1998), "The number of juvenile Violent Crime Index arrests in 1997 was 49% above the 1988 level. In comparison, the number of adult arrests for a Violent Crime Index offense in 1997 was 19% greater than in 1988." Violent Crime Index offenses include murder, forcible rape, robbery, and aggravated assault; juveniles are defined as those under 18.

The Bureau of Justice Statistics reported in 1994 that U.S. residents age 12 or older experienced approximately 42.4 million crimes. Of these, 26 per-

TABLE II
IMPACT OF CRIMINAL VICTIMIZATION

Occurrences	Yearly rate per 1,00 adults
Accidental injury, all circumstances	220
Accidental injury at home	66
Personal theft	61
Accidental injury at work	47
Violent victimization	31
Assault (aggravated and simple)	25
Motor vehicle accident injury	22
Death, all causes	11
Victimization with injury	11
Aggravated assault	8
Robbery	6
Death from heart disease	5
Death from cancer	3
Rape (women only)	1
Accidental death, all circumstances	0.4
Death from pneumonia or influenza	0.4
Death in motor vehicle accident	0.2
Suicide	0.2
Death from HIV infection	0.1
Homicide and capital punishment executions	0.1

cent were crimes of violence (10.9 million). More specifically, for every 1,000 persons age 12 or older, there occurred two rapes or attempted rapes, three assaults with serious injury, and four robberies with property taken.

Another view of the impact of criminal victimization on the United States population is seen in Table II from the BJS.

After accidental injury, victimization and assault together with personal theft occur more frequently than motor vehicle accidents or death from all illnesses or accidents. Seen in this light, the excited headlines about the decline in the U.S. crime rate offers scant hope to young males, especially blacks, living in urban centers. Beyond these youngsters, too many of us run the risk of being victimized or having somebody we love victimized on the street, at work, at school, or at home.

Based on 1997 data (Federal Bureau of Investigation), a violent crime currently occurs in this country every 19 seconds, an aggravated assault every 31 seconds, a robbery every one minute, a forcible rape every five minutes, and a murder every 29 minutes. Because only about half of all serious violent crime is reported, these numbers have to be considered significant underestimates. In addition, once reported, about two thirds of the violent crimes are cleared, with the perpetrator identified and brought into police custody. This means that only about 20 to 30 percent of all criminal violence will result in a criminal charge. Only a fraction of those charged are eventually convicted and fewer are imprisoned. Thus, out of 100 reported rapes, only a few will result in conviction, and only about half of those convictions will lead to imprisonment (Coleman, Butcher, and Carson, 1980).

Sexual offenders admit to committing two to five times more sexual assaults than they are apprehended for (Groth, Longo, and McFadin, 1982). Among sexual offenders, however, pedophiles are reported to have committed anywhere from 10 to 30 prior sexual assaults for each arrested offense (Furby, Weinrott and Blackshaw, 1989). It is not simply sexual offenders who deserve blame for one-person crime waves. Convicted robbers admit to arrests for only 30 percent of committed violent acts, and half of that group declare an intention to resume their criminal career once released (Petersilia, Greenwood, and Lavin, 1977). So much for the presumed beneficial effects of "correctional" facilities.

Perhaps more insidious than the analysis of the actual numbers of crimes committed and the rates at which one is likely to be victimized, is a qualitative change in the nature of the worst crimes. A majority of mass and serial murderers have lived in the past one-half century, as far as records can be believed (e.g., International Reference Organization, 1981). These horrific perpetrators have engaged in a wide assortment of sexual torture, dismemberment, bludgeoning, stabbing, and shooting. Certainly the development of cheap and easily available rapid-fire guns plays a role here. There are those who postulate that the broad reach of media reports of such violence stimulates "copy-cat" crimes. Others lay the blame at the foot of the entertainment industry with "Silence of the Lambs," "Halloween," and the "Freddy Kreuger" movies singled out.

A chilling example of new trends in mass murder is seen in an analysis of the school shootings in 1997 and 1998. In 1997 in Pearl, Mississippi, a 16 year old killed his mother and father and two classmates with a rifle. In October 1997, in West Paducah, Kentucky, a 14 year old killed three girls at his school with a .22 semiautomatic Ruger. An 11 year old and a 13 year old killed five in a schoolyard with handguns and rifles, after setting off a false fire alarm in Jonesboro, Arkansas. A 15 year old discharged 51 rounds, killing two students and wounding 18 others in Springfield, Oregon, at Thurston High School, after murdering his parents.

A trend toward violent crimes committed by strangers, rather than intimates or known assailants, has been identified in the National Institute of Justice reports (1993) with males much more likely to be victims of violence by strangers than by family members. Fifty-three percent of persons victimized by violence did not know their assailant and almost eight out of ten robberies were committed by strangers. Rapes and sexual assaults, on the other hand, were committed by strangers in only three out of ten cases. Robberies were committed by strangers 77 percent of the time (Bureau of Justice

Statistics, 1996). These figures concerning stranger violence are significant because in the past a larger proportion of such crimes was commited by assailants known to their victims.

Handguns are now used in about ten percent of all violent crimes and weapons are used in about four out of ten crimes committed. Offenders used or possessed a weapon in slightly more than half of all robberies, compared with 16 percent of rapes/sexual assaults. (National Crime and Victimization Survey, 1996). These statistics do not describe the type of weapon used, but it is likely that an increasing number of weapons are automatic, rapid-fire guns. Such weapons make it all the easier to kill or wound many people at one time, particularly when the assailant is immature, impulsive, or affected by a virulent substance such as crack cocaine.

In the years 1973 to 1993, an estimated 37 million victims were injured, and more than one third of those injured had no health insurance or were not eligible for other health benefits. Thus people are becoming victimized repeatedly when they suffer criminal attack.

Paralleling these changing trends in victimization is an apparent increase in family violence that includes spouse, child, elderly, and sibling abuse. This may reflect the breakdown of the primary family unit as the key determinant of values and interpersonal control in our society. Clinicians working with very young children are seeing increased fears about risk of harm, particularly as public media broadcast stories of violence in schools. Issues such as nuclear holocaust, auto accidents, kidnapping and sexual abuse are now taking a back seat to the fear that classmates or older children will arrive with weapons in school.

As if to echo the deterioration of societal values, an almost unending media focus on President Bill Clinton's extra-marital affairs during his presidency served only to underscore the sense of diminished national values through a public preoccupation with exposure of human foible. The popular cry to end the investigations by Independent Counsel Kenneth Starr may have had as much to do with a wish to avoid and deny society's diminishment, as it had to do with boredom and ennui.

Patterson and Cobb (1971) reported that in young children, 80 percent of their assaultive behaviors, across typical situations, produced rewarding consequences. This high level of intrinsic reinforcement remains stable over time. It may be that ordinary children, like violent adult offenders, exhibit such behavior in part because of their prior success in getting what they want. A list of childhood precursors to violence appears in the Appendix B, Checklist of Factors Associated with Violence.

A simple review of crimes described on a daily basis in newspapers and on television indicates more callousness and insensitivity toward the commission of violence and its effects upon victims, and more narcissism and indulgence towards oneself. Recent research (Donnerstein, 1993) into television violence shows that televised rates of physical aggression hold steady at 60 percent with increased numbers during prime time. Particularly important is that violence is portrayed as heroic with attractive role models committing nearly 40 percent of the violent acts. More than 70 percent of the aggressors show no remorse and receive no punishment or penalty. Importantly, there is no physical injury, blood, or suffering in about half of the violence portrayed. (Donnerstein, 1993).

Violence appears to be socially acceptable in the United States. Violence is widely regarded by the male population as necessary to maintain social order (Blumenthal, 1976). In this study, 80 percent of the male respondents felt police should use clubs to control crowds. About two thirds thought that the police should use guns, but only to wound or frighten, not to kill. Nearly one third of the low-income subjects scored high on an index that indicated a belief that violent protest is necessary to bring about vast social change. Blumenthal believes that violent attitudes are not confined to deviant individuals, but instead reflect positive attitudes toward violence deeply embedded in significant segments of our culture. This is why, he suggests,it is useless to take attitudes toward violence as a predictor of dangerous behavior.

A concrete example of our preoccupation with violence to manage violence can be seen in the exponential growth of prison beds across this country. Communities regularly and predictably vote down increased expenditures for schools, social services, and welfare, but easily support increased spending for prisons. At present, the United States incarcerates 1.8 million individuals, more than any other western culture. This is a doubling of the incarceration rate since 1985 and a six-fold increase since 1972 (Bureau of Justice Statistics census, 1998). It has been argued that very little of this growth is due to better police work, or even because more criminals are being imprisoned. Rather, a more punitive approach to sentencing and harsher parole boards are imposing longer sentences with less and less likelihood of earlier release (Blumenstein and Beck, 1999).

Lay persons reveal a general ignorance about violence is revealed when asked to describe how often and under what circumstances violence will occur. The public at large is dubious at best about whether violence can be predicted and tends to focus on irrelevant traits of the predictee. As we will see in Chapter 2, science laid the foundation for these misconceptions early. For example, in a pilot effort designed to assess the knowledge and attitudes about violence in the Hawaii community, 50 white-collar government workers were asked four basic questions (Hall, 1981) relative to (1) perceived clearance rates of violent crime; (2) possible backgrounds of violence; (3) description of the potentially violent person; and (4) favorite movies and heroes. The results show that subjects overestimate the clearance rates of violent crimes and underestimate the percentage of current violent offenders with a past history of violence. When asked to provide a description of a person who would be potentially violent, the vast majority of subjects list stereotypical physical traits, rather than triggering states or associated environmental events. For example, there was a great concern with eyes; the potentially violent person was described as having "beady" or "shifty" eyes or exhibiting poor eye contact. A prior history of violence was mentioned rarely, if at all.

Of particular interest was the pattern of favorite movies and heroes that emerged, specifically the attraction to males associated with inflicting violence (e.g., actors such as Charles Bronson, John Wayne, and Clint Eastwood) or men who had been victims of violence themselves (e.g., Martin Luther King, Jr., and John F. Kennedy). Not unexpectedly, the favorite movies were those that glorified war and socially sanctioned violence (e.g., *Gone with the Wind, Patton,* the *Star Wars* trilogy). This substantiates Blumenthal's earlier findings.

It is not just the lay public that misunderstands our ability to predict violence. An early study by Hellman and Blackman (1966) is widely referenced and used as a common test for the prediction of violence by many contemporary clinicians. Few who cling to their enuresis = fire setting = cruelty to animals "triad" theory are aware that the data is based upon a statistically insignificant sample of 21 prisoners who presented a history supportive of this theory. Later research has not supported the triad theory (Justice, Justice, and Kraft, 1974), and other attempts to replicate the study have been unsuccessful. Yet it is common today to observe clinicians asking about a history of bed wetting, fire setting, and cruelty to animals as part of a standard assessment of potential dangerousness.

In a tightly controlled empirical study of violence prediction yielding poor accuracy levels (R = +.34) (Menzies, Webster, and Sepejak, 1985, p. 67) stated, ". . . The point for zero 'sound barrier' for prediction–outcome correlations represent a more realistic parameter for competence. Given these considerations, a thorough going reappraisal of the 'policy of dangerousness' is long overdue." These authors might have been surprised to discover that some 15 years later, following numerous reappraisals, new approaches to violence prediction have given fresh life to the "policy of dangerousness" through more-accurate approaches to prediction.

Chapter 2 will provide a brief history of attempts to predict human behavior through the ages, moving toward a contemporary approach to violence prediction.

Chapter 2

HISTORICAL FOUNDATIONS

Ancient Roots

THE EARLIEST ATTEMPTS TO UNDERSTAND aberant and criminal behavior were rooted in the attempt to understand individuals and their special characteristics. Attempts have been made throughout the centuries to identify those individuals who are most likely to behave in strange or dangerous ways. The earliest written attempts to understand human behavior, especially aberant actions, tend to flow from descriptions of observed behaviors. The more bizarre the behavior, the more likely it was to be included in these categorizations. The earliest theorists tended to be classifiers with little appreciation or understanding of causitive factors. Nonetheless, one often sees glimmers of contemporary understandings, and great intellect, in these earliest writings.

Plato, in *The Dialogues*, wrote about the soul, which he believed had three parts, each residing in a different section of the body. The highest resided, logically, in the brain and provided the ability to reason. The central part of the soul was located in the center of the body, in the chest, and was responsible for emotional life. The bottommost part of the soul was located in the abdomen and was responsible for passion and other "base" appetites. In attempting to understand disorders of the soul, he wrote,

> We must acknowledge disease of the mind to be a want of intelligence; and of this, there are two kinds: to wit, madness, and ignorance. In whatever state a man experiences either of them, that state may be called disease; an excess of pains and pleasures are justly to be regarded as the greatest disease to which the soul is liable. . . . And in general, all that which is termed the incontinence of pleasure and is deemed a reproach under the idea that the wicked voluntarily do wrong is not justly a matterful reproach. For no man is voluntarily bad; but the bad become bad by reason of an ill disposition of the body and bad education, things which are hateful to every man and happen to him against his will. And in the

15

case of pain, too, in like manner the soul suffers much evil from the body. (Goshen, 1967, p. 3)

Hippocrates, perhaps contemporaneous with Plato, attempted to provide a medical understanding of human behaviors. His theory of balancing bodily "humors" extended even to an analysis of dreams. One practical advantage of his concept was a focus on treatments for problems caused by unbalanced humors. He writes in his *Regimen IV*,

> In a word, all the functions of body and of soul are performed by occurring naturally, just as they were done or planned during the day in a normal act—these are good for a man. They signify health, because the soul abides by the purposes of the day, and is overpowered neither by surfeit or by depletion nor by any attack from without. But when dreams are contrary to the acts of the day, and there occurs about them some struggle or triumph, a disturbance in the body is indicated, a violent struggle meaning a violent mischief, a feeble struggle, a less serious mischief. As to whether the act should be averted or not, I do not decide, but I do advise treatment of the body. For a disturbance of the soul has been caused by secretion arising from some surfeit that has occurred. Now if the contrast be violent, it is beneficial to take an emetic, to increase gradually a light diet for five days, to take in the early morning, long, sharp walks, increasing them gradually, and to adapt exercises, when in training, so as to match the gradual increase of food. If the contrast be milder, omit the emetic, reduce food by a third, resuming this by a gentle, gradual increase spread over five days. Insist on vigorous walks, use voice-exercises, and the disturbance will cease. (Goshen, 1967, p. 12)

If the contemporary reader notices a similarity between ancient prescriptions of exercise and diet as a curative for troubled thoughts and our contemporary approaches to stress, it is well to take a moment to appreciate the wisdom of our forefathers. Although we chuckle at the concept of balancing "humors," we can value the sageness of suggestions concerning manipulation of food intake and exertion as a means to exert a calming influence over external pressures. Perhaps future observers will chuckle at our misguided attempts to manipulate our environment to achieve psychological calm.

Moses Maimonides, a Jewish physician writing 1,000 years ago, introduced an ethical approach to the understanding of human dysfunctional behaviors. His writings remind us of Plato's in that he too supports the concept of learned behavior, yet he adds the significant concept of tabla rasa—a neutral starting point for human development. His thesis is that we learn our good and bad behaviors from the world around us, and thus we are capable of reeducation or achieving "cure" when our soul becomes "diseased."

Know, moreover, that these moral excellences or defects cannot be acquired, or implanted in the soul, except by means of the frequent repetition of acts resulting from these qualities, which, practiced during a long period of time, accustoms us to them. If these acts performed are good ones, then we shall have gained a virtue; but if they are bad, we shall have acquired a vice. Since, however, no man is born with an innate virtue or vice . . . and, as everyone's conduct from child-hood up is undoubtedly influenced by the manner of living of his relatives and countrymen, his conduct may be in accord with the rules of moderation; but then again, it is possible that his acts may incline towards either extreme, as we have demonstrated in which case, his soul becomes diseased. In such a contingency, it is proper for him to resort to a cure, exactly as he would were his body suffering from an illness. (Goshen, 1967, pp. 37–38)

Unfortunately, not all of the ancient thinkers were as humanistic or logi-cal. Paracelsus, a Swiss physician writing in the 1500s, was a product of his times and reflected darker, more mysterious approaches to human under-standing. He wrote about "truly insane people," relying on his belief in plan-etary and mystical influences.

There are four kinds of insane people: *Lunatici, Insani, Vesani,* and *Melancholici. Lunatici* are those who get the disease from the moon and react according to it. *Insani* are those who have been suffering from it since birth and then brought it from the womb as a family heritage. *Vesani* are those who have been poisoned and contaminated by food and drink, from which they lose reason and sense. *Melancholici* are those who, by their nature, lose their reason and turn insane. We must, however, note that apart from these four kinds, there is another kind: these are the *Obsessi* who are obsessed by the devil. . . . (Goshen, 1967, p. 51)

Pseudoscience: Phrenology and its Brethren

This sampler of historical theories designed to explain human behavior and abberations of such behavior offers a glimpse into human inventiveness in the face of the compelling mystery of strange and troubling behavior. The insufficiency of these theories and the inadequacy of the suggested treat-ments perhaps help to explain the remarkable public acceptance of phrenol-ogy, a pseudoscience that took over the nineteenth century as no explanato-ry theory before.

Franz Gall developed the "science" of phrenology in the early 1800s founding it upon the common sense assumption that all aspects of human behavior are located within the brain and thus can be observed or measured by the unique bumps and dents found in the skull. Although clearly based upon mistaken understandings of brain development and function as well as inaccurate appreciation of skull growth, this theory quickly became widely accepted and broadly popularized. It was not at all unusual for people in the nineteenth century to go to "phrenologists" to have their skulls measured and their characters diagnosed. The popular belief was that personality types or "propensities" could be measured by careful analysis of skull formation and the subsequent development of a personality diagnosis. Thus, bumps on the skull supposedly indicated a variety of emotional and cognitive faculties such as destructiveness and combativeness, and the calculated degree or intensity of these "propensities" could be combined to determine character. Following these concepts, a simple measurement of the skull would be able to determine an individual's propensity for criminality, or in the terms of phrenologists, "wickedness." Gall's writings were slim, but Gaspar Spurzheim elaborated on Gall's work and soon became the prime popularizer of this wildly popular "science." Spurzheim's *Phrenology*, published in London in 1826, demonstrated the techniques for character analysis. Following is his listing of "elements of a number of characters according to the common designations, in alphabetical order," each with a specific location (or bump) on the skull:

> Affable, Amiable, Ambiguous, Audacious, Austere, Avaricious, Booby, Brutal, Caballist, Calumniator, Capricious, Comic, Communicative, Conspirator, Corruptible, Credulous, Decent, Diffident, Discreet, Disputative, Dogmatist, Double, Eloquent, Extravigant, False, Flatterer, Gloomy, Hypocrite, Jacobin, Impertinent, Indiscreet, Industrious, Modest, Noble, Partial, Rash, Superstitious, Tyrant, Unequal, Unpolite, Vindictive, Wicked.

Quite a remarkable collection of characteristics—almost one for each letter of the alphabet—and certainly a thorough listing of human traits for the budding "scientist." Phrenology ruled contemporary thought for most of the 1800s. Darwin's collaborator, Alfred Hollis, wrote in 1899: "In the coming century phrenology will . . . prove itself to be the true science of mind. Its practical uses in education, in self-discipline, in the reformatory treatment of criminals, and in the remedial treatment of the insane, will give it one of the highest places in the hierarchy of the sciences."

George Combe was an exponent of the idea that all prisoners should be classified through phrenology, and his ideas were taken up throughout many prison systems. In 1847, the American Phrenological Journal reported that Sing-Sing was a "phrenologically conducted institution." (Goshen, 1967, p. 102)

The introduction of this pseudoscience into the world of criminology resulted in heretofore unrecognized moral dilemmas. If it was possible to classify prisoners based upon their brain function and skulls, it became clear that some individuals could be defined as not capable of rehabilitation because of their large "propensity for destructiveness," while others might be identified as easily curable because of "higher areas of morality or goodness." Clear distinctions could now be drawn between those who were "scientifically" incorrigible and those who were not, based entirely upon the skill of the phrenologist. Using this logic, society could now rely upon the phrenologist's objective "diagnosis" and separate criminals into those who are treatable and those who should be locked away for life. The only problem was that these decisions were based upon a theory that we know today is false and likely carried a heavy racial and social bias against those who were clearly "inferior." This moral dilemma is predictable whenever classification schemes are developed and should serve as a warning for today's forensic clinician, much as it should have served as a warning for Gall and Spurzheim's disciples.

The Italian physician Cesare Lombroso took phrenology to a newer level and searched for physical or bodily indices of criminal behavior. Although he developed numerous modifications of his early theories, he is primarily known for his initial belief that the physical appearance of criminals is directly related to that of prehistoric man and animals. His study of the skulls and brains of criminals persuaded him that there were clear resemblances to earlier, primitive cultures. This enabled him to develop the theory that criminals were Jurassic Park-like throwbacks to earlier, and therefore baser, creatures. This clearly elitist theory enabled him to characterize criminals as born to their way of life, unable to behave in any other than antisocial ways and thus irredeemable.

Although widely known for this rather cruel and segregationist theory, Lombrosso should be credited for his flexibility in that he was open to discrepancies and discontinuities in his data. Throughout his life, he modified his theories and ultimately came to the conclusion that some criminal behavior was without any inborn or organic basis. His later writings discuss the "criminal by passion" and the "occasional criminal," indicating an evolution of his concepts toward contemporary views. Unfortunately, his earliest writings had already gained a wide following, and his later modifications had little influence upon those who gratefully accepted the notion that "they" were innately different from the rest of us and should be locked away for life.

Although Lombrosso's theories were finally and carefully refuted by Charles Goring (Goring, 1913), there remained a popular need to see criminal behavior as predictable and tied to inborn factors. Ernest Hooton attempted to provide support for the Lombrossoian physical or structural approach by publishing a study in 1939 to demonstrate that criminal behavior was directly the result of "inherited biological inferiority."

> Thieves and burglars tend to be sneaky little constitutional inferiors . . . robbers lean to several variants of the wiry, narrow, hard-bitten, tough, not notably undersized. . . . It is a remarkable fact that tall, thin men tend to murder and rob, tall heavy men to kill and to commit forgery and fraud, undersized thin men to steal

and to burglarize, short heavy men to assault, to rape and to commit other sex crimes, whereas men of mediocre body build tend to break the law without obvious discrimination or preference. (Goring in Korn and McCorkle, p. 161)

Korn and McCorkle discuss analyses of Hooton's work that demonstrate that his sample sizes, his poorly selected populations, and his generalizations all leave much to question. They note that despite the "bad" science used and the inadequate conclusions drawn, Hooton's recommendations for "treatment" of these inferior populations are severe in their brutality. Thus they quote Hooton, "these hopeless constitutional inferiors should be permanently incarcerated and, on no account, should be allowed to breed. Nevertheless, they should be treated humanely, and if they are to be kept alive, should be allowed some opportunity for freedom and profitable occupation within their own severely restricted area" (Korn and McCorkle, 1961, p. 219).

To demonstrate the widespread acceptance of Hooton's "bad" science, only half a century ago in 1949 psychiatrist William Sheldon developed a theory of delinquency based upon the body shape of individuals or, as he called it, a theory of "constitutional psychiatry." He proposed the classification of "somatotypes" that allow the investigator to categorize people into one of three different types of body build. His assumption was that the predominant body build directly corresponds to the individual's psychological properties. The reader will note the theoretical pathway between this theory of body build, Gall and Spurzheim's theory of skull shape reflecting brain propensities, and Lombroso and Hooton's later physical theories. In these ways, not much had changed in 150 years.

Sheldon wrote about endomorphs, who were characterized by plumpness; ectomorphs, who in contrast, were thin; and mesomorphs who were athletic and muscular. His system argues that endomorphs are generally pleasant, happy, and social individuals while ectomorphs are nervous, easily agitated, and unpredictable. Mesomorphs, in contrast, are vigorous and assertive. Since it was not possible to categorize most people easily into one of these three groupings, he developed a scale rating body build on a one-to-seven ranking that would indicate the proportion of each individual's characteristics across these three categories, lending a more "scientific" calculation to arrive at a diagnosis. Thus, a person who received a 1-7-1 rating would be an extreme mesomorph; a person who was a 1-1-7 an extreme ectomorph, and finally 7-1-1, an extreme endomorph. Most often, assessments arrived at a more complex rating.

Sheldon next searched for a relationship between delinquency and his constitutional typology. He developed an index of "disappointingness" (D), which included the person's delinquent history as well as medical and psychological factors. The total D scale was then correlated with the somatotype scale. Analyzing 200 delinquents this way, he found a tendency toward mesomorph body types. An analysis of a smaller group of 16 seriously delinquent boys demonstrated a stronger mesomorph finding. These findings led him, as it had led others before him, to a rather simplistic classification schema, designed to sort out potential delinquents from the rest of the population. Yet, aside from his reporting of these early correlations, his findings have not held up upon replication. Sheldon was particularly critical of what he called "unscientific" measures being used by other professionals, referring to their approach as the "Babel" of psychiatry. Yet his discussions are no more scientific than those of the phrenologists who preceded him.

In 1956, Sheldon and Eleanor Glueck tested Sheldon's theory with the use of a control group and again found that delinquent boys were more mesomorphic than nondelinquent controls. Rather than look to social and environmental explanations, they arrived at the conclusion that a muscular appearance is causatively related to delinquent behavior. The Glueck's study probably represents the final gasp of the pseudoscientific attempts to correlate physical factors with human behavior. Although this 1956 analysis was roundly criticized for not attending to the likelihood that physical strength would reasonably be an intrinsic characteristic of boys engaged in aggressive male pursuits, the apparently intuitive and "common sense" strength of this mode of thinking carries forward to the present day. A brief scan of movies or television shows about violent individuals will demonstrate a predominance of physical types selected to play villains, with more than a casual nod given to the Sheldon-Glueck typology. Science aside, we clearly remain tied to the belief that dangerous and violent individuals need to look and be different from the rest of us. One need only watch the popular response to publicized shootings and other tragedies to observe the pressing public need to explain violent behavior in a manner that provides a sense of reassurance that the perpetrators are "them" and most certainly not "us."

Chapter 3

FIRST-GENERATION
SCIENTIFIC PREDICTION

A T EXACTLY 11:47 P.M. on April 15, 1982, Sergeant First Class (SFC) Robert Stryker, in front of more than 20 witnesses, killed a man by shooting him in the back.

Witnesses reported on events as follows: At about 10:30 p.m., SFC Stryker entered the Non-commission Officers (NCO) Club in Erlangen, West Germany, and ordered a beer. At a table about ten meters from the bar, Staff Sergeant Ralph Dolbert, the victim, was sitting with the perpetrator's wife, Hilda, and a battalion executive officer. Shortly thereafter, Sergeant Dolbert started slow dancing with Hilda; Sergeant Stryker began to dance with another woman. At a point about halfway through the musical score, the perpetrator left his partner standing on the dance floor and returned to the bar. He then threw a small object at the victim, later identified as a pocket dictionary, hitting him on the shoulder. In reaction, Sergeant Dolbert made a motion as if to attack Sergeant Stryker but was restrained by observers. Minutes later, he joined the perpetrator at the bar in what appeared to be intense conversation.

Throwing up his hands as if ending the discussion, Sergeant Dolbert laughed loudly and walked in the direction of his table. The perpetrator then yelled for the victim to stop, but the latter continued, his face set in a wide smile. From the back of his waistband, Sergeant Stryker pulled out a pistol, a nine-millimeter German Lugar, and fired in the direction of the victim. The first bullet went low and to the right, ricocheting into a juke box. Sergeant Dolbert, still smiling, did not slow his pace. He continued to walk. The perpetrator then assumed a "competition stance"—legs spread apart with both hands gripping the pistol—and fired twice more in rapid succession. It was never determined which bullet was fired first, the one that entered slightly above the right knee, or the bullet that entered the back and tore through the heart, but the victim lurched forward with his right leg crumpling noticeably before he fell on his face.

In this case, as in others to follow, the reader is asked to try his or her hand at predictive tasks with the information available. Please turn to Appendix A, Dangerousness Prediction Task #1, before you go on to the rest of this chapter.

Three major types of prediction emerged from the behavioral science literature in the 70s and 80s (Avanesov, 1981; Scheibe, 1978), all of which have some relevance to the prognostication of human violence. Each prediction process had particular strengths and weaknesses, and each had its proponents and detractors in this country and abroad. All three were used in various combinations to enhance predictive accuracy. The first of these types may be called Prediction by Control and Authority. This predictive process is characterized by the power to influence the predictee overtly or covertly. This is seen in a number of early social psychology studies such as Buss's (1961) "aggression machine" and Milgram's famous experiments (1963, 1965) to study obedience to authority. The potency of this mode of prediction can be illustrated by the fact that the large majority of Milgram's subjects administered what they believed were severe and painful shocks to confederates even in the face of their own personal discomfort. The parallel between the results of these studies and what occurred in the Nazi concentration camps was not lost either on Stanley Milgram or on the general public who learned of these studies. For many, particularly today, these early experiments that predicted violence by creating violence are considered unethical and probably cannot and will not be replicated. Yet their message about compliance to a higher authority remains significant, especially at the close of the violent 20th century.

The multitude of behavior-modification studies on aggression, especially those in institutions or otherwise restricted settings, attempted to predict violence by controlling it (e.g., Hall, Price, Shinedling, Peizer, and Massey, 1973; and Hall, Shinedling, and Thorne, 1973). Dangerousness prediction in these contexts is relatively easy through the use of a wide variety of aversive and/or rewarding consequences, from tokens, to praise, to inhalation of noxious fumes, to receiving electrical stimulation by a remote-controlled apparatus. Simply by controlling consequences, and in some cases by utilizing antecedents as in classical conditioning, or discriminative stimuli as in operant analysis, positive results can be observed. Impressive and sharply defined ABAB paradigms can be obtained; within subjects, differences can be demonstrated to show more and less violence as a result of baseline and treatment procedures, respectively. Such strategies have more recently been employed in clinical populations, especially with violent and self-abusive mentally retarded and autistic individuals as at the Judge Rotenberg Institute in Massachusetts and with sex offender populations. These strategies, while generally considered to be successful in reducing and eliminating violent behavior, are not without significant controversy and criticism.

In January 1990, the American Association of Mental Retardation Board of Directors produced a "position statement on aversive procedures" that condemned "inhumane" forms of such procedures in order to achieve modification of behavior. As reported in the Association's *News and Notes* of July/August 1990, "The policy urges elimination of aversive procedures which cause physical damage, pain, or illness. Procedures which are dehumanizing—social degradation, isolation, verbal abuse, and excessive reactions—are also condemned." This position statement was approved by the Board of Directors later that year.

Unfortunately, the power to predict using this mode of intervention evaporates with the loss of control over the predictee. Once a violent offender is freed into the open community, the power to predict violence through the use of control and authority can be described as episodic and negligible. "Proper" generalization of nonviolent behavior is very difficult to achieve. Most violent people don't respond to learning principles as we would like, and all they have to do to nullify this type of predictive accuracy is to escape, avoid, and in many cases, simply deny external control and authority. This problem is magnified when the predictee acts with impulsive violence rather than instrumentally, as do many individuals with organic and substance abuse problems, or when the predictee does not mind (or would prefer) a return to an incarcerated setting. Here events can be determined internally, rather than environmentally. Moreover, accurate prediction from one context of validation, say the psychological laboratory or the penal institution, is dubious when the predictee is in another context of validation, such as the general community.

Perhaps the area of greatest public concern in this regard is that of the sexual predator released to the community from the confines of an institution. Many states require that clinicians assess such individuals prior to release and determine whether they remain sexually dangerous. Any clinician who has been in such a position knows the difficulty of attempting to anticipate such violent behavior in an individual who has been incarcerated and without the opportunity to express such behavior for many years. In such cases, the clinician is well advised to indicate the limits of such predictive ability in statements to the court and in relevant reports.

Prediction by empathy (or clinical insight) is based upon understanding predictees from their individual perspective, so that their feelings, thoughts, and motives are more readily comprehensible. The most fragile of the prediction modes, prediction by empathy, can yield accurate results, as reported in the literature and by the reported experiences of many clinicians.

Showing support or affection to the predictee is distinct, a different issue, from attempting to place yourself in their perspective so that data can be yielded to illuminate their intentions and thoughts. Classic examples of prediction by empathetic understanding are illustrated in various parlor games. Players can know that another is bluffing in poker, for example, not by a giveaway cue but by the realization that the bluffer does not expect to be discovered. Illustrations of this mode in dangerousness prediction include criminal profiling, and clinical case assessment and management.

Prediction by empathy can easily be nullified by (1) poor clinical or empathetic ability of the predictor, (2) paranoid or other defenses to probing by predictees, and (3) situational characteristics of the examination context. The examiner should keep in mind that the predictees may very well be evaluating the examiner and modifying behavior in the direction of their vested interests. This certainly happens in clinical interviews, but is more likely in dangerousness prediction evaluations where the outcome stakes are high, oftentimes determining whether a predictee remains at, proceeds to, or is released from preventive detainment.

In addition to these three nullifying factors, countertransference by the examiner can nullify empathy. We may be turned off by the predictee even though empathy can produce valuable data or leads. It may be too painful for the examiner to sit empathetically with a murderer of a child or with a particularly deviant offender. The result is that the predictor is limited in prediction.

Prediction by association is the skill of seeing parts of a whole and picking out those parts of greatest apparent significance. The task is to decide whether each part is in fact associated with a particular type of event. Then all that is necessary is to observe the cue or association necessary to make predictions. When one has been able to identify the critical factors associated with each event are identified, it no longer is necessary to study the whole.

For example, prediction by association makes use of the datum that 75 percent of college Ss choose "3" when asked to pick a number between 1 and 4; 28 percent of Ss choose "7" when asked to pick a single digit number; most Ss say "blue" when asked to name a color; most Ss say "lion" when asked to name a wild beast; most Ss say "Paris" when asked to name a capital city on the European mainland; and most Ss say "rose" when asked to name a flower (Scheibe, 1978).

A plethora of associations with dangerousness have been reported in the behavioral science literature ranging from the so-called pathological triad (enuresis, fire-setting, cruelty to animals) to having violent friends, group membership in some subcultural groups within which violence is perceived as an acceptable solution to interpersonal problems and certain types of tattoos. Most violent offenders attribute the cause of their violence to outside forces (e.g., alcohol); projection of blame is usually followed by lack of acceptance of responsibility for their misdeeds. Unfortunately, many of these reported associations, such as the pathological triad, are not based upon replicable studies and often do not meet acceptable reliability criteria. As we will soon see, new research from the MacArthur group supports specific associations with a particular high-risk group of mentally ill individuals.

The problems with predicting violence by association are as follows: (1) The information is useful until shared by the predictee who then may attempt to disguise or otherwise distort it. Recall that you may be carefully scrutinized by the examinee in the typical dangerousness evaluation. Be aware also that many of the statistical and clinical associations to violence are available in the popular media; (2) There are hundreds of factors associated with violence, many of which are of low statistical weight, as shown in the next section. Given a large enough sample, it may be that most factors in life can be demonstrated to be associated in some way with other factors. Classes of violent behaviors, people, or situations like other broadband psychological phenomena may be statistically associated with a large number of other factors. Which factors should be chosen? How are weights assigned to each factor? How does one set of factors differ for a predictee compared to another person, or even within the same individual over time? Where does etiology to violence come into play, since association does not imply causation?

These questions and problems require that data to arrive at a best-case scenario. Borrowing from the MacArthur approach, carefully defined procedures and methods are strongly advised, and an organized approach to analysis is recommended. This requirement suggests both a general and a specific approach to violence where content and process factors must be taken into consideration. In short, we need a classification system that can be generalized and a set of decision rules to manipulate data content.

DEFINITIONS. Subsumed under rubrics such as *acting out* (Brown, 1965; Curnutt & Corozzo, 1960), *violence* (Toch, 1969; Hartogs, 1970), *aggression* (Bandura, 1973; Role & Nesdale, 1976) and *dangerousness* (Levinson and Ramsay, 1969; Shaw, 1978; Steadman and Cocozza, 1980), arguments over how to define the likelihood of future harm is the subject of endless professional quibbling. Yet, like the Supreme Court's definition of pornography, we know a violent act when we see it. Being shot by Sergeant Stryker was violent by any definition. Because we are often called upon to define our terms in court and in reports, the following is therefore offered as a guide.

Prediction of violence, aggression, or dangerousness all refer to a sequential posthoc decision-making *process* leading to circumscribed outcome statements concerning the future likelihood or risk of threatened, attempted, or consummated physical harm to oneself, others, or property within a specified temporal period. These considerations are in order:

(1) Violence prediction refers to the interaction of perpetrator, context, and victim rather than to characteristics of the predictee alone. Individual persons may have high-risk characteristics, motives, and intentions, but specific behaviors in interaction with environmental factors at a certain time, place, and setting make for dangerousness or nondangerousness;

(2) "Physical harm" means tissue injury, penetration, or destruction;

(3) Violence prediction assumes threatened, attempted, or consummated violence rather than the moral evaluation of violence. Thus, police officers may exhibit a set of dangerous behaviors in certain circumstances regardless of the legitimacy of their acts. This consideration often comes into play when evaluating war veterans for violence potential. War violence is a factor when evaluating basal violence;

(4) Violence prediction does not depend on first establishing a mental disturbance. The long-held belief that the mentally ill are no more dangerous than others is clearly not accurate however, as demonstrated by the MacArthur studies;

(5) The "decision-making process" refers to a sequential analysis of the database after careful information collection; awareness of possible misrepresentation or deception by the predictee; and identification of basal violence, triggering stimuli, and opportunities to aggress. The decision path assumes that all steps must be completed before a violence prediction can be made. Figure 1 presents the simplest version of the process in the form of key questions.

The basic concept of Figure 1 is that a sequential series of steps in the form of a decision tree should be applied posthoc to forensic evaluations of dangerousness. A formal decision tree will be presented later. Although each step contains testable hypotheses, all the steps represent a total process of prediction that can only be examined artificially in its component parts.

The first step involves determination by the predictor that a request for violence prediction is relevant, ethical, and appropriate given the referral source, setting, and status of the predictee, as well as the competence and training of the predictor. These are often defined by local, state, or federal laws, but in the final analysis, this is determined by the individual forensic professional. For Sergeant Stryker, a dangerousness prediction was requested by the court for sentencing purposes after he was found guilty of manslaughter.

The second step involves creating a valid and reliable dangerousness database, multisourced and interdisciplinary in nature, that forms the basis for all evaluative conclusions in regards to dangerousness. The content provided by looking at perpetrator, victim, contextual stimuli, current stress, and other data relevant to the predictee's past and present is the foundation of the forensic database. Sergeant Stryker was administered a complete battery of intellectual and personality tests in addition to several clinical interviews. All police investigation records were reviewed and significant/knowledgeable others were interviewed. Keep in mind that a wide forensic database is often the strongest part of the dangerousness prediction process, provides for flexibility and later shift in focus if necessary, and allows others to replicate your conclusions. This data collection will often provide the foundation for a forensic opinion to be provided to the court, and the value of this information to the court will be measured against the thoroughness and objectivity of the data gathering.

The third step necessitates awareness of the direction and magnitude of the predictee's retrospective distortion manipulation as well as possible misrepresentation at the time of the evaluation. For Sergeant Stryker, this consisted of determining whether he was attempting to deceive the examiner both for the time of the crime and for the time of the evaluation. Nondeliberate distortion caused by memory defects, stress, intoxication, and other factors must be taken into account. Deliberate distortion in terms of response styles employed by the examinee must be scrutinized and measured. Chapter 6 *The Forensic Distortion Analysis* probes malingering and the forensic distortion analysis in detail and presents guidelines for report writ-

1. Appropriate Referral?

↓

2. Adequate Forensic Database?

↓

3. Accounted for Distortion?

4. Basal Violence Examined?

↓

5. Triggering Stimuli Present?

↓

6. Opportunity Variables Operative?

↓

7. Inhibitory Factors Analyzed?

↓

8. Limited and Replicable Conclusions?

Figure 1. Dangerousness Prediction Process Questions

ing and presentation of results.

The fourth step involves a historical analysis of basal violence to include the comparison of previous violence to the type and quality of violence predicted. Previous significant violence *must* have occurred in order to proceed with the decision process. For Sergeant Stryker, as Appendix A suggests, there was no history of violence up to his entry into the U.S. Army and a nonremarkable developmental period was revealed. Serious violence was shown only after he reached adulthood, prior to the instant killing.

The fifth step requires careful analysis of the triggering stimuli, short term in duration and intense in impact, to set the violence into motion. This step also involves current factors such as cumulative stress within the last year or months that operate to lower the threshold for violence to occur and are directly associated with certain types of violence, such as spouse and child abuse. Reports by others such as family, employers, and therapists can be extremely useful in detailing the growing effects of such pressures. Momentary stress and intoxication must also be considered.

The sixth stage of the process necessitates analyzing of the presence of opportunity factors that support the occurrence of violence or expand the various ways it can be expressed. Proficiency in firearms as well as their availability at the time of the killing, for Sergeant Stryker was of significance. Other opportunity variables such as the availability of transportation to take Sergeant Stryker to the NCO club and the presence of the victim at that facility must be considered, for without these elements, the killings could not have occurred at that time. Opportunity variables, discussed later, appear to operate in an all-or-none fashion, in that similar, but not identical, means to inflict violence are usually not considered by the perpetrator. It is doubtful in the instant case that Sergeant Stryker would have used available knives in the NCO Club had his firearm malfunctioned, if other similar homicide cases provide any comparison. Stress and other factors may operate here to increase behavioral rigidity at a point of high arousal such that other options are not thought of or acted upon.

The seventh step calls for analyzing inhibitory variables that operate to lower the probability that violence will occur. Inhibitory variables fall into a lower range of frequency, intensity, and duration of the previous factors. The time since the last exhibited violence should also be considered. Sergeant Stryker, for example, may have become psychologically impaired as a result of the effects of prolonged depression or possible loss of his wife. Both may affect the likelihood of future violence. Practically speaking, there is no need to create a separate category for inhibitory variables because they will be included within history, opportunity, and possible triggers to violence.

The last step calls for limited and replicable conclusions in regard to estimated risk of future violence. These conclusions must be time limited with a specified direction of violence and a feedback mechanism. Other conclusion limitations must be presented and will be expanded upon later.

In general, the decision tree is applied posthoc after the data is gathered but before conclusions are drawn so that an evaluation of the process can be made. If any branches of the decision tree are missing, the dangerousness prediction cannot be made reliably. Each limb assumes more data than the previous and flows sequentially toward the forensic examiner's conclusions. Each limb contains its own set of inclusionary and exclusionary steps that must be met and will be expanded in subsequent chapters.

Dangerousness Typology

The dangerousness prediction scheme must be able to process basal violence. What is needed, without delving into the dozens of extant typologies of violence, is a content scheme that is quantifiable, replicable, and mutually exclusive in category. Because most violence is interactioned in nature, the relationship of the perpetrator to the victim should be addressed. Whether previous violence was perpetrated by a *stranger, acquaintance,* or *family member* is another fundamental division. A violent act is assigned to one and only one category depending on the relationship of the perpetrator to the victim. The perpetrator is a stranger if the victim identifies the individual as a stranger including those "known by sight," after blood and marriage ties are ruled out (National Institute of Justice, 1982). All others are acquaintances or family members, the last according to the blood or marriage criterion.

A second concern is whether the previous violence was towards *self, others,* or *property.* Although individuals often exhibit more than one direction of violence, what may occur in the future is likely to have been exhibited previously in similar circumstances. The focus of this book is on violence to others, but prediction of self-harm is certainly a crucial concern for most clinicians.

Third, the severity of past violence must be considered. Four primary categories were suggested by the U.S. Department of Justice (1985) based upon a survey of 60,000 Americans. These categories are whether (1) *minor harm* was sustained, (2) harm was experienced and the victim was *treated and discharged,* (3) *hospitalization* occurred, or (4) the violence was *lethal.* Since standardized point values are suggested in this categorization, the results of the analysis can be used in individual cases to determine whether violence, as in Sergeant Stryker's case, was escalating over time. Severity and violence acceleration is discussed in Chapter 6.

Based upon this analysis, a 3 x 3 x 4 factorial typology as shown in Figure 2 is offered for consideration.

Each of the 36 possibilities is mutually exclusive and may have a differential probability of reoccurring, as the literature suggests. Spouse and child abuse involving minor harm, for example, are both common and predictably recidivistic, frequently with gradually increasing severity of harm. Rape and other sex offenses and robbery involving serious injuries to victims are unfortunately, also, highly recidivistic. Homicide in all relationship categories is rare, comprising less then 2 percent of all violent crime (Uniform Crime Reports, 1985) and is rarely recidivistic, especially when between family members.

Factors Associated with Violence

What are the historical variables that should be considered in this violence typology? Table III presents two basal categories of historical factors.

Baseline Characteristics (Category Ia) describe past violence. Frequency, severity, type, recency, whether weapons were used in the commission of the crime, and other characteristics of violence are relevant here. Certain characteristics of past dangerousness (e.g., multiple, recent violence) are associat-

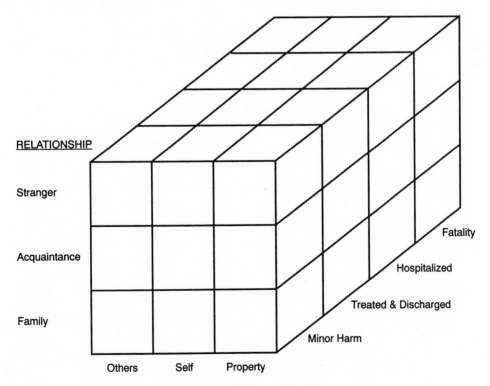

Figure 2. Basal Violence Typology

TABLE III
FACTORS ASSOCIATED WITH VIOLENCE

Category Ia Baseline characteristics

Condition or event	Range of confidence	Sample reference
Incidents of violence l.e. multiple	1	Wolfgang (1978); Petersilia et al. (1977)
Fatal or potentially fatal violence	2	Steadman & Cocozza (1974)
Rape, robbery, murder, or aggravated assault	1	Michigan Corr. Dept. (1978)
Recency immediate (less than one year)	2	Michigan Corr. Dept. (1978)
Firearm or other potentially lethal weapon	2	Kelly (1978); Berkowitz & LePage (1967)
Past violence maintained/intensified by pain cues from victim	2	Fort & Beech (1951); Dobonowsky (1980)
Serious institutional misconduct	3	Michigan Corr. Dept. (1978)
Felony arrest before 15th birthday	2	Michigan Corr. Dept. (1978)
Arrests for previous violence	2	Steadman & Cocozza (1974)
Convictions for violent crimes	1-2	Steadman & Cocozza (1974)

Continued on next page

ed with a higher probability of future violence when compared to other characteristics along similar lines (e.g., infrequent, remote acts of violence). The phrase *prepotent* violence history is reserved for frequent, severe, and recent violence when in combination. Research will show that, in general, historical variables account for the major portion of the statistical variance contributing to violent acts. Prepotent violence is the most influential factor in accurately predicting violence (true positives); nonprepotent violence accounts for most of the variance in accurately predicting nonviolence (true negatives). This may very well be related to the MacArthur findings of the significance of sociopathy in determining future risk.

Developmental Variables (Category Ib) are historical occurrences in childhood associated with later violence. Developmental events act as signals to the evaluator that the predictee may have a history of uncovered violence, or that the basal violence history is worse than supposed by the predictor. Child abuse as a perpetrator, for example, is known to be highly correlated with child abuse as a victim. Yet factors in this subcluster include self-reinforcement and praise for inflicted violence, violent parents or siblings, pref-

TABLE III—*Continued*

Category Ib Developmental variables

Condition or event	Range of confidence	Sample reference
Violent parental or sibling model (especially same-sex)	1-2	Bandura (1973)
Physical abuse	4	Hoffman (1960); Goldstein (1974)
Pathological triad (pyromania, cruelty to animals, enuresis)	4	Hellman & Blackman (1966)
Preference for violent TV shows	3	Lefkowitz, Eron, Walder & Heusmann (1977)
Alcoholism/drug-abusing parents	3	Bach-Y-Rita, Lion, Clement & Ervin (1971);
Juvenile record (nonviolent or status crimes)	4	Steadman & Cocozza (1974)
History of reinforcing results for aggression	3	Patterson, Cobb & Ray (1972); Dobonowsky (1980)
Praise or reward by parents for aggression	3	Loew (1967)
Evidence of self-reinforcement for aggression	3	Bandura & Walters (1959)
Spontaneous or concussion-related loss of consciousness before age 10	4	Bach-Y-Rita & Veno (1974)
School problems—assault on teachers, temper tantrums, threats	3	Justice, Justice & Kraft (1974)

Note: Confidence levels denote the degree to which condition/event is associated with violence:
1. Certain; 2. High to moderate; 3. Moderate to low; 4. Insufficient data

erence for violent films, certain types of brain trauma, and school problems such as fighting and truancy. These factors may have combined in some unknown way to reflect the first serious violent act. For example, a 15 year old may have committed an assault with a weapon, have a violent same-sex parental model, observed the method repeatedly on television, and received praise from others for violence. Factors in this subcluster are not necessary to know in detail, again acting as signals or cues. Unfortunately, they are often misconstrued as primary factors along with the predictee's assumed personality traits. Developmental variables are never sufficient in and of themselves to predict violence in the absence of actual basal violence. No one can predict the first act of violence for an individual; we can only, after the fact, look at possible causative factors. This means that violence prediction is limited to an analysis of previous dangerousness in the predictee. It should be noted that careful analyses of cases demonstrates that "first acts" of violence in adults are often simply logical steps along a prior violence-filled continuum of hidden or secret acts.

Other content variables that should be considered are current operating factors such as triggers and other more long-range events that are presumed to raise the likelihood that violence will occur. A list of some triggering stimuli (Category IIa) is presented in Table IV. Triggering stimuli are precipitating variables associated with the subject's behavioral repertoire. These are immediate causes, short term in duration, intense in impact, which set violence into motion. Factors in this subcluster include substance abuse and intoxication, command hallucinations, certain organic states, and other variables. These factors are considered internal causes of violence when they are not environmentally-induced stress. They include physiological and psychological states that cause quick deterioration of judgment and self-control, which may shortly afterward result in violence. Precipitating variables have high-impact effect and may also include environmentally induced stress, an *external* cause to violence. Breakup of the central love relationship for an adult or gross disruption in the primary family unit for a minor appear to be primary triggers in this subcluster. As with internal causes, the potential for triggering events must be established within the predictee's existing behavior patterns. Later research will show that although triggers are necessary for all but the most chronically violent individuals, they account for a small proportion of the statistical variance contributing to the violent act.

Cluster IIb, *Present Operating Conditions*, are those factors associated with increased interpersonal conflict and include the personality and behavioral traits usually associated with violence, such as high hostility, impulsivity, low behavioral control, projection of blame, poor verbal skills, and so forth. These variables are often associated with below-average intelligence and/or organic factors. Reinforcing variables include demographic variables that are current operating conditions or traits associated with violence. These are essentially defining features of the person (e.g., age, sex, race, socioeconomic status–SES) associated with violence as listed in Table IV. For example, the annual Uniform Crime Reports clearly indicate that robbery, rape, and aggravated assault are essentially crimes of young adult males. Even so, the number of incorrectly designated possible violent offenders (false positives) is extremely high either when demographic features of the predictee are used alone or even when coupled with a violence history except for certain classes of high-rate offenders. As a consequence, the life experience of young black males in urban environments involves frequent search and arrest by

TABLE IV
FACTORS ASSOCIATED WITH VIOLENCE

Category IIa Triggering stimuli

Condition or event	Range of confidence	Sample reference
Young adult	1-2	Kelly (1976)
Sex (male)	1-2	Kelly (1976)
Race (some minority groups)	2	Kelly (1976)
Residential mobility	4	Michigan Corr. Dept. (1978)
Overcrowding	4	Bandura (1973)
Socio-economic status (low)	3	Monahan (1981)
No current or sporadic employment	3	Brenner (1977)
Marital status (single or divorced)	4	Michigan Corr. Dept. (1978)
Subcultural acceptance of violence to solve problems	4	Blumenthal (1976)
Belief that certain types of violence will go unpunished (e.g., spouse, child abuse)	4	Monahan (1981)
Self-perception as dangerous	4	Webster, Slomen, Sepejak, Butler, Jensen & Turdal (1979)
Self-mutilation (especially arm scars)	4	Bach-Y-Rita & Veno (1974)
Violent content fantasies	3	Dix (1976)
Nightmares with violent thema	3	Yochelson & Samenow (1976)
Intellectual retardation	4	Hirschi & Hindeland (1977)
Low frustration tolerance	4	Geen & Berkowitz (1967)

Continued on next page

police who are mistrained or socially biased to focus primarily on demographic characteristics. Demographic variables are commonly used in forensic reports as a basis for predicting dangerousness because of face validity. In generally, however, reinforcing variables, much like developmental factors, are nothing more than indices of possible violence and do not constitute a basis for prediction in the absence of substantive data such as actual basal violence coupled with opportunity and triggering stimuli. When previous

TABLE IV—*Continued*

Category IIb Present operating conditions

Condition or event	Range of confidence	Sample reference
Sudden worsening of financial state	2	Webster, et al. (1979)
Placement in incarceration	2	Webster, et al. (1979)
Other intense, sudden, recent stressors involving sex dominance, survival and territoriality	2	Webster, et al. (1979)
Sudden pain	2	Bandura (1973)
Status threats in group context	2	Short (1968)
Insults to selfesteem	2-4	Toch (1969)
Instructions to aggress	2	Milgram (1963, 1965)
Alcohol intoxication	1-2	Wolfgang (1978)
Drug intoxication (especially PCP, LSD, amphetamines, and opiates)	1-2	Petersilia, et al. (1977)
Alcohol and drugs in interaction	1-2	Pritchard (1977)
Fired or laid off from work	2	Webster, et al. (1979)
Unfavorable change in reward structure	2	Webster, et al. (1979)
Central love relationship breakup	2	Bandura (1973)
Body space invasion	2	Kinzel (1970)
Feelings of helplessness and powerlessness	4	Webster, et al. (1979)
High hostility	4	Webster, et al. (1979)
Deficits in verbal skills	4	Toch (1969)
Weak community support base	3	Wolfgang (1977)
Violent peers	2	Bandura (1973)
Alcohol abuse or dependency	1-2	Wolfgang (1977)

Note: Confidence levels denote the degree to which condition/event is associated with violence: 1. Certain; 2. High to moderate; 3. Moderate to low; 4. Insufficient data violence is established and the predictee has a number of current operating factors, especially young age, male sex, low SES, mental illness, and current substance abuse, the chances may or may not be increased that violence will occur. The problem is that previous violence, especially recency of last violent act, may already take into account demographic features of the predictee and thus render these variables redundant. The base rate of violence to which the predictee holds membership, discussed later, is relevant here and can be added as a first estimate of violence probability, but should never serve as a substitute for thorough data collection.

The major drawback of some reinforcing variables such as personality traits, especially predictee hostility, is that the predictor often reacts emotionally, but covertly, and becomes subtly biased in his or her conclusions about dangerousness. This subcluster is rarely used as a sole basis for prediction, as courts accurately see it as inherently unfair to hold involuntary characteristics, genetic traits, or externally imposed conditions against a person, in spite of their possible actuarial veracity for certain classes of offenders.

Being aware of the current operating conditions of the predictee, besides providing information about the signaling function, provides additional information about the notion of topography or situational context. Usually long term in development, topography defines the form or style of later violence when combined with other cluster factors. An example is a divorced, unemployed, cocaine-abusing mother living in an inner-city slum, who correctly believes her chances of arrest for child abuse to be slim. The form and style of her violence to others may not be difficult to predict because we are aware of topographical features of the possible violence context. Appropriate interventions can then be proffered if requested.

A last category of content variables is *opportunity* or *availability factors*. As Table V illustrates, those include availability of accessible weapons and identified victims. The recent purchase of a firearm is an especially bad sign when combined with a prepotent violence history and high current stress caused by threatened breakup of the central love relationship. Add substance intoxication and the risk level soars. Much concern for opportunity variables is addressed by the courts and other control agencies when, in fact and as discussed later, most perpetrators appear either to find or create their own opportunity to aggress.

In examining Tables III, IV, and V, readers can see that the clusters cannot help but overlap; an arbitrary decision was made, however, that each factor is assigned to only one category. For example, substance dependence or abuse is a reinforcing cause of violence (Category IIb) but is also a stimulus trigger (Category IIa) when the individual is intoxicated. Further, these tables are not complete in that only a representative part of the literature is

TABLE V
FACTORS ASSOCIATED WITH VIOLENCE

Category III Opportunity variables

Condition or event	Range of confidence	Sample reference
Availability of weaker victim	1-2	Bandura (1973)
No peaceful response possible (e.g., trapped by mugger or rapist)	2	Monahan (1981)
Recent purchase of firearm	2	Berkowitz & LePage (1967)
Possession of firearm	2	U.S. Dept. of Justice (1983)
Situation presents opportunity for instrumental aggression (e.g., beating up drunk for money)	3	Berkowitz & LePage (1967)
Release from preventive detainment	3	Stone (1975)
Cessation of tranquilizing or stabilizing medication	3	Stone (1975)
Vehicular transportation	3	Monahan (1981)

Note: Confidence levels denote the degree to which condition/event is associated with violence:
1. Certain; 2. High to moderate; 3. Moderate to low; 4. Insufficient data

sampled. They are presented in an attempt to show the large variety of influences associated with human violence. Sample references have been provided for each factor and are recommended as excellent starting points for individual study.

A rating of the degree of confidence is presented for each factor and represents an arbitrary but empirically based judgment of the amount of confidence one can place on each factor. The highest rating (1) is reserved for replicated empirical findings or results from large epidemiological surveys of violence such as the MacArthur project. In these cases, the statistical association is high between the existence of the factor and the likelihood of risk for violence. There is no attempt to judge the weight of each factor in the violence equation, however. A 2 stands for a *high-to-moderate* association, 3 for *moderate-to-low*, and 4 is only a *suspicion* that a statistical association is operative, although the evidence is weak. Degree-of-confidence ratings for current operating conditions and opportunity factors always presuppose that basal violence has been established. Confidence range estimates may include a range within any one factor. For example, it is generally believed that insults to one's masculinity in juvenile gangs ,"dissing," provoke violence among the most dominant members when those remarks are directed at them. Yet there is only a suspicion that insults to self-esteem in general increase the risk of violence for most people. Some forensic professionals hold that there is no association at all. Their conflicting positions led to the assignment of a score of 2–4 for the insults to self-esteem factors.

A simplified checklist of violence factors is presented in Appendix B as a working tool. The predictor should note during or after a dangerousness evaluation, whether the factors were in place before arriving at his or her own decision process.

Degree of Certainty and Report Parameters

Dangerousness predictions have usually been proffered in terms of degree of confidence, because of scientific and liability issues, when in fact, future violent behavior will either occur or not occur (Meehl, 1974). Current terminology focuses on risk assessment as a means of stressing the probabilistic nature of forensic prediction. For purposes of consistency, the following degrees of certainty for dangerousness prediction/risk assessment are suggested in this book:

(1) *Negligible*–In your professional opinion, future violence will likely not occur within the specified period. This term is used for average people with no history of serious violence. Operationally, you mean and should be able to demonstrate that the probability figures are closely tied to base rate data. This degree of certainty is within the legal meaning of "nondangerousness" and assumes a zero or minimal risk assessment.

(2) *Low*–In your opinion, within the time period, violence will *not* occur or the likelihood is very unlikely. This degree of risk might be used for the average person who is perhaps under temporary high stress or who evidences some maladaptive behavior, but has no history of violence. You mean and should be able to demonstrate that the probability of occurrence is from 11 to 25 percent, within the predicted time span, but only when numerical probability is tied to base rate data. This degree of certainty is also within the legal meaning of "nondangerousness."

(3) *Mild*–In your opinion, serious violence may occur within the specified time period, although your evidence is weak. This term is used for people with or without a history of serious violence. You are saying there is a fair likelihood that violence will occur. This degree of certainty is again within the legal meaning of "nondangerousness." The suggested range of risk probability associated with this legal term is 26 to 50 percent but only when numerical probability is tied to base rate data (Frederick, 1978b; Stone, 1975).

(4) *Moderate*–In your opinion, it is more likely than not that violence will occur within the specified time frame, but you are aware of the difficulty of specifying certainty. This term is usually limited to people with a violence history. Treatment can occur in the community. Probability of occurrence is 51 to 75 percent, but only when base rate data is considered. This corresponds to the suggested legal definition of "preponderance of evidence." (Stone, 1975; Frederick, 1978)

(5) *Considerable*–In your opinion, there is a strong likelihood that violence will occur within the specified time period. Risk is high. This term is limited to people with a violence history. Control may be institutional combined with community interventions (e.g., residential facilities, transition houses). The probability of occurrence is 76 to 90 percent, but only when base rate data is considered. This corresponds to the legal meaning of "clear and convincing evidence."

(6) *Substantial*–In your opinion, violence will occur within the specified time period if measures for intervention are not taken. This term is limited to people with a violence history and a number of high risk factors such as mental illness, substance abuse, and possession of weapons. Institutional control is necessary if the expected violence is to be controlled. Probability of occurrence is 91 to 100 percent, but only when base rate data is considered. This corresponds to the suggested legal definition of "beyond a reasonable doubt" and, of course, represents the highest degree of risk. It is in such circumstances that a clinician is mandated to use a Tarasoff warning and must act to protect a third party.

For dangerousness prediction evaluations, Appendix C, Dangerousness Prediction Report Format, presents a fully developed report format. This sample demonstrates the posthoc decision process of the examiner with circumscribed conclusions provided to the referral source, identifying degree of risk and certainty.

Imminent Dangerousness Prediction

The following discussion is limited to organizational contexts and involves predictions of violence for up to several days after that prediction is rendered. Imminent dangerousness prediction is actually prediction from control and authority in that staff, and organizational behavior often is assumed to contribute to outcome.

This section is based entirely upon the clinical experience of the authors and clinical impressions reported in the literature. The Bill Green case described in Chapter 1 provided a focus for this discussion. No reliable base rate data or consensus exists in regards to the "proper" set of staff behaviors that would prevent or reduce physical injury, property loss, or post-traumatic sequelae in association with a violent outburst. Studies that have been conducted consist of questionnaires for mental health professionals in communities where violence has occurred in mental health settings (Madden, Lion and Penna, 1976; Vernstein, 1981; Faulkner 1990; and Romans, Hays and White, 1996). The findings of these surveys suggest that victims are usually young and relatively inexperienced (trainees, interns) and aggressors are those with a history of both suicidal and aggressive behaviors. Confounding the difficulty is the fact that many perpetrators appear to choose their own time and context within which to act out, especially the critical factors regarding the use of weapons, location of crime, and whether others are present. Recognize, therefore, that in predicting imminent dangerousness, the vast majority of perpetrator behaviors may be instrumental in nature, having a large element of self-control, rather than reactive, and spontaneous, and involuntary. Contextual cues therefore are not to be ignored. Some victims have reported that they clearly minimized and denied such cues.

A further problem in preventing violence is that staff behavior inside and outside the treatment facility may be quite different. Staff may have little influence, for example, over the selection of some events to which perpetrators choose to respond (e.g., organizational strictures, lines of authority, uniform wearing). Yet some guidelines are suggested, coming under the rubrics of prevention, practice, documentation, and informing authorities and/or other potential victims of possible violence.

Imminent dangerousness prediction necessitates rapid consideration and action based upon perpetrator, victim, and contextual characteristics of the potentially violent situation. A first step is to recognize that the quality of staff judgments varies inversely with degrees of physiological arousal experienced in the violent situation. Figure 3 illustrates this general phenomenon.

Poor decisions by staff when under threat of violence can be expected unless emergency routines are established, distributed, practiced, and reevaluated by all relevant parties. Prevention is the first priority; practice should be simple, concrete, applicable to as many clinical situations as possible, and overlearned. Denial is a common mechanism for all in crises and only ongoing practice and training can serve to break through this defense.

High-risk victims can include those possessing inferior physical status to the possible perpetrator, although those in high status can just as easily be targeted, as in Dr. White's case. Other victim traits are discussed in Chapter 6 *The Forensic Distortion Analysis* and include *similarity* to the possible perpetrator in terms of race, sex, perceived SES, and exhibited anger. Impulsive staff behaviors are often a trigger to violence during the escalation stage. The virtue of physical and verbal nonresponsiveness prior to violence may be considered in light of National Institute of Justice statistics indicating increased risk of victim harm when initial resistance is shown. Dr. White's attempt to wrestle the gun from Bill Green may very well have been a factor that increased the risk of later violent action.

Contextual stimuli to violence are also discussed in Chapter 6 and include the architectural features of the building in which the violence may take place; subdued lighting; time of day, with late evenings the prime time for violence; and noxious stimuli such as heat and aversive odors. The two contextual features of most importance, according to the writers' experiences, are whether the possible perpetrator has a weapon and if a public, rather than private, setting is the focus of confrontation.

Danton (1986) suggested the acronym "DEAD," admonishing treating staff (a) not to Deny that violence is always a possibility, (b) always to have an Exit accessible, (c) to avoid Aggressive displays of their own behavior, and (d) Don't make promises that cannot be kept. The basic conflict resolution strategy consists of de-escalating the conflict, clarifying communication, describing win-win outcomes, and setting a short time for action/resolution of conflict. This is partially based upon the notion of a perpetrator assault cycle consisting of a *triggering phase*, an *escalation phase*, where arousal mounts and the perpetrator becomes more threatening; to a *crisis phase*, where the actual violence occurs; to a *recovery phase*, followed by a *post-crisis depression*

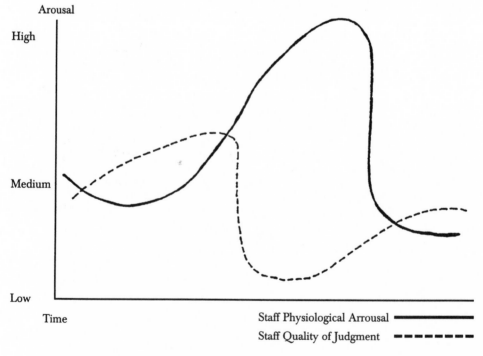

Figure 3. Staff Reaction to Violence

phase. Figure 4 illustrates the typical assault cycle and, again, parallels the Bill Green case.

The acronym "SCARED" is offered to insure that all violence issues within an institution are taken into consideration (Danton, 1986). It stands for safety, control, assessment, restraint, examination, and diagnosis. Continuing with alphabetic advice, the seven "A's" from the clinical literature suggest that possible perpetrators include those with *absent* roots, *authority* problems, an *arrest* history, prior *assaults,* causing *another's* harm or death, *alcohol* and *amphetamine* intoxication, and those with *access* to weapons. In addition,

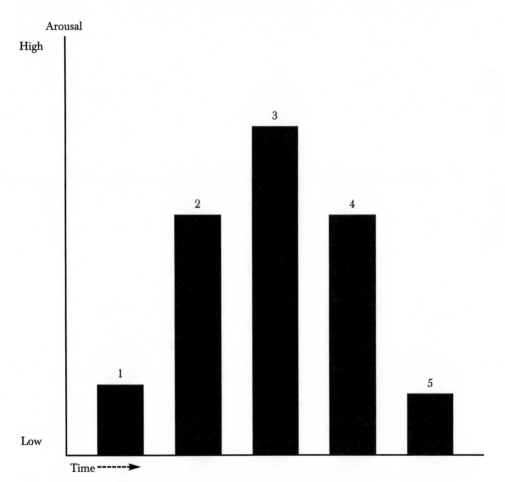

1. Triggering Phase: Decision is made to aggress
2. Escalation Phase: Preparatory behaviors are shown
3. Crisis Phase: Contact with victim effected
4. Recovery Phase: Somatic attempts to regain homeostasis
5. Post-crisis Depression Phase: Apologetic or remorseful behaviors often appear

Figure 4. Typical Assault Cycle

MacArthur high-risk factors add those with a diagnosed mental illness and antisocial personality.

The following are considerations culled from various sources regarding intervention tactics with potentially violent clients. Of course, individual application requires individual assessment due to unique circumstances. Staff may consider the following:

(1) Pay attention to your immediate environment. Know your facility's violence standard operating procedures (SOP). These may include routine use of multiple therapists with high-risk categories of clients, therapy sessions in large rooms with open doors, and telephone code words for assistance, or use of panic buttons.

(2) Minimize the risk of creating agitation by maintaining the self-esteem of the client. Set aside plenty of time and physically convey that you are listening. Maintain eye contact. Be polite, use Mr. or Mrs. or first name but not only last names, honor reasonable requests, and be willing to compromise. Remember that Bill Green's perception of Dr. Black's decision to pick up the fallen piece of paper was that the doctor had somehow injured his sense of self.

(3) Do not continue to work with a client who brings weapons, who threatens or who engenders fear. Pay attention to your countertransference: your nonverbal responses are probably finely tuned after years of experience with clients.

(4) Be interested, and convey the attitude of acceptance, with clear and direct questions when dealing with an already-agitated client. Don't interrogate or challenge, but do ask about current and previous violence, availability of weapons, operative stress, and likely victims. Observe body language to assist you in determining within what part of the assault cycle the client is functioning. *The value of simply allowing the client to ventilate is dubious* when that ventilation is coupled with threats and agitated behaviors toward the therapist. Be gentle but persistent in attempting to defuse the situation. Don't worry about saying the wrong thing, as the attitude of acceptance on the therapist's part is much more important than word content.

    (a) Point out immediate and ultimate aversive consequences of proposed action.

    (b) Be clear about your wish not to be hurt—help the client understand your humanity and the importance of your safety.

    (c) Emphasize and reinforce self-control and self-control processes.

    (d) Consider medication, isolation and/or seclusion, relaxation methods, role playing assertion, physical activity, and other distracting/redirecting techniques.

    (e) Point out options to violence or have the client do the same; help formulate an alternative plan to achieve the client's goals.

(f) Give permission to leave the session *prior* to the client becoming threatened or threatening.

(g) Give yourself permission to leave the session if imminent harm is suspected or threatened. Don't stick around if you can help it. Police can be called from another telephone line. It is a low priority as to whether the client engages in property destruction in the office compared to your safety.

(5) Recognize that transference toward the therapist and counter-transference toward the client are crucial to outcomes. Don't argue with the client about feelings. Affirm your own affect when appropriate, especially if you are feeling fear, and proceed with the interview if you are sufficiently comfortable. Acknowledge fear when necessary, for example. This may *not* hold true for cases where the client has a history of sadistic violence after the victim exhibits pain cues or distress. In the latter situation, feelings of your own fear can be reframed in terms of questions designed to make explicit the direction of client threat. Making the covert overt often defuses a threat of violence toward the therapist.

(6) Leave the area immediately when violence is threatened or initiated. If that is impossible, start with the least-restrictive strategies and go to the most restrictive, that is physical interventions. Never attempt to control an assaultive incident if sufficiently trained and available team members are not present. Your job description should not include sustaining physical injury or getting killed; you may be a good therapist, but you are not a superhero.

(7) Seek consultation promptly after the violence. Prime consultation issues include whether to issue Tarasoff-type warnings to intended victims, the amount of outside intervention necessary to contain violence, and obtaining knowledge of the client by that consultant, if appropriate.

(8) Document all the previous seven steps, and specify a feedback mechanism to evaluate results of the intervention. Discuss the case at staff conference in order to disseminate all needed information and to dilute the negative impact on other staff members.

Basic Concepts and Working Materials

CONCEPTS. A rudimentary phenomenological network appears to have emerged in terms of predictor/perpetrator characteristics and dangerousness prediction accuracy. This will be expanded in the next chapter.

Findings relevant to *predictor* characteristics include the following:

(1) Demographic features such as older age, female sex, and lower educational level are associated with *perceiving* more behaviors as dangerous (Monahan and Hood, 1978).

(2) *Level of training influences outcome,* with predictive skills descending in
order from faculty members, to actuarial tables, to less experienced
clinical staff, to students (Shapiro, 1977).

(3) In their acceptance by referral sources who make predictions themselves (e.g., judges, probation officers), the value of the prediction
depends on how relevant data-forming conclusions were gathered
(i.e., with degree of impact descending from information obtained by
test-retest comparisons, citation of relevant recidivism statistics, to
the sole use of the clinical interview) (Hall and McLaughlin, 1981).

Findings relevant to *perpetrator* characteristics include the following:

(4) The predictee must have a *past history of violence* in order for the
examiner to forecast dangerousness, since base rates for violence
among previously nonviolent persons are low (Kozol, 1972; Bandura,
1975).

(5) This means the most accurate dangerousness predictions may be
toward repeat violence offenders, who as a subgroup, account for the
majority of violence-related arrests (Wolfgang, Figlio and Sellin,
1972; Petersilia, Greenwood and Lavin, 1977). These studies suggest
that up to 70 to 80 percent of cleared violence is perpetrated by a
small core of subjects that represents a minority of the criminal population. These persons may also account for violence that does not
result in arrest (Shinnar and Shinnar, 1975).

In the absence of other information, *base rates* are held to be the
best single predictor of dangerousness. For example, for those individuals convicted of a serious violent act, within four years, 70 percent are rearrested for rape, robbery, or aggravated assault (Kelly,
1976). With five or more arrests for violent crimes, the probability of
similar future arrests approaches certainty (PROMIS Research
Project, 1977). Unfortunately, clinicians must remember that base
rate information is available for very few target groups.

(6) Factors relevant to base rates include age, sex, and race, which are
generally disregarded by the courts and other criminal justice agencies for social-moral reasons, although some feel they are important
for an accurate prediction (Wilson, 1977).

(7) Since dangerousness is a nonunitary phenomenon, the direction of
violence (i.e., to others, property, self) must be specified since each
may have different probabilities of occurrence (Stone, 1975).

(8) Dangerousness prediction may be as good, or as bad, as future estimates of other low-base-rate violence phenomena such as suicide and

child abuse (Mischel, 1968; Heller and Monahan, 1977).

(9) Methods for establishing true basal violence and possible deception should be included in the dangerousness process (Ziskin, 1981; Hall, 1986).

(10) In their accuracy, first-generation dangerousness predictions ran around 25 percent for true positives. True negative accuracy averages about 85 percent, reflecting the easier task of predicting nondangerousness (e.g., Kozol, Boucher and Garofalo, 1972; Steadman and Cocozza, 1974; Cocozza and& Steadman, 1976; Steadman, 1977; Thornberry and Jacoby, 1979). The best predictor of true positives ranged from 35 to 40 percent (Kozol et al. 1972) Second-generation dangerousness predictions have pushed the true positive accuracy rate to about 70 percent with about the same batting average for true negatives as first-generation studies (e.g., Perkins, 1980; Hall, Catlin, Boissevain and Westgate, 1984). The new MacArthur findings have increased prediction rates by allowing us to focus on risk assessment, rather than on yes-no predictions.

MATERIALS.

(1) Be sure to use the dangerousness prediction cases provided in the appendices. Only by going through actual cases and examining your decision-making process can you hope to improve dangerousness prediction skills.

(2) The checklist of dangerousness factors in Appendix B is a handy tool to content analyze present and current behavior of the predictee. It can be used during actual examinations for dangerousness or when going over the individual prediction cases in this text. The checklist is a critical learning device in this book. Please refer to it frequently in your determinations. Included are relatively strong signs of possible future dangerousness, such as recent and serious past violence and a juvenile felony record, as well as unversified suggestions from the clinical literature. We are interested in the factors you choose, which in combination yield the highest degree of accuracy, and how you use these factors in a decision path to arrive at your prediction.

(3) The dangerousness prediction process factors as set out in Figure 1 should be referred to until the component parts are memorized. A full-blown version of the tree is presented in Chapter 6.

(4) The verbatim format for reporting of dangerousness presented in Appendix C will save the predictor much evaluation time while addressing most of the important issues in the evaluation. This format has been identified as one of the most important byproducts of violence-prediction training.

Chapter 4

TOWARD DECISION ANALYSIS
AND VIOLENCE PREDICTION:
SECOND GENERATION AND BEYOND

S OCIAL CHANGES FOLLOWING THE CIVIL RIGHTS REVOLUTION in the United States in the 1960s had unintended impact upon all levels of society, including mental health treatment and hospitalization, and indirectly increased the need for mental health professionals to become skilled in the prediction of violence.

Concepts of equal justice and the use of law to obtain relief for disadvantaged populations quickly spread from battles over desegregation in the schools and in public life to unequal treatment and life-long incarceration for disabled populations. For years in the 1970s, legal redress was applied to overcrowded and inhumane conditions in institutions housing both mentally retarded and mentally ill inmates.

Wyatt v. Stickney (1971) , a major lawsuit against the State of Alabama, began when a cut in the Alabama cigarette tax resulted in the layoff of almost 100 state personnel at Tuscaloosa's mental hospital. The subsequent suit claimed that the staff cuts meant a loss of treatment for involuntarily committed patients. The court of appeals agreed, but more importantly held that civilly committed mental patients have a constitutional right to treatment in order to reduce the danger to themselves or to others.

Only one year later, in *Lessard v. Schmidt,* the U.S. District Court held that Wisconsin's civil commitment procedures denied due process safeguards when Alberta Lessard was committed based solely on a finding of mental illness. The court concluded that the state must use the same due process safeguards when deciding civil commitment as those used when determining incarceration for a crime.

O'Connor, a patient in Florida for 15 years, had regularly requested release and was just as regularly turned down. He filed suit (*O'Connor v.*

Donaldson, 1975) claiming that he had been deprived of a constitutional right to freedom as well as a lack of proper treatment. The court supported O'Connor's right to treatment, but protected the public official (Donaldson) from liability because he was acting under state statute.

These cases, and others, became landmark rulings that served to redefine civil commitment practices to replace earlier life-long hospitalization without due process. As new state statutes defining civil commitment spread across the nation, the untested assumption that mental health professionals could determine dangerousness as one of the prongs for such commitment became a daily necessity for the staffs of such facilities.

In 1969, Tatiana Tarasoff was murdered by Prosenjit Poddar, a graduate student at the University of California, and after years of litigation, the now famous Tarasoff standard was made law (*Tarasoff v. Regents of the University of California*, 1976). Poddar once dated Ms. Tarasoff and quickly became obsessed with her. When she traveled to South America, he entered therapy at the University counseling office. The intake psychiatrist was quite concerned and prescribed a neuroleptic, telling his patient that he felt Poddar was quite troubled. He referred Poddar to a psychologist for ongoing treatment, where on August 18, 1968, the student revealed fantasies of killing Tatiana.

After learning of Poddar's plan to buy a gun, the therapist consulted the supervising psychiatrist. They agreed hospitalization was appropriate, and the therapist contacted the campus police by phone and letter, asking their assistance in commitment. Unfortunately for all, especially Ms. Tarasoff, a new commitment law had recently passed in California, and different procedures should have been followed. Rather than campus police, the local police were the appropriate authority, and they should have transported Poddar to a psychiatric facility for evaluation. Instead, the campus police interviewed Poddar in his apartment, where he denied any intention to harm. They warned him to stay away from the victim and left. He dropped out of treatment and moved in with the victim's brother. Two months later, Poddar confronted Tatiana Tarasoff after her return and killed her.

Following this horrific act, the family sued claiming negligence on the part of the police and the clinicians: the police for not detaining Poddar and the clinicians for not warning Tatiana. After the court dismissed the complaint, a 1974 appeal to the California Supreme Court concluded in the Tarasoff's favor. The court found a duty to warn: "When a doctor or a psychotherapist, in the exercise of his professional skill and knowledge, determines, or should determine, that a warning is essential to avert danger arising from the medical or psychological condition of his patient, he incurs a legal obligation to give that warning" (*Tarasoff v. Regents of the University of California*, 1976, p. 914).

This legal finding stung mental health professionals as no other yet. The professional organizations filed briefs with the court asking for a rehearing, arguing that therapists' predictive abilities were nil and that breaching confidentiality would harm, if not destroy, the therapeutic relationship. Because of the strength of these arguments, the California Supreme Court reheard the case and issued a second Tarasoff finding in 1976. This opinion again found a duty by the therapist to the victim, but the duty was defined more broadly and shifted the focus from a duty to warn to one that protects the intended victim: "When a therapist determines or pursuant to the standard of his profession should determine, that his patient presents a serious danger of violence to another, he incurs an obligation to use reasonable care to protect the intended victim against such danger. The discharge of this duty may require the therapist to take one or more of various steps depending upon the nature of the case. Thus it may call for him to warn the intended victim or others likely to apprise the intended victim of danger, to notify the police, or take whatever steps are reasonably necessary under the circumstances" (*Tarasoff v. Regents of the University of California*, 1976, p. 346).

Not only did mental health professionals now have to predict the dangerousness of their patients for purposes of commitment, but they had to anticipate the likelihood that a dangerous patient could act to harm a third party. Once they determined (or should have determined) this, they were required to take action to protect that third party. Thus, the assessment of dangerousness had shifted from an esoteric, questionably valid event to one legally required by all community based clinicians. Just as civil commitment legislation spread across the land state by state, so now Tarasoff-like cases began to proliferate in different jurisdictions (e.g., *McIntosh v. Milano*, 1979; *Davis v. Lihm*, 1981; *Jablonski v. U.S.*, 1983 and *Peterson v. Washington*, 1983). Case law invariably affirmed the California Supreme Court's view that clinicians have a duty to warn and to protect third parties. In anticipation of future judicial mandates, some states took a preemptive road and developed Tarasoff-like legislation with the aid of professional associations. In Massachusetts, for example, the state psychiatric association and the state psychological association took the unusual step of joining hands to develop and advocate for such legislation. Thus, by the mid-1980s, whether through court order, legislative mandate, or voluntary action, psychologists, psychiatrists, and social workers became united in the awareness of their need to be able to predict and prevent the dangerousness of their patients, whether inpatient or outpatient.

If Tarasoff was not sufficiently compeling, *Gregg v. Georgia* (1976) served to intensify the need for valid means of predicting dangerousness when capital punishment was deemed constitutional under certain circumstances. Now the need for mental health professionals to predict future dangerousness carried a different sort of life-or-death implications—the prediction of future dangerousness might serve to support capital punishment. Hardly had clinicians begun to digest this troubling news, when a case in Texas provided powerful evidence of how questionable clinical testimony could affect capital murder cases. *Barefoot v. Estelle* (1980) involved the embarrassing spectacle of a clinician predicting future dangerousness without ever having interviewed the individual, and this occurred in a hearing that resulted in a determination that the predicted likelihood of future violence justified execution. Not insignificantly, the unsuccessful appeal of this case noted that the body of professional literature argued against the ability of clinicians to predict dangerousness at a better-than-chance level.

John Monahan wrote a now-classic 1981 monograph, *The Clinical Prediction of Violent Behavior* in which he reviewed the research to date concerning the ability of mental health clinicians to predict dangerousness. As Randy Otto notes in his 1992 review *Prediction of Dangerous Behavior: A review and analysis of "second generation research*:

> The findings were not encouraging. Perhaps the most discouraging findings cited by Monahan were those from studies in which mental health professionals' predictions of dangerousness were compared to actual outcomes (e.g., Cocozza and Steadman, 1976; Kozol, Boucher, and Garofalo, 1972; Steadman, 1977; Steadman and Halton, 1973; Steadman and Keveles, 1972; Thornberry and Jacoby, 1979). The subjects in these studies were typically individuals who had been institutionalized (in forensic, psychiatric, or penal settings) and then released, either in accordance with or against the recommendation of one or more mental health professionals. In his review of these studies, Monahan concluded, "The 'best' clinical research currently in existence indicates that *psychiatrists and psychologists are accurate in no more than one out of three predictions of violent behavior over a several year period among institutionalized populations that had both committed violence in the past (and thus had high base rates for it) and who were diagnosed as mentally ill* (1981, emphasis in original).

Despite these gloomy findings, Monahan was optimistic that clinicians could improve the accuracy of their predictions by focusing on actuarial methods and increasing their sensitivity to environmental variables. Thus, Monahan's stand was not that clinicians could not accurately predict violent behavior, but rather that tools were at hand and were being developed that would increase the accuracy of such predictions, if clinicians opened themselves to such data gathering. He additionally indicated that short-term predictions were likely to have a higher rate of accuracy than were the long-term predictions, based upon the research he cited. Yet, the "soundbite" concerning inaccurate predictions two thirds of the time became a siren call for those who attempted to close the doors on such predictions. Fortunately the debate that raged as a consequence of Monahan's monograph led not only to the predictable criticism and calls for abolition of civil commitment, but, importantly, to increased research that took into account Monahan's original discussion of the shortcomings of earlier research.

Otto's 1992 article reviewed the results of 10 years of post-Monahan research, labeling it "second generation" research (post-1980 work that incorporated Monahan's 1981 suggestions). He divided these into studies that examined base rates of dangerous behavior among the mentally ill and studies that examined predictive issues.

He concluded his analysis by expressing surprise that only a small number of relevant studies had been published in those ten years. Yet he noted optimistically that because these studies had incorporated a number of Monahan's suggestions, the picture "looks somewhat brighter than it did ten years ago." (Otto, 1992, p. 129) He pointed out that the changes in methodology now suggested that dangerous behavior was not a very low base-rate behavior, as had commonly been thought, particularly among mentally ill people with a prior history of such behavior. Not only did these findings ease the task for clinical prediction by reducing the likelihood of error rates, the research also strengthened the argument for predictive abilities among mental health professionals. He was now able to conclude "mental health professionals do better than chance when trying to identify people who may go on to threaten or hurt themselves or others." (Otto, 1992, p. 129) Thus, in ten years the ability of mental health professionals to predict dangerousness had risen from one in three to better than one in two. No longer could it be said that the mandates of the courts in Tarasoff and in Lessard were unjustly placed on the shoulders of professionals unable to carry out these duties; rather therapists now had to brace themselves to carry the weight of society's demands.

Importantly, a new understanding of prediction was taking place. It was now clear that it was necessary to distinguish between short-term and long-term prediction and to focus on limiting prediction to subsets of the population, such as mentally ill individuals with a history of aggression.

Writing in the same 1992 issue of *Forensic Reports* as Otto, Norman G. Poythress focused on expert testimony concerning dangerousness, given the many prior calls for abolition of such testimony. He noted the satisfying progress reported in the literature to date and recognized the potential of actuarial approaches to improve accuracy of prediction; he also felt, however, that it was premature to limit expert testimony solely to statistical studies, as some argued. He supported the role of mental health clinicians in providing "descriptive clinical and anecdotal information" (Poythress, 1992, p. 145) as experts and suggested that testimony concerning research findings on behavioral correlates of violence recidivism would be helpful as well. He recommended that mental health testimony could address risk-management precautions based upon an analysis of individualized risk factors. In sum, although his presentation argued for caution and awareness of our limitations, seen in the context of the prior years of calls for abolition and restriction of mental health professionals from the courtroom, this came as a breath of fresh air for those laboring in the trenches.

John Monahan and Henry Steadman edited *Violence and Mental Disorder: Developments and Risk Assessment* in 1994, pulling together the new trends in dangerousness prediction and laying the foundation for what was to become the MacArthur Risk Assessment Study. Seven methodological principles were identified that were to shape the design of this newest approach to risk assessment research:

(1) "Dangerousness" must be disaggregated into its component parts—the variables used to predict violence (risk factors), the amount and type of violence being predicted (harm), and the likelihood that harm will occur (risk).

(2) A rich array of theoretically chosen risk factors in multiple domains must be chosen.

(3) Harm must be scaled in terms of seriousness and assessed with multiple measures.

(4) Risk must be treated as a probability estimate that changes over time and context.

(5) Priority must be given to actuarial research that establishes a relationship between risk factors and harm.

(6) Large and broadly representative samples of patients at multiple, coordinated sites, must participate in the research.

(7) Managing risk as well as assessing risk must be a goal of the research. (Monahan & Steadman, 1994, 297)

Henry Steadman led the talented group of professionals who conducted this remarkable "new generation" multiple-site study. A total of 1,136 male and female patients were carefully selected from populations at the Western Psychiatric Institute and Clinic at the University of Pittsburgh, the Western Missouri Mental Health Center in Kansas City, and the Worcester State Hospital and the University of Massachusetts Medical Center in Worcester, Massachusetts. One hundred and thirty different variables were included for study, and these were grouped into four areas: personal factors, historical/developmental factors, contextual/structural factors, and clinical factors.

This multi-year project produced rich and important results, both for public policy and for clinical practice. For example, Steadman et al. (1998) demonstrates "no significant difference between the prevalence of violence by patients without symptoms of substance abuse, and the prevalence of violence by others living in the same neighborhoods who are also without symptoms of substance abuse." Thus, the common belief that mentally ill individuals pose a higher risk of danger than those without mental illness is shown definitively not to be based on fact in comparisons of populations who are not abusing substances. Importantly, substance abuse significantly raises the rate of violence in both samples. It drove the one-year prevalence rate from 17.9 percent for mental patients without substance abuse to 31.1 percent for those with combined major mental disorder and substance abuse. The rate soared to 43.0 percent for patients with "some other form of mental disorder" (e.g., character disorder) as well as substance abuse.

Of predictive interest is that people at highest risk of assault by such patients were family members in their homes or in the patient's home. The form of violence was interestingly similar, whether committed by discharged patients or by community members. Thus, this aspect of the MacArthur Risk Assessment study served to clarify that discharged mental patients are generally not likely to be more dangerous than their community neighbors. The study underscores the need to see such people not as a homogeneous group but rather as members of discrete subgroups and to recognize the significant impact of substance abuse and other mental disorder (e.g., personality disorder such as antisocial personality) when imposed upon *major mental illness.*

Based upon this work, the most salient factors among the 130 variables studied as posing increased risk for persons hospitalized for treatment of a mental disorder are, in order of salience:

1.   Psychopathy or antisocial personality disorder diagnosis;
2.   Prior arrests as an adult in terms of seriousness and frequency;
3.   Substance abuse history;
4.   No major mental disorder;
5.   Anger as measured by the Novaco Scale;
6.   Father's use of drugs or arrests;
7.   Violent fantasies as measured by the schedule of imagined violence;
8.   Serious abuse as a child.

Importantly, only psychopathy and prior-arrest factors were strongly correlated for increased risk. The remaining factors had a positive but low (less than 0.2) correlation.

It should be noted that eligibility criteria for the patients sampled included civil admissions, ages 18 to 40, English speaking, white or black ethnicity, and a medical record diagnosis of major mental illness, alcohol or drug abuse, or a personality disorder.

Surely future research will grow from this carefully structured work to search out those factors that are predictive of violent behavior in other discrete populations. Until that time, the forensic clinician will do well to learn the lessons of the past years of research of predictive studies, to examine carefully and closely those variables known to have high predictive validity, to narrowly focus on subpopulations, to be aware of the value of actuarial approaches, and to be ever so careful to not broaden conclusions beyond available data.

Chapter 5, *Violence Prediction and Risk Analysis: Empirical Advances, Guidelines, and Report Sample,* outlines the quantitatively derived methods that have been developed to date that increase prediction analysis to levels previously thought to be impossible.

Chapter 5

VIOLENCE PREDICTION AND RISK
ANALYSIS EMPIRICAL ADVANCES,
GUIDELINES AND REPORT SAMPLE

THIS CHAPTER FOCUSES ON ADVANCES in violence risk analysis and provides a sample report for use with clinical-forensic settings and situations. The focus is on quantitatively derived methods and decision analysis. Little doubt exists that violence risk assessment based on statistically derived empirical factors and decision analysis is superior to a purely clinical assessment (Breiman, Friedman, Olshen, and Stone, 1984; Gottfredson and Gottfredson, 1988; Grove and Meehl, 1996). In regard to sex offender recidivism across various studies and investigations, for example, Hanson (1998) found strong support for statistical assessment ($r = .46$) as opposed to clinical assessment ($r = .10$), the latter not much better than chance. Hanson's finding actually reflects a trend favoring quantitative methods regarding violence prediction over the last five decades involving a wide variety of subpopulation groups (Bonta and Hanson, 1994; Bonta, Law, and Hanson, 1998; Borum and Otto, 2000; Gardner, Lidz, Mulvey, and Shaw, 1996; Hall, 1987; Quinsey, Rice, and Harris, 1995).

Let's consider the evolution of risk analysis. The first generation of violence prediction methods from an applied perspective consisted of unstructured clinical opinion, a method that did not come close to meeting the rigorous standards demanded in forensic settings and situations. A second generation consisting of structured clinical opinion did not fare much better due to the low reliability and validity of the methods employed. A proliferation of research in the 1980s provided the basis for a third generation of violence prediction methods–empirically guided evaluation (Becker and Coleman,

---

This chapter is based upon one that will appear in Hall, H.V., *Workplace violence: Effective prediction and intervention strategies.* Kamuela, HI: Pacific Institute for the Study of Conflict and Aggression (2001).

1988; Hall, 1987; Hall, Catlin, Boissevain, and Westgate, 1984; Klassen and O'Connor, 1989; Menzies, Webster and Sepejak, 1985; Nuttfield, 1982; Webster, Harris, Rice, Cormier, and Quinsey, 1994). A variety of findings were empirically established relating to history (e.g., multiple, recent violence; a past history of different kinds of violence; reinforcing results from violence; child abuse; violent parent or sibling models), opportunity factors associated with violence (e.g., recent purchase of a lethal weapon, cessation of psychotropic medication, release into the community) and triggering stimuli (e.g., substance intoxication, breakup of the central love relationship). Many, if not most, forensic professionals currently utilize empirically guided evaluation methods for a variety of reasons. Not only are the methods mantled in scientific methodology, and in fact more accurate than clinical opinion, they are also in the author's experience usually well received by referral sources and the criminal courts.

A fourth generation consisting of pure actuarial measures began to appear in the mid-1990s and continues to this day (Hanson and Thornton, 2000; Quinsey, Harris, Rice, and Cormier, 1998; Quinsey, Rice, and Harris, 1995). These scales yielded quantitative degrees of certainty for violent recidivism, ranging from one year to 10 years. As such, the actuarial measures represented a quantum advancement in violence prediction. Researchers are no longer vexed by violence representing a low base-rate phenomenon. Rather, the problem has been resolved through the use of statistical methods such as Receiver Operating Characteristics (ROC), first developed in communications technology and in signal detection theory in psychophysics, that looks at the tradeoff between hit rate and false alarm rate in predicting violent events. ROCs permit estimating the true test accuracy to yield an effect size that is unaffected by different selection ratios and base rates; ROCs have been utilized extensively in the creation of actuarial devices to predict violence. Some test developers allow forensic professionals to clinically adjust the fourth-generation actuarial measure (e.g., due to the predictee developing a sudden debilitating illness, incorporating verified violence that did not result in arrest or conviction), as long as the modifications are slight and do not violate the measure's underlying statistical assumptions (e.g., see Hanson, 1998; Hanson and Bussiere, 1998). Others discourage this practice if the predetermined probabilities associated with given scores are to be utilized (e.g., see Quinsey, et al., 1998).

A recent fifth generation consists of combinations of the earlier work, and is commonly advocated by leading forensic practitioners who routinely predict violence in the course of their forensic work (Meloy, 2000; Salter, 1988). A variety of actuarial and other empirically based methods are typically employed along with reporting the findings for each measure in the risk analysis report. The evaluator then usually opines on the overall risk of violent recidivism within a given time period, citing the basis for the proffered conclusion.

A projected sixth generation may consist of violence prediction measures that attempt to reflect the real-life clinical thinking and the overall, sometimes mind-boggling, complexity in individual cases. Prior to 2000, only two such empirically derived decision paths were available: The Assaultive Risk Screening Sheet of the State of Michigan, reported by Monahan (1981a), for use in prison assignment and parole decision making, and the Dangerousness Prediction Decision Tree (Hall, 1987), which offers a short-term violence prediction for a three-month period and will be discussed in Chapter 6.

The Michigan group obtained a 40 percent accuracy, denoting a 40 percent recidivism (true-positive) rate for 4.7 percent of the sample of 2,200 inmates released on parole simply by noting whether (a) the crime description fit robbery, sex assault, or murder; (b) the inmates showed serious institutional misconduct; and (c) the inmates were first arrested before their 15th birthday. A 98 percent (true-negative) rate, denoting a very low risk, was obtained by 19.7 percent of the sample by noting (a) no serious type of crimes committed—robbery, sex assault, or murder; (b) no juvenile felony; (c) no assaultive felonies; and (d) if the inmate was ever married. This decision analysis is simple to utilize, merely following the path to its assigned risk category (Monahan, 1981a, p. 61).

This sixth-generation classification tree approach for decision analysis, rather than a main-effects regression approach, may thus provide an opportunity to assist the forensic professional in a user-friendly, direct fashion. Steadman, Silver, Monahan, Appelbaum, Robbins, Mulvey, Grisso, Roth, and Banks (2000) elucidated how the classification tree approach can employ two decision thresholds for identifying high- and low-risk cases. Their approach is congruent with findings from the MacArthur Violence Risk Assessment Study. In this way, conclusions can be directly tied into proposed treatment and risk management strategies in terms of differential intensities of treatment and monitoring of the two classifications. The classification tree approach is also highly compatible with artificial intelligence methodology. Table VI presents the extant empirical methods.

The empirically based violence prediction systems from Table VI, which are available in the mental health-law interface today, are presented in the following pages. Again, keep in mind that development of empirically based violence prediction scales has been vigorously addressed by investigators only since 1986 (e.g., Hall, 1987; Hanson, 1998; Hanson and Bussiere, 1998; Monahan and Steadman, 1994; Quinsey, et al., 1998). At this stage, statistical analyses in validation studies show that the systems are far less than perfect in terms of *sensitivity* (e.g., percentage of true positives) and *specificity* (i.e.,

TABLE VI
PROMISING EMPIRICALLY BASED VIOLENCE PREDICTION SYSTEMS

Test or method	Predictor variables	Application or findings	References
Seriousness scoring system	History of harm/injury, sex acts, and intimidation (based on survey responses of 60,000 Americans)	Identifies high seriousness scores for possible intervention; demonstrates escalation over time for individuals	Wolfgang, Figlio, Tracy, & Singer (1985)
Meta-analysis of predictors of general and violent recidivism	Objective risk assessment, juvenile delinquency, family problems, other factors (based on 52 studies; 16,191 persons)	Recidivism factors for mentally disordered offenders same as for nondisordered offenders; criminal history best predictor; clinical factors, worst	Bonta, Law, & Hanson (1998)
Psychopathy Checklist–Revised (PCL–R)	Factors suggesting exploitation of others and chronically unstable lifestyle, few violence-related items	PCL–R scores the best single predictor of violence, although scale was not designed for such; for adult males only	Hare (1991)
Violent Risk Appraisal Guide (VRAG)	Developmental, personality, nonviolent and violent history items; includes PCL–R score	Predicts for 7 and 10 years the risk of violent (non-sexual) acts, yielding percentiles; for adult males only	Quinsey, Harris, Rice, & Cormier (1998)
Sex Offender Risk Appraisal Guide (SORAG)	Development, personality, nonviolent and violent history, deviant sexual preferences	Predicts for 7 and 10 years the risk of violent (sexual) assaults, yielding percentage score; for adult males only	Quinsey, et al. (1998)
Meta-analysis of predictors of sexual violence	Deviant sexual arousal, violence history, personality factors (based on 61 studies; 28,972 persons)	15–30 year follow-up showed 77% chance of reoffending for previous sex offenses, boy victims, and never married status, as one finding	Hanson & Bussiere (1998)

Continued on next page

percentage of true negatives). Using multiple measures and methods to predict violence is therefore strongly recommended, along with presenting the appropriate caveats and limitations in the forensic report.

TABLE VI–*Continued*

Test or method	Predictor variables	Application or findings	References
Rapid Risk Assessment for Sexual Offense Recidivism (RRASOR)	Includes victim and victim-relationship factors, prior sexual offenses, age of release (total sample size of 2,592 persons)	Predicts recidivism rates for 5- and 10-year periods based on four factors gleaned from review of administrative records	Hanson (1997)
Minnesota Sex Offender Screening Test–Revised (MnSOST–R)	History, victim, substance use, other factors	Predicts for 6 years high-versus low-risk sex offenders	Epperson, Kaul, & Huot (1995)
Static and dynamic risk-assessment tools	History of sex offenses, demographic factors, attitudes	Provides for low, medium, high risk of sexual offenses	Hanson (1997); Hanson, & Steffy (1992)
Dangerousness prediction decision tree	Remote/recent History of violence, Opportunity, Triggers (HOT) after inhibitions taken into account	Predicts for 3 months whether individual is more likely to be high risk for violent acting out, using a 5-step decision path	Hall (1987); Hall & Ebert (in press)
Spousal Assault Risk Assessment Guide (SARA)	Spousal assault, criminal history, psychosocial adjustment, alleged most recent (based on 2,309 adult male offenders)	Summary ratings include risk of violence toward partner, as well as toward others in general; risk management strategies associated with SARA scores	Kropp, Hart, Webster, & Eaves (1999)
Sexual, Violence, Risk (SVR–20)	Professional guidelines for assessment of risk for sexual violence	Researched in Europe, translated into several languages	Boar, Hart, Kropp, & Webster (1997)
Historical, Clinical, Risk Management (HCR–20, Version 2)	Risk factors include 10 Historical, 5 Clinical, and 5 Risk Management items presented within a set of professional guidelines	Researched in Europe, translated into several lanaguages	Webster, Douglas, Eaves, & Hart (1997)
California Actuarial Risk Assessment Tables (CARAT)	Victim and sex-offense history factors	Yields percent reoffenses within 5 years for child molesters, rapists	Schiller & Marques (1999)

Continued on next page

TABLE VI–*Continued*

Test or method	Predictor variables	Application or findings	References
Level of Service Inventory–Revised (LSI–R)	Risk/needs assessment tool prompts data in most areas of offender's life	Score related to institutional problems, likelihood of early release, recidivism, self-reported criminal activities; parole outcome, halfway house success	Andrews & Bonta (1995)
The Workplace Violence Risk Assessment Checklist (WVRAC)	Risk factors include historical, recent critical events, work attitudes and traits; yields guidelines rather than representing test or scale	For use in workplace or vocationaly-related areas	Hall & Pritchard, 2001

Discussion of Methods

Seriousness Scoring System

The seriousness scoring system shows the degree of harm resulting from violence by adding up the statistically derived values for each act of previous violent behavior within a given time period. The scoring system stems from the U.S. Department of Justice's National Survey of Crime Severity by Wolfgang, Figlio, Tracy, and Singer (1985). Based on the responses of more than 60,000 Americans, this system, for the first time, provides an easily derived, quantitative score for the amount of harm that an individual has perpetrated during a particular act, a circumscribed time period (e.g., one, five or ten years), or even over the lifetime of the individual, if that is of interest. The following sections, summarized in Table VII and described by the U.S. Department of Justice in their publication (1985), demonstrate how to calculate point values and utilize the system.

I. NUMBER OF PERSONS INJURED. Each victim receiving some bodily injury during an event must be accounted for. Physical injuries typically occur as a direct result of assaultive events, but can be caused by other events as well. The four levels of bodily injury are:

(a) Minor harm–An injury that requires or receives no professional medical attention. The victim may, for instance, be pushed, shoved, kicked, or knocked down, and receive a minor wound (e.g., cut, bruise).

(b) Treated and discharged–The victim receives professional medical treatment but is not detained for further medical care.

(c) Hospitalized–The victim requires inpatient care in a medical facility,

TABLE VII
SEROUSNESS SCORING SYSTEM[1,2]

Score sheet_____

Name and identifcation number(s):_____

Component scored	Number of Victims	x	Scale Weight	=	Total
I. Injury					
(a) Minor harm	____		1.47		_____
(b) Treated and discharged	____		8.53		_____
(c) Hospitalized	____		11.98		_____
(d) Kille	____		35.67		_____
II. Forcible sex acts	____		25.92		_____
III. Intimidation					
(a) Verbal or physical	____		4.90		_____
(b) Weapon	____		5.60		_____
IV. Premises forcibly entered	____		1.50		_____
V. Motor vehicle stolen					
(a) Recovered	____		4.46		_____
(b) Not recovered	____		8.07		_____
VI. Property theft/damage (optional)	____				_____
				TOTAL SCORE	_____

[1] U.S. Department of Justice (1985)

[2] $\log 10Y = .26776656 \log 10X$ where Y = crime severity weight
W = total dollar value of theft or damage

regardless of its duration, or outpatient care for three or more clinical visits.

(d) Killed–The victim dies as a result of the injuries, regardless of the circumstances under which they are inflicted.

II. SEXUAL INTERCOURSE BY FORCE. This event occurs when a person is intimidated and forced against his or her will to engage in a sexual act (e.g., rape, incest, sodomy). Such an event may have more than one victim, and the score depends on the number of such victims.

A forcible sex act is always accomplished by intimidation. Thus, the event must also be scored for the type of intimidation involved as described in subitem III. Intimidation is scored for all victims in a forcible sexual act. The victim of one or more forcible sexual acts is always assumed to have suffered at least minor harm during the event. Even when medical examination may not reveal any injuries, the event must be scored for minor harm. This level of injury should also be scored when the victim is examined by a physician only to ascertain if a sexually transmitted disease has been transmitted or to collect evidence that the sexual act was completed.

III. INTIMIDATION. Intimidation occurs when one or more victims is threatened with bodily harm or some other serious consequences for the purpose of forcing the victims to obey the request of the offenders to give up something of value or to assist in a criminal event that leads to someone's bodily injury, the theft of or damage to property, or both. Ordinary assault and battery, aggravated assault and battery, or homicide are not to be scored for intimidation merely because someone was assaulted or injured. The event must also have included the threat of force for intimidation to have been present. With the exception of forcible sexual acts, criminal events involving intimidation are scored only once, regardless of the number of victims who are intimidated. The types of intimidation are:

(a) Physical or verbal–Physical intimidation means the use of strong-arm tactics (e.g., threats with fists, menacing gestures). Verbal intimidation means spoken threats not supported by the overt display of a weapon or by body language.

(b) Intimidation by weapon–This involves display of a weapon (e.g, firearm, cutting or stabbing instrument, blunt instrument) capable of inflicting serious bodily injury.

IV, V, VI. THEFT RELATED. Use of the categories on theft is optional. To retain the severity system as a pure measure of violence, the evaluator may wish to delete these categories. The other scores will remain the same.

The relevance of a total severity score (net harm) for global sentencing considerations should not be overlooked. Total net harm represented by an instant offense, for example, can be linked to victim restitution criteria or to sentencing procedures, thus adding a quantitative dimension to a notoriously subjective task.

Forensic professionals may wish to determine if an individual's violence is escalating over time. A declining slope suggests deceleration, much as an upward slope suggests escalating violence. The senior author has used acceleration/deceleration data in court but always in conjunction with other predictive methods (Hall, 1987; Hall and Pritchard, 1996; Hall and Sbordone, 1993). The key question is whether the violence act under scrutiny represented an ongoing trend or the last gasp of a fading propensity. Only additional clinical-forensic information can answer this question.

Violence Meta-analysis

The meta-analysis by Bonta, Law, and Hanson (1998), involving 52 studies and 16,191 persons, was conducted to determine whether the predictors of recidivism for mentally disordered offenders were different from the predictors for nondisordered offenders. They were the same. Effect sizes were calculated for 27 predictors of violent recidivism. Criminal history variables were the best predictors and clinical variables the worst. Bonta et al. suggested that risk assessment of mentally disordered offenders can be enhanced with a focus on the criminological literature and less reliance on notions of psychopathology. The predictors for violent recidivism are presented in Table VIII. The authors use predictors of effect sizes equal to or greater than .10 or -.10, a practice with some statistical support.

Psychopathy Checklist–Revised (PCL–R)

Because Hare's (1991) well-received Psychopathy Checklist–Revised (PCL–R) is commonly embedded in several validated predictive systems (e.g., see VRAG, SORAG, HCR-20, SVR-20 in Table VI), the abbreviated and other versions of the PCL will not be discussed in this chapter. The PCL–R yields information on two main factors that make up psychopathology. Factor I–the selfish, callous, and remorseless use of others (e.g., items reflecting superficial charm, pathological lying, manipulation, lack of remorse, failure to accept responsibility for own actions); and Factor II–a chronically unstable, antisocial, and socially disruptive lifestyle (e.g., items reflecting a high need for stimulation, early behavior problems, parasitic lifestyle, poor behavioral controls). Hare recommends a cutoff score of 30 to diagnose psychopathy. Others use a lower cutoff score, such as 26, to operationally define a high PCL–R score and therefore determine whether psychopathology is present (e.g., Grann, Langstrom, Tengstrom, & Kullgren, 1999).

According to Zinger and Furth (1998), Canadian courts have encountered three problems with the PCL–R, all of which the author has observed in American courts. First, experts frequently render substantially different PCL–R scores for the same defendant. Defense experts typically present lower scores on the PCL–R for the defendant compared to their prosecution counterparts. Second, some forensic mental health professionals use the PCL–R on populations other than the normative base (e.g., women, adolescents). Third, Canadian courts have been provided with PCL–R scores based solely on a records review, which generally underestimates the total scores slightly. Hare (1991, 1996) points out that omitting the interview is acceptable only if "extensive" collateral information is available.

Violence Risk Appraisal Guide (VRAG)

The best extant measure of violent recidivism is the Violence Risk Appraisal Guide (VRAG) (Quinsey, et al., 1998). The VRAG is the culmination of 25 years of research with mentally disordered offenders at a psychiatric facility at Penetanguishene, Ontario, Canada. The sample of more

TABLE VIII
PREDICTORS OF VIOLENT RECIDIVISM[1]

Predictor	Violent recidivism	N	k
Objective risk assessment	.30	2,186	9
Adult criminal history	.14	2,163	8
Juvenile delinquency	.20	985	3
Antisocial personality	.18	1,634	3
Nonviolent criminal history	.13	1,108	4
Institutional adjustment	.14	711	4
Hospital admissions	.17	948	3
Poor living arrangements	NR		
Gender (male)	NR		
Substance abuse (any)	.08	2,013	4
Family problems	.19	1,481	5
Escape history	NR		
Violent history	.16	2,878	9
Drug abuse	NR		
Marital status (single)	.13	1,068	4
Weapon	.12	716	2
	Mixed relationships		
Days hospitalized	-.09	850	4
Alcohol abuse	NR		
Employment problems	.22	1,326	5
Clinical judgment	.09	786	3
Education	-.02	1,066	4
Intelligence	-.02	1,873	4
Socioeconomic status	NR		
Race (minority)	.09	999	3
	Negative relationships		
Mentally disordered offender	-.10	2,866	6
Homicide index offense	NR		
Age	-.18	1,519	5
Violent index	-.04	2,241	6
Violent index (broadly defined)	.08	1,950	7
Sex offense	.04	1,636	3
Not guilty by reason of insanity	-.07	1,208	3
Psychosis	-.04	3,891	11
Mood disorder	.01	1,520	3
Treatment history	NR		
Offense seriousness	.06	1,879	5

[1] Adapted from Bonta, Law, & Hanson (1998).

than 600 males, all of whom had a basal history of serious violence, were followed over a ten-year period after release. Correlation between VRAG scores and violent recidivism was .44 and, by utilizing the 80th percentile, classification accuracy was 74 percent, with a sensitivity of .40 (true positives) and a specificity of .88 (true negatives). Probabilities of violent recidivism are presented by the authors both for seven and ten years.

The 12-item measure consists of the following predictors, with score weightings available in the Quinsey, et al. (1998) text:
• Lived with both biological parents to age 16
• Elementary school maladjustment
• History of alcohol problems
• Marital status
• Criminal history score for nonviolent offenses
• Failure on prior conditional release
• Index offense
• Victim injury in index offense
• Any female victim in index offense
• Meets DSM–III criteria for any personality disorder
• Meets DSM–III criteria for schizophrenia
• Psychopathology Checklist-Revised score

Support for the VRAG's reliability and validity, as well as its applicability to other populations, continues to mount (e.g., see Barbaree and Seto, 1998; Grann, Belfrage, and Tengström, 2000; Hanson and Harris, 1999; Kroner and Mills, 1997; Nadeau, Nadeau, Smiley, and McHattie, 1998; Nichols, Vincent, Whittemore, & Ogloff, 1999).

The forensic clinician should note that the VRAG for adults can be used without directly measuring psychopathy through PCL–R scores. The PCL–R is simply scored zero and the same probability table is utilized to calculate risk of violent recidivism (Quinsey, personal communication, 2000).

If the predictee is a psychopath, however, the obtained probability of risk may be lower than expected. In cases where psychopathology is suspected, therefore, the actual PCL–R score should be derived and included in the VRAG scoring. Alternatively, the Child and Adult Taxon Scale–CATS–discussed in the following paragraph, can replace the PCL.

The PCL–R score in the VRAG can be replaced in its entirety by the Child and Adolescent Taxon Scale (Quinsey, et al., 1998). The CATS illustrates the static nature of the VRAG and supports the authors' speculation that psychopathology is a life-history strategy. Importantly, such replacement allows the forensic clinician to calculate risk from the same probability table used in the original measure. The univariate correlation for the CATS is essentially the same as the PCL–R (d = 1.04, ROC area = .75; in a separate study, $r = .975$, with 54 mentally disordered offenders). The CATS has many of the same items, with the CATS more heavily loaded on Factor 2 of the PCL-R, reflecting a disruptive, conflictual lifestyle. The CATS items, with illustrated scoring in Quinsey, et al. (1998) include several VRAG items and, in addition, more than three DSM-III Conduct Disorders symptoms, ever suspended or expelled from school, and arrested under the age of 16.

Quinsey et al. (1998) stated the following (pp. 167-168):

> The practical and theoretical significance of this result (if borne out in cross validation) is profound. First, from a practical point of view, actuarial appraisal of the risk of violent recidivism may be accomplished without reference to a restricted psychological test which, in some jurisdictions, requires a licensed professional for its administration. We would argue that a more appropriate approach to qualifying risk appraisers lies in the evaluation of the reliability and validity of predictions, irrespective of general professional certification. Second, from a theoretical perspective, we would argue that a measure of psychopathy might be necessary for the prediction of violent recidivism, but that the PCL-R might not be. That is, although the two PCL-R factors are highly correlated ($r = .50$, approximately; see Harpur, Hakstian and Hare, 1988), there is considerable theoretically motivated debate about which PCL-R factor better predicts violence. The results showing that the entire PCL-R can be replaced by variables pertaining only to antisocial childhood behavior imply that PCL-R Factor I items reflecting apparently adult personality (e.g., glibness, grandiosity, lying, conning, remorselessness, shallowness, callousness) do little or nothing to reduce uncertainty about the likelihood of violent recidivism. This is not to say that these characteristics are not associated with psychopathy. It is also possible that our record-based measurement was not the ideal way to measure these interpersonal behaviors.

The reader is encouraged to use the CATS whenever gathering information necessary to derive a PCL-R score is not practical or warranted.

The possibility—even likelihood—that the VRAG can be accurately calculated without directly interviewing the predictee is raised by the foregoing discussion. Items on the VRAG can be obtained from a records review and/or significant/knowledgeable others. The authors strongly recommend, however, interviewing the predictee whenever possible. The courts and other forensic entities not surprisingly assign greater credibility to those experts who have met with the predictee. The notion of fairness—allowing the predictee to explain past behavior and events—may be inextricably bound up with the perception of accuracy of the instrument.

The forensic professional who is limited to predicting violence in the absence of interviewing the assessee is well advised to obtain a strong multi-sourced database. Possible sources of information include, but are not limited to, the following:

- Interviewing and/or testing of previous victims and significant/knowledgeable others;

- Behavioral observations of the predictee in both social and nonsocial contexts;
- Behavioral observations of the predictee in both structured and non-structured situations;
- Behavioral observations in both stress/intoxicated (e.g., alcohol EEG) and tranquil/nonintoxicated circumstances;
- A functional analysis of previous violence-related responses;
- Environmental assessment to include culture-bound stimulus factors;
- Description of probable but unknown behavioral traits from actual demographic traits observed by others;
- Use of relevant violence base-rate data;
- Medical, neurological, and laboratory examination results by others;
- Inspection of crime scenes or sites where violence was previously exhibited;
- Various intrusive medical procedures (e.g., alcohol EEG);
- Semantic and transcript analysis, if available;
- Results from instrumentation such as the polygraph;
- Records produced by the predictee (e.g., diaries, letters);
- Records produced by others (e.g., military, school, job);
- "Expunged" records usually available to court examiners in the state or federal archives;
- Relevant psychological-mathematical models that are then used as a basis for further inquiry (e.g., geographic profiling).

Sex Offender Risk Appraisal Guide (SORAG)

The Sex Offender Risk Appraisal Guide (SORAG) predicts for seven and ten years and was developed with the same methodology as the VRAG (Quinsey, et al., 1998). The 14 items in the SORAG consist, in part, of similar factors as the VRAG (i.e., living with biological parents to age 16, elementary school maladjustment, history of alcohol problems, marital status, criminal history of nonviolent offenses, failure on prior conditional release, age at index offense, meeting the DSM–III criteria for any personality disorder or for schizophrenia, and the PCL–R or CATS score). In addition, the score is computed from new items (i.e., criminal history of violent offenses, number of previous convictions for sexual offenses, history of sex offenses only against girls under 14, and phallometric test results).

The SORAG has a greater-than-chance, yet only modest ability to predict sexual recidivism, with a correlation of about $r = .20$ between predictor and criterion variables (approximately 4.5 percent of the variance accounted for). Still, the SORAG has done as well as other sexual recidivism scales that other investigators have produced (e.g., see Firestone, Bradford, Greenberg,

Nunes, and Broom, 1999; Hanson and Thornton, 2000).

Quinsey (2000), importantly, observed, "We developed the SORAG as an enhancement of the VRAG for sex offenders but have been *unable to show so far that the SORAG is more accurate than the VRAG for sex offender subjects in predicting violent or sexual recidivism.* We ordinarily do not score both because they are highly correlated. The omission of the plethysmograph item slightly degrades accuracy on the SORAG but, as I mentioned above, these instruments are quite robust. Missing data move the estimated probability of a subject toward the base rate of the construction sample." (Emphasis added)

These points made by Quinsey (2000) are far reaching in their implications. The VRAG may be more accurate than the SORAG because sexual assaults may reflect a propensity and desire to harm rather than seek sexual gratification, an argument long raised by feminists and those who treat sex victims. Alternatively, the extra items in the SORAG relating specifically to sexual assaults may not be all that sensitive, despite the research findings upon which their inclusion was based. The finding that omitting the plethysmograph only slightly degrades accuracy on the SORAG, together with the finding that the VRAG is more accurate than the SORAG, suggests that the plethysmograph may not be necessary in order to accurately predict sexual recidivism. Yet research findings show that the plethysmograph is the single best predictor of sexual violence. Hanson & Bussiere (1998), with $r = .32$, determined that there was a 46 percent chance of reoffending with deviant arousal and a 14 percent likelihood without deviant arousal. The answer may lie in the higher correlation of the VRAG with both physical and sexual recidivism ($r = .44$). Until more cross-validation is available, the forensic professional is advised to utilize the VRAG to predict sexual recidivism.

Sexual Recidivism Meta-analysis

The meta-analysis of predictors of sexual recidivism by Hanson & Bussiere (1998) stands as a superb statistical achievement in sex offender research, involving 87 articles, 61 datasets, a median follow-up period of four years, and 28,972 sexual offenders. The base rate for reoffending was about 30 percent across all offenders. Among other findings, a combination of previous sex offenses, boy victims, and never married, equaled a 77 percent chance of sexual reoffense in the 15-to-30-year follow-up period. The likelihood of any new offense for this group was 42 percent. For the 4-to-5-year follow-up period, the likelihood of any offense was 37 percent and 13 percent for a new sex offense. Importantly, treatment did not reduce the chances of sexual recidivism.

Forensic professionals can include from this meta-analysis the following useful factors, with correlations on the right side, into their risk analyses (i.e., correlations equal to or greater than +.10 or -.10):

• Phallometric preference for children	.32
• Masculinity/femininity scale of MMPI	.27
• Deviant sexual preference	.22
• Prior sexual offense	.19
• Personality disorder	.19
• Negative relationship with mother	.16
• Paranoia Scale–MMPI	.16
• Low motivation for therapy	.15
• Stranger versus acquaintance victim	.15
• P-graph preference–boys	.14
• Antisocial personality	.14
• Victim female child	-.14
• Age	-.14

Evaluators should realize that there was no scientific basis for Hanson & Bussiere's (1998) meta-analysis for the following, and should gear their reports and court testimony accordingly:

• Classified mentally disordered sex offender	.07
• Degree of sexual contact	-.03
• Empathy	.03
• Social skilled	-.04
• Prior violent behavior unrelated to sex offenses	.05
• Young child versus older child as victim	.05
• Phallometric arousal to rape scenes	.05
• Alcohol abuse	.05
• Prior non-violent	.00
• Force/injury	.01
• Psychological problems	-.01
• Sexually abused as a child	.02

Some of these factors strongly correlate with sexual offenses in actuarial devices (e.g., nonviolent behavior, alcohol abuse on VRAG). In such cases, the evaluator should utilize factors from both approaches and report upon the contradictions in the forensic report.

Rapid Risk Assessment for Sexual Offense Recidivism (RRASOR)

The Rapid Risk Assessment for Sexual Offense Recidivism (RRASOR) was based on a sample size of 2,592 persons and predicts recidivism for five- and ten-year periods. The measure does not require interviewing the predictee, and knowledge of the measure's four factors is commonly available from a review of administrative records. The RRASOR has a modest correlation with recidivism (.27). The factors and their scoring are presented here:

Prior Sexual Offenses
None = 0
1 conviction and/or 1–2 charges = 1
2–3 convictions and/or 3–5 charges = 2
4 or more convictions and/or 6 or more charges = 3

Age at Release
25 or more years of age = 0
Under 25 years old = 1

Victim Gender
Only female victims = 0
Any male victims = 1

Relationship to Victim
Only related = 0
Any non-related = 1

The totals of these four factors are broken down into five- and ten-year periods. For 5 years, the estimated recidivism rates by obtained score (in parentheses) are: 0 (4.4%), 1 (7.6%), 2 (14.2%), 3 (24.8%), 4 (32.7%), and 5 (49.8%). For 10 years, the likelihood of recidivism is 0 (6.5%), 1 (11.2%), 2 (21.1%), 3 (36.9%), 4 (48.6%), and 5 (73.1%). The finding that roughly three-quarters of sex offenders who score positive on all four factors recidivate within 10 years should serve as a caution to those who recommend interventions. These indications are that sexual offending, especially with boy victims, is generally recalcitrant to change.

Minnesota Sex Offender Screening Test–Revised (MnSOST–R)

The Minnesota Sex Offender Screening Test–Revised (MnSOST–R) by Epperson, Kaul, and Huot (1995) and Epperson, Kaul, and Hesselton (1998) predicts for sux years using a contrived base rate of reoffense of 35%. The 16 factors are as follows:

- Sex-related convictions
- Duration of sex-offending history
- Supervisory status when committed a sex offense for which they were charged or convicted
- Whether the sex offense was in a public place
- Threat of force in any sex offense for which they were charged or convicted
- Multiple acts on a single victim during one contact event
- Age groups victimized
- Offenses against a 13-to-15-year-old victim (perpetrator more than five years older than victim)
- Stranger victim for any sex-related offense
- Adolescent antisocial behaviors
- Substance abuse in the year preceding index offense
- Employment history
- Documented discipline or infractions while incarcerated
- Substance abuse treatment while incarcerated
- Sex offender treatment while incarcerated
- Age at release or discharge from incarceration

These investigators provide cutting scores from +8 to +17, using their scoring on the above factors. Cutting scores correspond to percent correctly classified as High Risk, ranging from 70–92% to Low Risk, ranging from 68–75%.

Static and Dynamic Risk Assessment Tools

Static and dynamic risk assessment tools yield low, medium, and high risk predictors for sexual offenses (Hanson, 1997; Hanson, Scott, and Steffy, 1995). Static measures consist of factors that cannot be altered–history, demographic variables (except for age), and characteristics of past offenses. Hence, static factors cannot be utilized by programmers and treaters either to gauge change over time or as a basis for intervention. Dynamic risk assessment, on the other hand, consists of sexual interests, socioaffective functioning, response to treatment, and other factors that can be used for risk/reduction/management.

Dangerousness Prediction Decision Tree

One of the authors and his colleagues developed a measure of both dynamic and static violence risk factors with adequate sensitivity (75 percent) and specificity (75 percent) for a three-month predictive period (Hall, 1987; Hall et al., 1984). In this prospective project, young adult males in the military were followed over the 90 days in their on-post and off-duty behavior. The following five categories of prediction were yielded by data analysis.

The best predictor of short-term violence was at least two stimulus triggers, short term in duration (less than one month), high in impact, superimposed on multiple acts of past violence, one act of which occurred recently within the preceding year. This prediction presupposes victim availability and a context within which to act out.

(a) The most potent external trigger seemed to be environmental stress, particularly actual or threatened breakup in the central love relationship. The second most potent external trigger was a deteriorating work environment or work conflict. Peer pressure to aggress, institutional commands to perform sanctioned violence, and other factors emerged from the literature as potential triggers but were not isolated in this study.

(b) The most potent internal trigger was substance intoxication. The trigger was considered likely if substance abuse occurred within the month previous to the prediction using DSM–III criteria. Other important internal triggers from the literature were command hallucinations, some organic and paranoid states, and obsessive thoughts of revenge or violence.

Predict up to substantial short-term violence based on the strength of your data for the above category.

The second best predictor of short-term violence was one trigger superimposed on a past history of violence. The literature suggests that conditions that are associated with violence should also be noted in the forensic report or expert testimony. These could be long-term in nature and define the form (topography) of violence. Numerical probability factors are always tied to base-rate data (Frederick, 1978b; Hall, 1987; Monahan, 1981a; Stone, 1975). For *Negligible*, the probability of violence is 0 to 10 percent within the predicted time span, for *Minimal*, the probability of occurance is 11 to 25 percent, *Mild* refers to a 26 to 50 percent range, *Moderate* references 51 to 75 percent, *Considerable* utilizes a 76–90 percent probabilty, and *Substantial* 91 to 100 percent.

(a) The most important dynamic conditions were age (young), socioeconomic status prior to the military (lower class, lower middle class), and substance abuse or dependence (particularly alcohol and opiates).

(b) Other important static and dynamic conditions were sex (male), subcultural acceptance of violence, belief that certain types of violence will go unpunished (e.g., child abuse, spouse abuse), deficits in verbal skills, violent peers, and a weak community support base.

Predict moderate to considerable risk depending on the strength of your data for the above.

The third best predictor of short-term dangerousness was relevant personality traits superimposed on a history of violence. These traits included current high hostility, low frustration tolerance, hypersensitivity, and high distrust of others.

Predict mild risk, at most.

The fourth best predictor of short-term violence, in the absence of having current information on the subject, was past violence standing alone.

(a) Relevant dimensions were severity, frequency, recency, and a history of reinforcing results for violence.

(b) Associated developmental events included abuse as a child, relevant school problems (e.g., fights, threats, fire setting, vandalism, insubordination), and spontaneous or concussion-related loss of consciousness before age ten.

Predict minimal to mild dangerousness at most unless the base rate for recidivism exceeds this degree of possible violence.

The fifth best predictor of violence was stress and intoxication, without a history of past dangerousness to others.

Predict negligible dangerousness.

Spousal Assault Risk Assessment (SARA)

The Spousal Assault Risk Assessment Guide (SARA) by Kropp, Hart, Webster, and Eaves (1999) was developed in Canada using more than 2,300 male offenders, including criminal-court referrals, probationers, and inmates. The similarity of factors compared to those obtained in the U.S. suggest that users of the SARA in that country can rely on the provided norms. Like the HCR–20 and SVR–20, the SARA is not a test with cutoffs, but simply a clinical checklist of risk factors for assault identified in the empirical literature. Nevertheless, norms were obtained on two large groups totaling 2,309 offenders with probation and correctional staff making the SARA ratings. Generally, probationers had lower scores than inmates. Many inmates had a known history of spousal assault. Overall, about 20 to 35 percent of offenders were judged by evaluators to be at high risk for spousal assault. Structural reliability analyses suggested this SARA has at least moderate internal consistency and item homogeneity (e.g., Cronbach's Alpha for corrected item-total correlations = .78 for total scores and .75 for number of factors present). Interrater reliability was impressive (e.g., $r = .84$ and .91 for the two subsamples and $r = .83$ and .91 for number of factors present). Criterion-related validity was examined in three ways, with the analyses offering strong support and a multitude of significant findings for the overall validity of the measure. SARA ratings of inmates can be proffered for those with and without a history of spousal assault, and it has concurrent validity with the PCL–SV.

The SARA can be used for comparing men who did and did not recidivate following referrals for group treatment.

Presented in a condensed fashion, the risk factors from the SARA included items regarding (1) past assault, (2) violations of conditional release or supervision, (3) problems in work or primary relationship, (4) victim of abuse, (5) substance abuse, (6) psychological problems or conditions to include suicidal behavior and personality disorder, (7) use of weapons, (8) violation of no-contact orders, or minimizing/denial of violence history, and (9) attitudes that support spousal assault.

Sexual, Violence, Risk (SVR–20)

The Sexual, Violence, Risk (SVR–20) was developed by Boar, Hart, Kropp, and Webster (1997) for professionals rather than researchers as a set of guidelines to evaluate risk of sexual offending. No probability of recidivism is generated.

Factors in the SVR–20 include those reflecting *psychosocial adjustment* (e.g., presence of mental disorders, victim of child abuse, relationship problems), *sexual offenses* (escalating in frequency/severity, and physical harm to victims), and *future plans* (e.g., presence of future plans, attitude toward intervention). Scores above the median (19) show an incremental chance of reoffending.

The SVR–20 can be utilized for intervention, according to the authors, as it contains both static and dynamic factors.

Historical, Clinical, Risk Management (HCR–20)

The Historical, Clinical, Risk Management (HCR–20) was developed by Webster, Douglas, Eaves, and Hart (1997) as a set of guidelines to prognosticate violence. Factors include historical items (e.g., previous violence, early maladjustment, substance use problems), clinical items (e.g., lack of insight, negative attitude, and impulsivity), and risk management items (e.g., exposure to destabilizers, lack of personal support, noncompliance with remediation efforts). Research demonstrated increased risk associated with more items (e.g., scores above the median) (Webster, et. al.) show four times the likelihood of future violence. The HCR–20, like some other measures of risk, contains both dynamic and static factors. This means that outcomes can be linked to risk management strategies.

California Actuarial Risk Assessment Tables (CARAT)

The California Actuarial Risk Assessment Tables (CARAT), developed by Schiller and Marques (1999), present the base-rate percentage of reoffenses within five years for both child molesters and rapists. For rapists, the range is from *minimal* risk (e.g., 21.5 percent for average IQ, acquaintance victim, prior felonies, age 25–35 at release from incarceration) to *substantial* (91.8 percent for average IQ, acquaintance victim, sexually abused as a child, under 25 at release). For child molesters, the range is more restricted, from a mild risk (46.3 percent for stranger victim, victim age < 6, has prior felonies, age 25–35 at release) to *moderate* risk (e.g., 70.4 percent for one prior sex offense, prior felonies, molests boys only, age 15–35 at release). Keep in mind Hanson's (1997, 1998; Hanson & Bussiere, 1998) overall estimate that child molesters base rate for reoffense is about 30 percent. Thus, the use of these combinations of factors can significantly improve accuracy of prognostication beyond that expected by the base rate. Further, the base rates for both rapists and child molesters do *not* include offenses for which the perpetrator avoided detection/apprehension, where the charges were dropped, or where a judicial alternative was imposed, such as mental health treatment in lieu of prosecution. Thus, a deception analysis should be performed to avoid either an underestimate or overestimate of basal violence and therefore, future risk (Hall, 1986, 1987, 1994a; Hall & Poirier, 2000; Hall & Pritchard, 1996).

Level of Service Inventory–Revised (LSI-R)

The Level of Service Inventory–Revised (LSI–R) by Andrews and Bonta (1995), considered a risk reduction/management tool based on information about almost all areas of an offender's life—criminal history, education/employment, financial, family/marital, leisure/recreation, companions, substance use, emotional/personal, and attitudes. For both individual and programmatic change, the LSI–R can assign *a priori* risks for institutional maladjustment, likelihood of early release, recidivism and self-reported criminal activities, parole outcome, and halfway-house success. The presence of dynamic factors makes the LSI–R a particularly appealing management tool.

The Workplace Violence Risk Assessment Checklist (WVRAC)

The Workplace Violence Risk Assessment Checklist (WVRAC), developed by the senior author (2001), includes factors from the clinical-empirical literature on history, recent events, and work attitudes and traits, as reported in Table IX.

TABLE IX
THE WORKPLACE VIOLENCE RISK ASSESSMENT CHECKLIST (WVRAC)

Historical items
Previous attempted or consummated violence toward others
Previous damaging of work-related property
Previous direct or veiled threats to harm other employees
Substance abuse or dependence (alcohol and/or drugs)
Poor compliance with company attempts to remediate worker
Belligerence toward customers or clients
Reckless or hazardous behavior on job
Past use or threatened use of weapons outside work

Recent events
Physical violence to others unrelated to work
Stress or desperation in family, domestic, or financial matters
Acquires firearm or related equipment
Signs of rehearsal (e.g., practices at the shooting range, assembles weaponry)
Exposure to, or increase of, destabilizers (e.g., alcohol, drugs)
Fascination with, or statements about, other incidents of workplace violence
Poor compliance with remediation attempts or directives by management
Lost job or perceives job will soon be lost
Stalking, including repeated harassment of other employees
Threats of suicide or homicide
Shows behavior suggesting a wish to harm coworkers or management

Work attitudes and traits
Sees self as victimized or treated unfairly by other employees
Sense of identity wrapped up in job
Does not take criticism well, including projection of blame to others
Authority issues regarding control from others present
Tends to be a loner on and/or off job
Hostile attitudes toward aspects of work
Perceived intrusions into private life (e.g., believes monitoring by management is excessive).

The WVRAC comprises factors associated with workplace violence (Vanden Bos & Bulatao, 1996; Feldmann & Johnson, 1996; Hall and Whitaker, 1999). Additionally, the WVRAC has been applied by the senior author to clinical-forensic cases of workplace violence with a general finding that increased violence potential is associated with a greater number of endorsed items. The items are not exhaustive, fixed or mutually exclusive, and the entire checklist should be considered a work in progress and a list of warning signs. Differing from other measures of risk, the checklist is meant for an interdisciplinary audience such as human resource managers, probation officers, and mental health personnel.

Readers are cautioned that a simple sum of risk factors and the use of specific cutoffs does not automatically equate to varying degrees of risk. This must be determined by cross-validating research. Importantly, some form of previous threatened, attempted, or consummated violence to others, self, or

property must be present to predict future violence reasonably from the predictor variables. The final summary ratings are judgments by assessors,
which may lead to comprehensive assessment and intervention, if appropriate. The inclusion of both dynamic and static factors suggests that the
WVRAC may be utilized as a management/risk-reduction tool.

Other Measures

Some extant methods of determining violence recidivism were not
included in this discussion. The STATIC–99, designed to predict sexual
recidivism by using a stepwise regression approach to classify offenders as
high, medium, or low risk, was developed from a merging of the database for
the RRASOR and a tool called the SACJ from a British database (Grubin,
1998). The STATIC–99 was not, however, significantly more accurate than
either the RRASOR or the SACJ, and was outperformed by the VRAG
(Kramer and Heilbrun, 2000).

Other measures were not included that lack of a norm base, or that fail
to report either reliability/validity data or even a listing of empirically-based
factors for those devices. The Analysis of Aggressive Behavior (e.g., see
Kramer and Heilbrun, 2000) falls into this category. Likewise, no objective
or projective psychological test (e.g., MMPI–2, MCMI–III, CPI, BPI,
Rorschach) is listed, as Megargee's (1970) observation still holds true that no
psychological test or subtest will postdict, let alone predict, violence.

Practice Guidelines

These practice guidelines are presented in the form of suggestions to violence predictors in forensic settings and situations. They evolved from several decades of investigation and include the following:

1. Be prepared to demonstrate that you are professionally competent to
   render a violence prediction and that no issues of ethics are involved.
   Know the literature on risk assessment, and be able to document that
   you have been trained in the methods.
2. Ascertain the referral question—whether the task is assessment, intervention, consultation, or some combination.
3. Start with the most valid information first; do not be biased by recent
   data or by hindsight bias.
4. Never predict violence in the absence of previous significant threatened,
   attempted, or consummated violence. Most extant actuarial devices
   assume a previous history of violence and hence are really measures of
   violence recidivism. Predicted violence will not occur if no significant
   basal violence is uncovered.

5. Remember that the perpetrator, victim, and context must all be analyzed in order to understand a particular violent event. Also use a multisourced database such as multiple actuarial devices, standardized testing, review of records, and interview of knowledgeable/significant others for each of these interactive factors.

6. Retain validated decision rules even when tempted to abandon them for a particular case. This is particularly true when your referral source desires a different conclusion other than the findings generated by your decision rules.

7. Use multiple, empirically derived, predictive measures or factors, such as those listed in Table VI, and present the finding for each individually prior to a synthesis of all the data into a risk judgment.

8. Remember to rule out or account for unintentional distortion as well as deliberate deception on the part of the predictee for both the time of the evaluation and previous violence. You must also take into account possible deception and distortion by witnesses and other third parties if they are utilized in your database.

9. The sequence of violence–baseline behavior, acceleration stage, the violent act, recovery, return to baseline–should be analyzed for all previous acts of violence in order to determine commonalities and differences, as well as trends over time, for a particular individual.

10. Think in terms of base rates unless using predictive devices that focus on decision analysis (e.g., classification-tree method), at which point you will still pay attention to base rates, but attend to whether the decision path is followed.

11. You can use empirically supported clinical opinion so long as it is identified as such (e.g., pain cues from the victim acting as a positive reinforcer for predictee violence). In fact, there is no escape from judgment in violence prediction (even purely actuarial devices like the VRAG comprise items involving clinical judgment).

12. Avoid falling prey to illusory associations, unsupported by the empirical literature, between evaluation data and supposed violence potential (e.g., poor cooperation or antagonism toward evaluator, physical stigmata, poor self-esteem, nonviolence during institutionalization, white space responses in the Rorschach).

13. Consider triggers to possible future violence based on previous triggering stimuli. Keep in mind that triggers contribute only slightly to the violent act (e.g., <5% in Hall, 1987; Hall, et al., 1984). Some classes of offenders, such as psychopaths, appear not to need triggers in order to perpetrate violence, only the opportunity to do so without being caught.

14. Consider opportunities for future violence given availability of weapons, victims, and other factors.

15. Consider inhibitions to violence based on past inhibitory stimuli and responses for that individual.
16. List alternative hypotheses to explain exhibited violence, and seek evidence for each, especially those contrary to your own interests or the vested interest of your referral party.
17. Synthesize your conclusions and account for discrepant findings. Keep in mind that your synthesis is essentially a clinical-forensic judgment.
18. Operationalize your conclusions and make them capable of replication.
19. Present contingent predictions, if possible; avoid dichotomous conclusions unless using a classification-tree approach.
20. Limit the temporality of the predictions to avoid the perception of an interminable prediction. Give the level of risk for different portions of the time period if variation is to be expected (e.g., a greater risk of violent recidivism within two years of release from prison).
21. Specify in summary form the factors that formed the proffered conclusions. The factors that lower the risk of violence, as well as the positive aspects of the predictee, should be presented in order to achieve a balanced report.
22. Suggest feedback mechanisms to assist future predictors of violence potential (e.g., reevaluation in one year with the same instruments).
23. Given your database findings, be prepared to fairly and accurately represent both the predictee's possible violence potential, as well as practical and effective interventions that are linked to the findings. Link recommended interventions with discrete dynamic predictor variables as presented in the Serious Scoring System of Table VIII.
24. Avoid recommending aversive interventions if at all possible. In particular, punitive interventions to violent behavior often lead to aversive cycles between perpetrator, victim, and unfortunately, other innocent parties.
25. Communicate effectively. Kramer and Heilbrun (2000) present guidelines for effective risk communication to include (a) using plain language and avoiding jargon; (b) describing the results of risk assessment in regards to consistency with other sources; (c) identifying dynamic factors that can be used for management of intervention; (d) distinguishing imminence, risk and nature, frequency, and possible severity of violence; and (e) referring to the language of the report when asked if the predictee will act out or is dangerous, thus preventing the misrepresentation of report findings.

TABLE X
EXAMPLES OF PROPOSED INTERVENTIONS
ASSOCIATED WITH PREDICTOR VARIABLES

Predictor variable	Intervention
1. Past violence	• Intensive supervision • Family treatment • Parenting skills training • Anger management • Correctional treatment for violence
2. Any violations of conditional release or community supervision	• Incarceration • Intensive supervision • Correctional recidivism program
3. Central love relationship problems	• Divorce counseling • Dispute resolution • Spousal assault group therapy • Couples counseling
4. Employment problems	• Vocational counseling • Drug/alcohol treatment
5. Substance abuse/dependence	• Transitional house placement • Drug/alcohol treatment (OPC) • Court-ordered abstinence • Urine or blood screening
6. Recent homicidal ideation/intent	• Crisis counseling • Psychiatric hospitalization • Psychotropic medication • Cognitive behavioral therapy • Weapons restrictions • Individual treatment • Drug/alcohol restrictions
7. Mental illness	• Hospitalization • Psychotropic medication • Individual treatment • Drug/alcohol restrictions
8. Personality disorder with anger, impulsivity, or behavioral instability	• Group/peer approaches • Intensive supervision • Specialized therapy for personality disorders
9. Past use of weapons and/or credible threats of death	• Incarceration • Intensive supervision • Weapons restrictions • Notification of intended victims • Crisis intervention
10. Extreme minimization or denial of violence history	• Peer/Group treatment • Psycho-educational group
11. Attitudes that support or condone violence	• Group treatment • Psycho-educational group

A blinded report using several of the empirically guided methods and the listed practice guidelines is presented in Appendix D, *The Honorable John Smith.*

Degree of Certainty and Report Parameters

Violence predictions are usually proffered in terms of degree of probability when, in fact, future violent behavior will either occur or not occur. As a convention, the following degrees of probability for violence prediction are suggested for synthesized data used in the forensic report.

Negligible–In your professional opinion, future significant violence will not occur within the specified time period. This term is used for average people with no history of serious violence. The probability of violence is 0 to 10 percent within the predicted time span. Numerical probability figures are always tied to base-rate data (Frederick, 1978; Hall, 1987; Monahan, 1981; Stone, 1975). This degree of certainty is within the legal meaning of nondangerousness.

Minimal–In your opinion, within the time period the likelihood of violence is very low. This term is used for average people, perhaps under high stress or showing some maladaptive behavior, with no significant history of violence. The probability of occurrence is 11 to 25 percent within the predicted time span, but only when numerical probability is tied to base-rate data (Frederick, 1978b; Hall, 1987; Monahan, 1981a; Stone, 1975). This degree of certainty is also within the legal meaning of nondangerousness.

Mild–In your opinion, significant violence may occur within the specified time period, but your evidence is weak. This term is used for people with or without a history of serious violence. You are saying there is a fair likelihood that violence will occur. This degree of certainty is within the legal meaning of nondangerousness, even though there is some chance it will occur. The suggested range of probability associated with this legal term is 26 to 50 percent, but only when numerical probability is tied to base-rate data (Frederick, 1978b; Hall, 1987; Monahan, 1981a; Stone, 1975).

Moderate–In your opinion, it is more likely than not that violence will occur within the specified time period. This term is limited to persons with a violence history. The probability of occurrence is 51 to 75 percent, but, as usual, only when base-rate data is considered. This corresponds to the suggested legal definition of preponderance of evidence (Frederick, 1978b; Hall, 1987; Monahan, 1981a; Stone, 1975).

Considerable–In your opinion, there is a strong likelihood violence will occur within the specified time period. This term is limited to people with a violence history. Control may be institutional combined with community programs (e.g., residential facilities, transition houses). The probability of occurrence is 76 to 90 percent, but only when base-rate data is considered. This corresponds to the legal meaning of clear-and-convincing evidence (Frederick, 1978b; Hall, 1987; Monahan, 1981a; Stone, 1975).

Substantial–In your opinion, violence will occur within the specified time period if measures for intervention are not taken. This term is limited to people with a violence history. Institutional control may be necessary if the expected violence is to be controlled. Probability of occurrence is 91 to 100 percent, but only when base-rate data is considered. This corresponds to the suggested legal definition of beyond a reasonable doubt.

CONCLUSION AND RECOMMENDATIONS

Violence risk analysis has evolved considerably in recent years. The measures presented in this chapter will hopefully be revised in concordance with new findings and new methodologies in this fascinating area. Certain findings regarding risk analysis will steadfastly remain. Among these is that empirically based decision analysis is superior to clinical judgment, reversing a trend in forensic mental-health practice over the last century. The practice guidelines for violence prediction, which are largely independent of theoretical views and specialized concerns, should remain durable as they pertain to the positive features of any risk analysis.

Violence prediction is a process that always involves, regardless of which measures are utilized, questions regarding the comprehensiveness of the database, whether deliberate deception and voluntary distortion were taken into account, if basal history was present, and the presence of recent factors associated with violence, such as triggers and opportunity factors. In addition to keeping abreast of the empirical literature, which should modify and refine one's evaluation of risk, this approach will serve to keep the violence predictor humble. As a standard practice when testifying in court on a risk analysis, the predictor is encouraged to share with the trier of fact their own percent of true positives and negatives in previous cases involving violence prediction.

Chapter 6

THE FORENSIC DISTORTION ANALYSIS: EXTANT SYSTEMS AND DECISION TREE

Summary of Dangerousness Prediction Task #2 : John Brown

TANYA P. WAS AN ATTRACTIVE, 22-YEAR-OLD university student who was brutally raped, sodomized, and beaten while on a vacation in Hawaii. During the assault, the perpetrator, John Brown, shoved a bottle into her vagina and attempted to break the object with a rock. Unable to accomplish this, he dragged her to a nearby cliff and shoved her over. Remarkably, she landed on a narrow outcropping below and only broke several ribs, instead of hurtling several hundred feet to her death, as he apparently had planned. Because of the severe mental and physical trauma that she sustained in the crimes, she was hospitalized for many months.

The police arrested her assailant after he was overheard in a bar bragging of his exploits. He later maintained that he was amnesic for the crimes due to the ingestion of drugs. At the trial, the defendant was found not guilty by reason of insanity because the judge accepted his claim that he was high on PCP, a powerful animal tranquilizer, during the instant offenses and the prosecutor had failed to prove otherwise. Of interest is that the alibi of chemical incapacitation was never medically substantiated, nor did the defendant have a history of mental illness or hospitalization.

He did have an extensive arrest record for previous violent crimes. These prior arrests, of course, could not be admitted into the court record during the trial. His juvenile record consisted of arrests for robbery (2), larceny (3), inlawful inhalation, paint sniffing, and burglary (2). His adult record consisted of arrests for drunk and disorderly conduct, assault in the third degree (2), harassment (2), burglary in the first degree, attempted homicide (2), possession of prohibited firearm, and carrying a firearm without a permit as well as robbery.

Following the finding of not guilty by reason of mental illness, Mr. Brown was committed to a psychiatric hospital. Ward notes during this hospitalization contain examples of serious prevarication that include lying to get off the forensic ward after permission had been denied by staff of an earlier shift. Significant distortion of facts by Mr. Brown appeared to have occurred since his initial hospitalization. When questioned a year later about alleged previous suicide gestures, he stated that the only such gesture occurred while he had been in custody pretrial as a ruse to change cells. The forensic hospital social worker, during an intake noted ". . . He has been observed in animated interaction and activity with other patients, but when speaking to staff assumes a 'depressive' attitude." This depressive attitude had been observed for at least a half a year. During that time, Dr. Smith observed that "the MMPI findings strongly indicate that the patient is faking the symptoms of isolation and impoverishment of emotional experience."

Other indications of faking from psychological, intellectual, neuropsychological, and achievement testing included the following:

He obtained better scores on some intellectual subtests than would fit with his allegation that he was mentally retarded. His Weschler Adult Intelligence Test IQs rose from 57 to 116 from a mentally defective range to bright normal, over three separate administrations, in only 5 months.

During administration of different tests in the same general time period, he showed the ability to perform multiplication and other complex mathematical manipulations on one test, while exhibiting an inability to correctly do simple addition on another test.

He correctly identified words such as "kayak," "descend," "bereavement," "appraising," "amphibian," while demonstrating an inability to define simpler words such as "winter," "slice," "conceal," and "enormous."

He exhibited inconsistent memory skills (digits forward, digits backward) over time instead of a generally suppressed performance.

There was a reversal of performance in verbal IQs as the superior mode of functioning over time, instead of a relative improvement within the dominant modes upon retesting.

He obtained MMPI profile results that were grossly inconsistent with his ward behavior. During forensic examinations conducted by one of the authors, other instances of distortion were observed that included outright prevarication and minimizing of past behavior, especially for events that involved threatened or actual violent behavior.

Four superimposed MMPI profiles obtained over the years revealed little personality change had occurred, and the diagnosis of Anti-Social Personality Disorder (DSM–IV R, code 01.7) (1994) was the most compatible condition given test results and the chronicity of historical violence. Coupled with serious distortion during recent years, Mr. Brown should be considered an unreliable source of information; psychometric tests or instruments used in the future to assess Mr. Brown's condition should include built-in devices to detect misrepresentation. These results suggest that Mr. Brown may have pretended to be insane and mentally retarded during his incarceration and during the early portion of his stay at the forensic hospital, following the finding of not guilty by reason of mental illness. It appears that he then shifted to a strategy of minimization and denial in order to obtain a conditional release. Requests for release were denied for several years. Currently, his request to the court for release awaits a hearing. If granted, he will be released within one month following the court hearing.

Your task for this case is to analyze the forensic distortion response style, both for the time of the forensic evaluation and for the reporting of historical violence, and then to use this material in your estimate of future dangerousness. Will he aggress towards others if released into the community in the near future? Does he remain a danger to his most recent victim? Data is available for six years following the evaluation as presented in Appendix E, *John Brown's Previous Criminality and Current Hospital Progress.*

Review of Distortion Literature

Forensic distortion analysis can be broadly defined as a first-generation set of interlocking operationalized procedures designed to detect possible misrepresentation of previous violence or other maladaptive behaviors, determine its direction and appropriate magnitude, place clinical findings and documented mental problems into clearer perspective, communicate the decision path of the examiner, and generate hypotheses for future inquiry. Put another way, forensic distortion analysis is an attempt to induce meaning from nebulous forms within shadows, an effort to measure validly and reliably nonverifiable response styles within equally nonverifiable and assumed mental conditions and psychological patterns. It is subsumed under such rubrics such as *malingering*–the pretense of disease or disability that does not exist; *partial malingering*–the conscious exaggeration of symptoms of disease or disability; simulation or positive malingering; *dissimulation*–the concealment or minimization of actual symptoms; *false imputation*–knowingly associating a condition to an untrue cause; *faking bad*–creating or amplifying conditions that are normally construed as undesirable to achieve desirable goals; and *faking good*–denying or downplaying existing, usually undesirable conditions according to perceived favorable outcomes; evaluative situations where forensic examinees deliberately misrepresent previous or current behaviors/events.

These various forms of distortion have received increased attention over the past 20 years (Adelman & Howard, 1984; Sierles, 1984; Hall, 1982, 1985;

Cavanaugh and Rogers, 1984; Faust, and Hart, 1988; Schretlen, 1988; Rogers, 1988, 1997; Ekman and O'Sullivan, 1991; Weissman 1990, 1991). Recognized as a key concept in the mental health-law interface, included within and looming in importance only after dangerousness and perhaps criminal responsibility, the notion of forensic distortion has wide applicability within both civil and criminal law arenas (Lorei, 1970; Ziskin, 1981; Rogers 1984, 1988; Hall 1986; Ekman & O'Sullivan 1991). Forensic distortion is significant in competency hearings, sexual abuse cases, child custody evaluations, violence prediction, determination of criminal responsibility and subsequent treatment potential, witness credibility assessment, personal injury litigation, secret service investigation, and institution/community monitoring of proscribed interventions. Social pressure, and in some cases legislatively mandated requirements to conduct forensic evaluations, reviewed by others (e.g., Stone 1975; Monahan, 1981) have in effect obligated the forensic professional to conduct an assessment of client misrepresentation to the extent to which knowledge of basal violence and other maladaptive behavior is conceived as necessary to justify conclusions derived from relevant database sources.

Legal Guidelines to Determine Distortion

It is instructive for forensic mental health professionals to understand what jurors in courts of law may use as factors in deciding believability of witnesses. In one California jurisdiction, jurors were told to consider the following:
- Whether the witness had the opportunity to see, hear, touch, smell, or otherwise become aware of the matter about which the witness had testified;
- The ability of the witness to remember or communicate the content of events;
- The general character and quality of the testimony;
- The demeanor and manner of the witness while testifying;
- Whether the witness had a biased, vested interest in a given outcome or had other relevant motive;
- Whether matters testified to can be or have been corroborated by other evidence;
- The attitude of the witness toward what he or she had testified to and toward the giving of the testimony itself;
- Inconsistency or consistency of previous statements made by the witness;
- The witness's prior conviction of a felony.

Review of instructions from other jurisdictions reveal generally similar legal standards for determining the believability of witnesses (Hall, 1983). Serious problems with such lists include a lack of specificity, leaving jurors or others to create a standard of believability for themselves.

A second problem is just as serious—even if valid, the listed standards are not presented in the form of ordinal factors so that a rough estimate can be made as to whether one factor is more important than another. Assuming that general believability is established, a global set of factors further does not take into account that many people selectively distort in presenting information and that no testimony can be entirely free of bias. They may not help to determine whether a witness was believable for a particular issue.

A third problem is that many of the factors just do not correspond to psychological realities. Take a potent determinant of believability in rape trials: the demeanor of the alleged victim while testifying. Real victims in many cases become emotionally aroused, and embarrassed, and they often contradict themselves. They tend to feel guilty about their lack of assertion and submission for the time of the crime and often blame themselves for the outcome. Further, facing their rapist in court for the first time since the crime, they may show avoidant responses with immobilizing fear and other emotional by-products. The victim may experience a symbolic reenactment of the rape itself, not only from the intrusive nature of the legal proceedings but also by reexperiencing the trauma through testimony and cross-examination. The victim's own background is subject to scrutiny. In short, an authentic rape victim may appear to be a confused, emotional, and nonbelievable witness.

Compare this to a victim who falsely testifies about being raped. That testimony may be dramatically different from the true victim, characterized in some cases by confidence and a lack of anxiety. The alleged victim will not feel guilty for behaviors during a rape that did not occur. Rehearsal of a believable story may have preceeded the testimony and may be delivered in court with directness and feeling. In short, an alleged victim who was not raped may make a better witness than the genuine counterpart.

Finally, the listed standards do not take into account that the existence of a prior conviction may be irrelevant to whether the witness distorted previous events. Prior convictions of the accused may not be presented at all during the trial unless insanity is asserted.

The court may use different criteria regarding distortion when compared to the forensic mental health professional who testifies on the same issue. None of the guidelines proffered in this list refer to a mental condition or disorder except in a very general sense. This does not imply mental conditions are necessary in order for a testifier to describe behavior accurately, but the court and the expert witness may communicate in two different languages in cases where mental disorders are seen to influence representation of events, an observation well established in the forensic literature.

Nondeliberate Distortion

A value in considering the perspectives of jurors and judges on distortion, besides highlighting possible miscommunication, is the focus on both deliberate and nondeliberate distortion in determining believability. Behavioral scientists and mental health professionals tend to focus on one type of distortion to the exclusion or minimization of the other. Yet the referral question may assume that differentiating deliberate from nondeliberate distortion will be addressed within the evaluation.

It is critical to know whether a child who is alleged to have been sexually abused is distorting due to developmental deficits and other factors, or to get out of trouble, or both. A focus on deliberate distortion may create invalid conclusions unless nondeliberate sources of distortion are considered. On one hand, developmental deficits can be reliably reproduced and are expected to occur given the child's age and other factors. On the other hand, in the case of deliberate distortion, the assault may not have occurred—with the risk of incorrectly accusing an individual for the alleged crime.

Well-publicized cases of alleged sexual molestation in daycare centers have raised the strong possibility that some children have been coached to provide false accusations (e.g., Curtois, 1998). A combination of deliberate and nondeliberate distortion may also occur. In adult cases, it is imperative to know whether a victim in an alleged robbery is overestimating the height of the perpetrator, the distance between the victim and perpetrator, and duration of the assault (often outcomes of second-stage General Adaptation Syndrome responses) or is deliberately exaggerating these factors to achieve a desired outcome, or both. The relevance to reconstructing the crime and apprehending the perpetrator are important in addition to the false positive issue once an alleged perpetrator is caught. Some common causes of nondeliberate distortion presented by Buckhout (1980) are presented in Table XI in terms of the reporting person, reported event, and evaluation errors.

A special concern is raised with children who may experience nondeliberate memory errors in reporting events as victims of violence. These may include or be separate from certain types of thinking errors, á la Piaget, for specific stages of cognitive development. Memory problems are usually due to (a) encoding errors involving acquisition of new perceptual events, (b) retention and processing errors during the time memory is stored within the brain, and (c) decoding or retrieval problems when attempts are made to utilize the information. Clinically noted nondeliberate errors in children and some adults include the following:
• Type of stimulus event (visual, auditory, etc.) changes distortion in that visual sequences may be remembered better by children than adults (Duncan, Whitney and Kunen, 1982);

TABLE XI
NONDELIBERATE DISTORTION FACTORS

Reporter:
  (a) Selective perceptions due to interactive history with predictee
  (b) Prior experience in regard to crime-specific events
  (c) Stress at time of reported events
  (d) Impaired physical condition of input source
  (e) Mental disorder of input source
  (f) Memory deficits: short term, intermediate term, long term
  (g) Inattention due to sleep or focusing on other events
  (h) Particular expectations in regard to stimulus figures

Reported event(s):
  (i) Too brief to notice
  (j) No opportunity to perceive (e.g., physical barriers)
  (k) Insignificant in intensity, contextual qualities, etc.
  (l) Sensory interference (presence of distractors)
  (m) Diluted or weak figure/ground differentiation (e.g., due to nightfall, rain)

Evaluation errors:
  (n) Invalid or unreliable measuring devices
  (o) Leading questions/leading procedures
  (p) Distant time from reported event
  (q) Creating an evaluation context of fear and conformity

Within the brain, and (c) decoding or retrieval problems when attempts are made to utilize the information. Clinically noted nondeliberate errors in children and some adults include the following:
  (1) Type of stimulus event (visual, auditory, etc.) changes distortion—visual sequences may be remembered better by children than adults (Duncan, Whitney & Kunen, 1982);
  (2) Presence of sensory interference reduces focal recall; e.g., presented words similar in meaning tend to interfere with recall of other words (Adams, 1967);
  (3) Simple time duration creates trace decay reducing original-material recall (Erickson & Collins, 1968);
  (4) Children may retain stimulus fragments; when representation detail is scant, children and adults are more apt to exhibit memory distortion (Loftus, 1993);
  (5) Children have more difficulty retrieving long-term memory events (Brown, 1979).

- The presence of sensory interference worsens focal recall. Presented words that are similar in meaning, for example, tend to interfere with recall of other words (Adams, 1967);
- Simple duration of time creates a trace decay resulting in less ability to recall original material (Eriksen and Collins, 1968);
- Children may retain fragments of the stimulus. When the representation is scant in detail, both children and adults are more apt to show memory distortions (Loftus, 1983);
- Children have more difficulty in retrieving long-term memory events (Brown, 1979);
- Once a distortion occurs, it appears to be accepted as part of reality and is difficult to change in favor of an original memory of an actual event (Loftus

and Davis, 1984);

- The presence of a postevent interviewer with strong preconceived notions of what happened may lead interviewees (Dent, 1982);
- Leading questions in general increase the chances that memory will be distorted (Marin, Holmes, Guth and Kovac, 1979);
- Postevent questions themselves may distort memory (Cohen and Harnick, 1980);
- Dramatic memory may be quite different from ordinary memory (Terr, 1991);
- Both enhanced memory (hyperamnesia) and amnesia have been shown to occur in traumatized children. Single or brief traumatic episodes often result in enhanced memory, while chronic trauma often results in denial, suppression, and dissociation (Terr, 1991).

In sum, nondeliberate distortion may be overlooked in the quest to uncover deliberate assessee misrepresentation. The reverse also may be true. The literature on eyewitness identification, for example, seems to assume an honest responder and largely ignores the possible interactive effects of deliberate with nondeliberate distortion. For many forensic professionals, clinical notions of cognitive intent may be inextricably intertwined with an assumed interplay of internal behavioral and affective experiences. For them, this may forever render moot the question of differentiating nondeliberate distortion from that which is intended. Finally, practical difficulties may be more formidable than theoretical leanings. The American Psychiatric Association in DSM–III (1980, p. 285) stated, "The judgment that a particular behavior is under voluntary control is made by the exclusion of all other possible causes of behavior." Easier said than done. It is simply impossible, given the state of the art, to rule out all nonvoluntary contributions to distortion even if forensic mental health professionals had sufficient time. Yet coming to conclusions regarding deliberate misrepresentation assumes differentiation from other sources of distortion.

Maladaptive Conditions and Misrepresentation

Historically, the literature is replete with instances of individuals faking almost all forms of maladaptive conditions including physical symptoms, thought disorders, organic conditions, mental retardation, dissociative reactions, and more-focal symptoms to include hallucinations, suicidal behaviors, and violent tendencies. Those with genuine pathognomic conditions have been found to create or exaggerate symptomatology and/or dangerousness, clearly suggesting that the existence of true maladaptive conditions is not preclusive of faking and may in fact provide an experiential basis for elaboration when needed. It should be noted that people with genuine clinical conditions may also deny or minimize their pathology to avoid treatment or labeling.

Faking maladaptive behavior appears to have been seen by clinicians throughout much of the historical and current literature as psychopathological itself. DSM–IV is among the sources saying that an assumption of psychopathology, for example, is made when factitious disorders are operative (American Psychiatric Association, 1994). This often involves a personality disturbance with voluntary symptom control involving no ostensible goal other than to assume the patient role. In Munchausen syndrome, for example, the patient's goal direction is to consciously fake symptoms, often both dramatic and acute in nature (e.g., lower quadrant pain, bleeding secondary to anticoagulant ingestion), in order to obtain or retain hospitalization status. In Ganser syndrome, often seen in prisoners awaiting trial, a wide complex of psychological symptoms may be present, including "Vorbeireden," the symptom of talking past the point or giving approximate answers. There may be a pronounced Vorbeireden during probes about a particularly violent crime. It is almost always superimposed upon a severe personality disorder with a frequently changeable and broadband set of simulated symptoms. The goal of assuming a patient role is paramount. A factitious disorder is considered a mental disorder in DSM–IV (300.16) (1994) and therefore can theoretically be the basis for a finding of no criminal responsibility in insanity trials. Munchausen syndrome, for example, can be extremely incapacitating in terms of (a) effects on work and interpersonal relationships due to hospitalization; (b) an association with positive medical findings in many cases; (c) frequent iatrogenically induced physical illness; (d) an association with drug abuse, analgesics being the most commonly abused drug of choice; and (e) a suspected association in many cases with brain damage, most particularly to the right hemisphere (Pankratz, 1981).

Factitious disorders must be differentially diagnosed from malingering. These are behaviors in the service of attaining an obviously recognizable goal other than to assume the role of a patient (e.g., escape from war duty, prison, or work responsibility). The distinguishing feature in DSM–IV (1994) appears to incorporate the notion of an attempt to maintain the sick role due to presumed intrapsychic conflicts (factitious disorders) versus blatant lying to attain a recognizable and usually socially disapproved goal (malingering). Clinicians are cautioned to be alert to malingering in (a) medical-legal contexts, (b) cases where there is a substantial difference between claimed symptoms and objective findings, (c) noncooperative evaluatees, and (d) when the examinee is an Antisocial Personality Disorder who usually has a history of violence (as in the case beginning this chapter).

Certain syndromes besides factitious disorders have been empirically demonstrated to incorporate misrepresentation as part and parcel of pathological behavior patterns. These especially include the psychopathic and substance abuse/dependent disorders (e.g., Sierles, 1984). Unfortunately, this is not very helpful, as persons outside these diagnostic categories are quite adept at distortion, given motivation to do so. These include:

• Those with psychotic, neurotic, or organic disorders as already discussed;

• Normals gaining admission to mental hospitals (Rosenhan, 1973). Congruent with the literature, his findings on misrepresentation suggest predictor false positive errors where persons who were not psychotic have successfully gained entrance into treatment facilities. False negative errors also appear to be operative, as illustrated by the second portion of Rosenhan's 1973 study. Here, pseudopatients would attempt to gain admission to a hospital where the professional staff, hearing of Rosenhan's earlier success, claimed they could not be fooled. Out of 193 patients admitted during the test period, 41 were judged with strong confidence to be faking by at least one staff member, and between 19 and 23 patients were considered suspect by at least three other staff members, including two psychiatrists. Actually no pseudopatients were sent to the facility.

• Normals on projective and objective psychological tests (Carp and Shavzin, 1950; Irvine and Gendreau, 1974; Krug, 1978). The limitations of psychological testing are well documented (Megargee, 1970; Ziskin, 1981; Rogers, 1984; Schretlen, 1998) and include the finding that virtually every psychometric device devised to detect misrepresentation can itself be faked to some degree.

• Normals instructed to fake neuropsychological deficits (Heaton, Smith, Lehman and Vogt, 1978; Faust, Hert and Guilmotte, 1998). In the Heaton, et al. study, volunteer malingerers were paid $25 for participation with a $5 bonus for successfully faking brain injuries. Malingering subjects were instructed to play the role of a victim of an accident caused by others in order to litigate financial compensation. They were to imagine that their daily lives had become worse with their earning power substantially reduced and that they deserved any compensation awarded. Ten neuropsychologists provided independent blind ratings regarding their belief as to whether the subject was faking on the Halstead-Reitan Battery and other measures. Results showed that the malingerers did as badly as those afflicted with genuine head injuries, and no significant difference emerged between WAIS IQs or on two of the neuropsychological summary measures. The ten neuropsychologists incorrectly classified from 31 percent to 50 percent of the subjects with a true-positive rate for actual injured subjects ranging from 44 percent to 81 percent and a true-negative rate for malingerers ranging from 25 percent to 81 percent. In general, the success of the judges ranged from chance expectations to about 20 percent better than chance.

In the Faust et al. study (1998), children between the ages of 9 and 12 were told to perform less well than usual, but not to be so obvious that the person assessing them would know that they were faking. They were offered $15 for participating and an extra $5 if they concluded their performance without detection (apparently it was assumed that children will lie for less money than the adults in Heaton). The children completed the Weschler Intelligence Scale Children–Revised and the Halstead–Reitan Neuropsychological Test Battery for older children. Of the 42 clinical neuropsychologists who reviewed the cases, 93 percent diagnosed abnormality and 87 percent of these clinicians attributed the results to cortical dysfunction. No clinician detected malingering, yet three-fourths of the respondents said that they were at least moderately confident in their judgment, and almost two-fifths were highly or very highly confident that their judgments were correct.

- Normals and those of mixed diagnostic categories exposed to intrusive procedures such as forensic hypnosis, sodium amytal/sodium pentothal, and the polygraph (Adelman & Howard, 1984).

- Normals and those of virtually every diagnostic category when clinically interviewed (Ziskin, 1980). The validity and reliability of the traditional clinical interview is so poor for example, that individual examiners are hard pressed to repeat their own performance (Hall, 1982, 1985, 1986).

In general, no reliable and valid method or procedure exists within the mental health or criminal justice systems that by itself adequately measures basal violence or other types of distortion. Most extant measures of distortion were derived in artificial laboratory situations or were clinically developed in a largely uncontrolled fashion. Further, there is no unified theory of misrepresentation in general or of forensic distortion in particular. Moreover, in practice settings, clinicians appear disinclined to acknowledge successful client misrepresentation for both theoretical and practical reasons, as previously discussed, and they tend to ascribe an underlying pathological process accounting for its occurrence. Few studies examine the ability of mental health professionals to detect deception and those that do are disappointing in nature. Clearly, the state of the art in detecting misrepresentation is rudimentary.

Several considerations are in order, however. First, a distortion analysis must occur in each forensic evaluation if one wishes to account for misrepresentation in proffering conclusions. Second, measures of forensic distortion have been developed and are of some utility, thus reinforcing continued use of such methods. Useful methods include objective psychological validity subscales that have built-in cutoff scores (e.g., Rogers, 1988 and 1997; Schretlen, 1998) and neuropsychological measures to detect faking bad (K. Freeland and J. Craine, personal communication, 1981). Controversial methods such as hypnosis have been found to refresh memory, "truth drugs" have lowered resistance to conscious deception in some cases, and the polygraph is claimed to be found accurate above chance levels. The exact percentage of polygraph accuracy is unknown, especially when procedures such as the concealed knowledge test are utilized, where only the perpetrator could know particular crime-specific events. These controversial methods are not usually accepted in court due to their lack of compliance with established scientific standards. The forsaken interview has even yielded positive results in terms of uncovering deception and generating hypotheses for further inquiry.

Generally, extant deception-detecting methods seem to fall into five categories: (1) clinical methods such as interviewing, hypnosis, and observation in controlled settings; (2) psychological and neuropsychological testing; (3) psychophysiological methods such as the voice stress analyzer and the polygraph; (4) statistical distortion baselines such as studies on Munchausen syndrome coping behaviors (e.g., Pandratz, 1981); (5) detection methods from other fields such as cultural practices reported in the anthropological and sociological literature.

Two of these categories, clinical methods and psychometric testing are the focus of this book. A direction of search in this difficult area is offered up by Resnick (1984) who stated, "The decision that an individual is malingering is made by assembling all the clues from a thorough evaluation into an integrated whole." The assumption here is that detection of distortion is possible, perhaps as a demonstrable and replicable phenomenon in which relevant conclusions can be decision-analyzed.

Faked Maladaptive Conditions: Clinical and Psychometric Methods

It is helpful to the examiner to look for assessee strategies of distorting information. This includes determining whether there is an *underreporting* of known significant historical or violence-related events. Nonfaking examinees usually have no difficulty reporting previous violence, for example, as these events tend to stand out in memory, unless they have suffered chronic trauma (e.g., Terr, 1991). Difficulty in reporting may be encountered by those with chronic, frequent histories of violence with too many acts of aggression to recall and/or from perpetrators suffering from violence-related memory deficits caused by gross intoxication, blackouts, or other conditions. Many fakers, especially those who minimize a violence history, seem to assume that requested recall of one's violence history or arrest record involves a large degree of acceptable error and omissions. Others, especially career criminals, may hope their arrest record is incomplete or simply unavailable in a particular jurisdiction.

Determining that the examinee has *amplified* pathological past conditions associated with violence, when compared to known conditions, may support a finding of distortion. A common ploy is to attempt to reduce criminal culpability, say from murder to manslaughter, by claiming ingestion of intoxicating substances far greater than indicated by blood alcohol concentration (BAC) or other tests. Amplification almost always indicates prevarication as compared to underreporting. It is much more difficult to establish deliberate distortion when the defendant claims, for example, less intoxication than instruments indicate, since nondeliberate memory factors may genuinely impair accurate recall—distortion is known to have occurred, but may genuinely be nondeliberate.

Suspect paradoxical motives are sometimes reported for the time of the exhibited violence or other maladaptive behavior. Actual incidents include raping a stepdaughter in order to "teach" her not to have sexual inhibitions and to be a sensuous wife, or assaulting others "for their own good" so they will not persist in their inappropriate behaviors. Such motives also included convenient memory lapses involving violent behavior that the assessee is ostensibly motivated to remember when no reasonable factor (e.g., high stress, intoxication, substance-induced blackouts, psychosis, retardation, dissociative states) accounts for the lack of recall and all indications are that the perpetrator acted willfully rather than defensively.

Various sets of guidelines for detection of misrepresented behaviors have been offered. Resnick (1984), for example, presented 16 clinically derived cues for the detection of psychosis. The signs seem to be on a consistency model in that the apparent clinical task is to detect behaviors incompatible or unlikely to be seen in genuine psychosis. They are presented in Table XII.

Feigned hallucinations are discussed by Resnick (1984), and involve the assumption that some fakers of hallucinations may not be aware of the true nature and quality of the reported aberrant perceptual processes. They may not know that hallucinations, for example, are usually

- Related to some psychic purpose.
- Associated with delusions.
- Eliminated or reduced when the individual is involved in activity.
- Perceived as emanating from outside the head; many schizophrenics affirm that the voices could have been due to their imagination.
- Either or both female and male voices with clear messages. Talking back to voices and perceiving the voices as accusatory occurs a minority of the time. Schizophrenics usually perceive voices speaking directly to them.
- If visual hallucinations, consist of normal size people and are in color.
- If olfactory, perceived as unpleasant odor.
- If gustatory, onset of peculiar tastes is often seen in acute schizophrenia.
- If alcohol-induced, the hallucinatory figures are vivid, often discussing the

TABLE XII
RESNICK'S CLINICAL SIGNS OF SIMULATED PSYCHOSIS

Sign of simulation	Relevant factor for client
1. Overplaying psychotic role	Attempt to behaviorally act congruent with ideosyncratic view of psychosis
2. Calling attention to symptoms	Rare in schizophrenia and some other psychotic conditions
3. Difficulty in imitation of form and style of psychosis	Often focuses on content of psychosis
4. May fit no diagnostic category	Unaware of DSM–III inclusionary and exclusionary criteria
5. Sudden onset of delusions	Unaware that delusions usually take several weeks to develop
6. Unlikely to conform to delusional content	Discrepancy between delusion content and behavior may not occur to examinee
7. Far-fetched story	Often seen in naive simulators
8. Contradictions in crime account more likely	Misrepresentation involves multiple attempts at consistency on several levels (crime events, mens rea, affective states)
9. Presentation of self as blameless	Desire to achieve favorable evaluation outcome
10. Long latency of response and/or repetition of questions	Stalling to formulate best response
11. More suspicious if accomplice involved	Sane accomplices usually do not associate with insane perpetrators
12. Nonpsychotic alternative crime explanation given	More likely to give psychotic alternatives to crime if genuinely psychotic
13. Perseveration of responses rare	More likely due to organicity or other genuine disorder
14. Description of hallucinations in stilted manner	Unaware that this is unlikely in genuine hallucinations
15. More unlikely to exhibit residual signs of schizophrenia	Ignorance of typically occurring prodromal and residual signs in schizophrenia
16. Genuine schizophrenics may fabricate hallucinations	Attempt to escape punishment for crime

substance abuser in the third person, and are more easily shared than are the hallucinations experienced by schizophrenics. The alcoholic's actions are rarely the result of command hallucinations and most often seem motivated by a desire to avoid threat or disgrace.

Resnick (1984) postulated that in some alleged conditions such as simulated post-traumatic stress disorder (PTSD), there is an attempt to avoid psychotic signs in an attempt to obtain desired outcomes. DSM–IV that PTSD consists of almost entirely subjective symptoms, and simulators may avoid all but necessary examinations in order to establish a claim. When interviewed, they may seem evasive, sullen, anxious, greedy, or uncooperative while presenting themselves as blameless. Many times there is a spotty history of employment and a claimed lack of ability to work with concurrent involvement in recreation and persistence toward the award of a claim. There is often a refusal to do work of which they are capable. There may be a history of alleged incapacitating conditions.

Several other considerations regarding faked PTSD are in order (Newman, 1985). First, distortion behaviors can range from the abject liar who did not experience any trauma to those who were continually exposed to severe, heavy stress (e.g., in combat, as a long-term hostage) and those who are pathological liars. Clinical signs include bringing up the traumatic event early, versus reluctance to discuss the phobia. Moral indignation or anger instead of surprise may be witnessed when the client is confronted with suspicions of distortion. A key difference is that with the genuine PTSD client issues will eventually emerge around impulse control whereas with fakers, control, and social manipulation of others is often not a problem.

The Structured Interview of Reported Symptoms (SIRS) was developed by Richard Rogers in 1992 and is increasingly being used to measure deception. The instrument uses a structured interview, with items culled from a number of other instruments. Component features rare symptoms that occur infrequently in a patient sample. Other scales include absurd symptoms, that rarely occur together in the same individual and blatant symptoms that would appear as obvious to an unsophisticated examinee. Scores are tallied, and each primary scale produces a response along a continuum from honest responding to definite malingering. The SIRS has high inter-rater reliability and good predictive validity, making it a sound instrument.

Non-verbal Signs of Distortion

Freud addressed nonverbal signals relating to detection when he stated, "He that has eyes to see and ears to hear may convince himself that no mortal can keep a secret. If his lips are silent he chatters with his fingertips; betrayal oozes out of him at every pore." (Freud, 1959). This appears to be an overstatement. The literature on "body leakage," represented in part by Ekman and Friesen (1969, 1972); Ekman, Friesen, and Sherer (1976); Kraut (1978); Depaulo and Rosenthal (1979) does, however, reveal a wide array of non-verbal behaviors that have been associated with deception. Table XIII presents a sampling of the literature. Knapp (1978) interpreted the "body leakage" literature as follows:

> Scholarly investigations have found a variety of nonverbal behaviors associated with liars rather than truthful communicators. According to these studies, liars will have a high pitch; less gaze duration and longer adaptor duration; fewer illustrators (less enthusiastic), more hand-shrug emblems (uncertainty), more adaptors—particularly face play adaptors; and less nodding, more speech errors, slower speaking rate and less immediate positions relative to their partners. Findings have not always been consistent, and researchers have used many methods of creating a deception to study. Furthermore, we don't know which, if any, of the cues just listed are used by observers when attempting to detect deception. We do know, however, that most studies show that untrained human observers can detect deceptive communication by strangers at about chance level—about 50% of the time.

Paul Ekman and Maureen O'Sullivan published the study "Who can Catch a Liar?" in 1991 in the *American Psychologist* and demonstrated an increase in the likelihood of catching liars, but only by a very specific, highly trained group: the U.S. Secret Service. Ekman and O'Sullivan used videotapes with known behavioral differences between honest and deceptive samples. They showed the tape to "professional eye-catcher groups" including the Secret Service, federal polygraphers, judges, police, psychiatrists, self-selected people who enrolled for a course on deceit, and students. Only the Secret Service group did better than chance in detecting deceit, and in this group alone, experience and age accounted for heightened accuracy. Secret Service lie-catchers used different information than did inaccurate lie-catchers. They listed different and more varied behaviors, emphasizing nonverbal more than verbal cues. They seemed better able to interpret subtle facial expressions as well. However, the study is limited in that the deception focused upon the concealment of strong negative emotions, and this is, of course, a very narrow form of deception.

Despite the difficulties, guidelines have been proffered. The face, arms/hands and legs/feet, in that order, have the capacity to send information with a reverse pattern in representing availability of leakage. The feet/legs are considered a good source of leakage when it occurs, with the face so easily controlled for many people that it may serve primarily as a distracter to the evaluator. Further, the face reveals deception from so called "micro-facial" movements, often very difficult to detect (except for Secret

TABLE XIII
POSSIBLE NONVERBAL SIGNS OF DECEPTION

1. High body tension shown by movement responses

2. General appearance of face; prevaricators show more emotion; honest responders are more pleasant

3. Gaze aversion allows examinee to gather thoughts

4. Less assertive and dominant within the evaluation context

5. Higher voice pitch, whining sounds

6. Longer latency of verbal responses

7. "Nose-up" associated with expressing an opinion; "rubbing" the nose while affirming positive past event is suspect

8. Hand over mouth or facial shielding means insecurity

9. "Steeple configuration" with the fingertips associated with speaking from a position of confidence

10. Clasping hands in order to hide movement

11. Sitting back; leaning forward associated with eagerness to answer

12. More speech errors

13. Less clear and more circumstantial

14. Shorter, terser answers

15. Posture incongruent with portrayed emotion

16. Self-grooming responses involving the hands

17. Smiling for inappropriately long periods

18. Less confidence

19. Nonrevealing of self-experiences

20. Higher in disparaging remarks, especially toward the victim

21. Holding less closely to the task at hand

22. Greater interest in test results and use thereof

Service experts) but which represent the true, brief facial emotions before they are disguised. Finally, the evaluator may be able to detect distortion in the face and other sites, but is often inaccurate in determining the underlying affective state.

Following from this discussion, most persons concentrate on self-control of facial behavior when attempting to deceive but tend to neglect limb movement. Peripheral movement is rarely involved in positive deception; one would look for lies of omission rather than commission in the hands, for example.

Examination of verbal content when compared to studying nonverbal attempts at deception may be more revealing of actual events. This finding has implications for forensic training and practice in that reading transcripts of examinees or listening to voice tapes may yield more information than attending to available visual cues. This would address the frequent finding that those who "ham" or histrionically exhibit verbal lying behaviors are more apt to deceive. The criminal justice system is replete with examinees of this description. Finally, the accuracy of detection seems to bear no relationship to ability to deceive others. People are generally more consistent at successful lying than they are as lie detectors. Clear sex differences have not emerged on any of those parameters.

Statement Reality Analysis

A clinical method to detect and testify about misrepresentation of crime accounts, termed "Statement Reality Analysis," has been developed by Udo Undeutsch (e.g., see 1982, 1984 reviews). The key assumption here is that truthful crime accounts differ "significantly and noticeably" from those that are deliberately distorted, minimized, or fabricated. Witnesses, victims, and perpetrators usually relate their stories a number of times after an alleged crime, first to family, friends, and acquaintances; then to police; then perhaps to the psychological expert called in on the case. The various versions of the same event presented to different parties are analyzed to note differences over time. The basic account should be the same even though there may be parts that have changed, depending on the type of questions asked, demand characteristics of the setting, the mood of the interviewee, and a host of other factors. An observation here is that sex cases, upon which the Statement Reality Analysis was formulated, are often elaborated upon without misrepresentation as the witness overcomes embarrassment and because subsequent questioning may be regarded as supplemental. Reversals in the other direction, for example, denying events affirmed earlier, is less frequent and more suspicious.

Undeutsch holds that the manner of delivery is important in that the

TABLE XIV
UNDEUTSCH'S STATEMENT REALITY ANALYSIS

Fundamental criteria:
- Concreteness (clarity and definiteness; vividness, individual depiction)
- Wealth of detailed description
- Originality (free of formalization, cliches, and stereotypy)
- Inner coherence and consistency
- Mention of details of the criminal-victim relationship known to be typical for the respective type of offense
- Embedding the reported crime in the actual life situation of the defendant and alleged victim

Special manifestations:
- Reference to details that exceed the capacity of the witness to fabricate
- Report of subjective experiences
- Trankell's "Bilateral Emotion Criteria"
- Mention of unexpected complications
- Mention of socially disapproved demeanor on the part of the witness before, during, or after the occurrence reported
- Spontaneous corrections, improvements, additional information

crime account should be delivered in a way congruent with the witness's educational level, sex, age, and other factors. Spontaneous and lively deliveries are held to be good signs of honest representations, with less importance attached to losing the conceptual train of the account. Note how this finding may conflict with deception-related "hamming" reported in the nonverbal leakage literature. In any case, the various related elements about the crime account are seen to fit into a pattern suggesting basic truthfulness or prevarication. The major criteria for the reality analysis are presented in Table XIV.

Elaborating on Table XIV, a typical crime relationship refers to the usual role each partner played in a crime case played to initiate, maintain, or conceal of the activities. Concealment on the part of the child sex victim, for example, is expected behavior, at least temporarily, in response to an adult offender introducing a pact of secrecy or threats. Embedding the crime into the actual life situation of the relevant parties is considered so important by Undeutsch that when fulfilled, it is seen to minimize the chance that the account was fabricated from imagination or really is a transplanted version of what occurred with other people.

Reference to details that exceed the mental capacity of the victim includes precautionary measures taken by the perpetrator and disarming statements designed to lure the victim into the act. Reporting of subjective feelings includes ambivalences, changes in the emotional feeling between relevant parties after the instant offense, victim indignation over perpetrator acts caused by exposure to the crime, and changes in behavior such as developing startle responses when touched or approached by others similar in some characteristics to the perpetrator. Avoidance of similar contextual settings when given the opportunity may be observed. Trankell's "Bilateral Emotion Criterion" is operative when the witness's personal situation must be considered (e.g., phobias) to understand an emotion that is described relevant to the crime (e.g., fear and avoidant responses). "A necessary condition is, however, that the emotion has been evoked by two independent stimuli, one of which emanates from the event under investigation" (Undeutsch, 1982, p. 47). Mentioning unexpected complications would include interruptions and changes from the anticipated sequence of crime events.

Undeutsch (1982, 1984) noted that it is virtually impossible in criminal cases to obtain the "ground truth;" that is, obtain an independent, valid, and reliable criterion of actual crime events. He nevertheless claimed a 90 percent case outcome as truthful in approximately 1,500 cases with a 95 percent conviction rate for the offenders. Cases consisted primarily of European defendants. Although none of the convicted parties were determined to be innocent by new conflicting evidence when the Statement Reality Analysis was utilized, the authors suggest extreme caution when attempting to validate such remarkable claims.

Response-style Taxonomies

A different approach to detect misrepresentation of maladaptive conditions by focusing on exhibited response styles was independently reported by Rogers (1984, 1988) and Hall (1985). Rogers (1984) presented a clinical heuristic model, designed to identify what clinicians use in distortion detection, and an empirical model based upon the literature. The two models are quasi-independent since some clinicians are aware of the research literature. The first response style of the empirical model is reliable, meaning that the examinee answered in a forthright, honest manner. Behaviors associated with this style include (a) consistent self-report, (b) unlikely rare symptoms, (c) sequence of symptoms congruent with diagnosis, (d) balance of obvious and subtle symptoms (e.g., as shown by MMPI item endorsement), (e) gradual onset of symptoms, (f) likely admission of common foibles, (g) likely endorsement of idealistic self-attributes, (h) no random pattern of responses, (i) likely that reported symptoms are consistent with clinical observations, (j) unlikely to show improbable failure rate, (k) unlikely to show responses that are nearly, but not totally, correct, and (l) unlikely to show endorsement of "stereotypes" of neurosis. This and the next two response style presupposed intentionality.

The second response style is malingering, involving the deliberate creation or exaggeration of symptoms. It includes (a) consistent self-report, (b) likely rare symptoms, (c) sequence of symptoms inconsistent with diagnosis, (d) increased obvious-over-subtle symptoms, (e) sudden onset of symptoms,

(f) likely admission of common foibles, (g) unlikely endorsement of idealistic self-attributes, (h) no random response pattern, (i) improbable failure rate, (k) possible that many responses are nearly or approximately correct, (l) often very willing to discuss symptoms, and (m) a small percentage endorse "stereotypes" of neurosis. Differences between the honest responder and the malingerer emerge on about one-half of these signs.

The third response style is defensive, referring to the denial or minimization of psychopathology. It includes (a) a consistent self-report, (b) a decreased obvious-compared-to-subtle items, (c) unlikely admission of common foibles, (d) likely endorsement of idealistic self-attributes, (e) no random pattern of responding, and (f) unlikely endorsement of "stereotypes" of neuroses. Notice that the only indicators that clearly distinguish this response style from the previous two are (b), (c), and (d), reflecting in part the dearth of research for this particular distortion pattern.

The fourth response style is irrelevant, signifying inconsistency and nonengagement in the assessment. It is characterized by (a) inconsistent self-reports, (b) rare symptoms likely, (c) obvious symptoms may increase, and (d) very likely a random pattern of responses. This fourth response style may not be intentional, instead resulting from brain damage, psychosis, confusion, or other factors.

A fifth response style of unspecified deception is offered by Rogers (1984) as a catchall category. He recognizes that a combination of styles is possible, such as shown by the examinee who inadvertently invalidates testing by attempting to appear psychopathological. The use of test cutoff scores for deception is strongly recommended by Rogers. Finally, there is the important recognition that no single indicator is indicative of any particular response style.

Hall (1985) presented a similar taxonomy to Rogers (1984), but focused on possible motivation for given distortion styles under two time conditions. This was based upon the notions that (1) some examinees tend to present evaluation responses with the goal of obtaining desired outcomes, and (2) response styles may be differentially employed for presented data relevant for the time of the crime compared to the time of the evaluation. The four response styles are faking good (i.e., denying or minimizing maladaptive behavior), faking bad (i.e., exaggerating or creating maladaptive behavior), no perceived distortion (i.e., responding honestly from the perspective of the examinee), and invalidating results. This means at least 4 or 16 distortion styles may be employed, corresponding to the four distortion styles under two time conditions. Table XV presents possible motivational sets for the 16 response styles using basal violence (i.e. historical) versus recent violence (e.g., crime related) as the maladaptive responses.

Faking good for the present and the past may occur when denial and/or

TABLE XV
DISTORTION STYLES:
POSSIBLE MOTIVATIONAL SETS FOR DANGEROUSNESS EVALUATIONS

	Fake good	Fake bad	No distortion	Invalidating results
Fake good	Evidence seen as weak; demand characteristicsa unusual and severe	Desires treatment most recent violence due to	Violence-free present coupled with concealed	Unknown
Fake bad	Desires to be seen as rehabilitated with previous violence due to due to environmental events	Desires to be punished, depressed, psychotic	Violence-free present coupled with no past violence	Unknown
No distortion	Benign past with attempt to cover up current violence	Violence-free past coupled with desire to receive help	violence-free present, violence-free past	Unknown
Invalidating results	Unknown	Unknown	Unknown	Unknown

minimization is the best perceived strategy due to insufficient evidence, unavailable documentation (e.g., juvenile records, expunged records), or other factors leading to the examinee's conclusion that an evaluator's determination of dangerousness rests on weak supports. This pattern may also occur to some extent due to the demand characteristics of the evaluation or particular personality traits of the examinee. Determination of this distortion style may lead to further evaluator inquiry such as examination of the database upon which the violence may rest, or attempts to correct or account for demand characteristics of the evaluation setting (e.g., multiple evaluations in different contexts).

Faking good for recent violence coupled with faking bad or no distortion for previous violence may occur when the examinee does not desire sanctioned intervention and wishes to convey that there is no present danger to others even though previous violence may be present. This strategy, if successful, may be useful at sentencing in order to obtain a reduced sentence. This may also occur in prison in order to obtain release, furloughs, or special privileges. It is advantageous in some incarcerated settings to have a violent past and a benign present. This may communicate to the staff that their interventions have been effective, while keeping the more predatory inmates at a distance because of an established violent reputation. In such cases, staff are well advised to conduct interviews with the most recent victim and witness to obtain more-accurate descriptions of violent behaviors.

Faking good for the past and faking bad or presenting no distortion for the present is often seen in individuals with a history of serious violence who committed a recent violent crime for which they were caught, and who would rather be committed to a mental hospital than go to prison. There may be a switch to faking good for the present when the individual is ready to leave the treatment facility. Personality disorders in recent years appear to involve this response style more frequently as more psychopaths enter the mental health arena. There are usually efforts to cover up lack of responsibility, impulsivity, manipulation of others, and outbursts of rage, often temporarily successful once in the treating facility. Here, the value of carefully documented observations by nursing staff is invaluable. A quick reversion to baseline behavior may be seen in unstructured situations.

Faking bad both for the present and the past is a poor prognostic sign and may be due to a cry for help, psychotic decompensation, overriding guilt, or other pathological, nonadaptive factors.

Psychometric Testing

Suspecting that the examinee is utilizing a particular strategy presupposes use of particular assessment methods that give data on the direction and magnitude of distortion. Psychometric methods to assist in detecting misrepresentation may be relevant in this regard. Table XVI presents some psychometric methods found helpful in determining the four basic response styles. Most of the results found using these methods are relevant to current distortion; however, some methods (e.g., parallel intelligence testing), may reveal information about the past when other data is available (e.g., a previous similar IQ test; clinical behaviors before, during, or after the violence indicative of a certain level of mental functioning).

No one method, even with positive results, confirms that distortion has occurred. Findings from a combination of methods, selected for particular deficits/excesses the defendant is claiming, may demonstrate but never prove a particular response style. Some psychological and neuropsychological test methods for determining misrepresentation follow, the first six of which were adapted to violence prediction from Freedland and Craine's (1981) attempt to detect faking bad in worker's compensation and criminal assessment cases.

PARALLEL FORMS. This involves retesting on a similar form at a subsequent temporal evaluation point (e.g., several hours later; the next day). When tested for intelligence, the defendant may want, for example, to excuse his past violent behavior by appearing intellectually subnormal but not so retarded as to appear obvious. The problem for the defendant is to

TABLE XVI
PSYCHOMETRIC METHODS TO DETECT POSSIBLE CLIENT MISREPRESENTATION

Detection method	Response style			
	Fake good	Fake bad	No distortion	Invalidating
• Parallel forms		X	X	
• Regression equations		X	X	
• Illusory difficult items		X	X	
• Easy vs. difficult versions of same test		X	X	
• Instrasubtest scatter on graduated scales		X	X	
• Learning curves		X	X	
• Validity scale analysis	X	X	X	X
• Test item analysis (e.g., subtle vs. obvious items)	X	X	X	X
• Goodness of fit	X	X	X	X

replicate the same quantitative degree of intellectual deficit upon retesting. Short forms of parallel tests such as the Peabody Picture Vocabulary Test (PPVT) and the Weschler Memory Scale (WMS) are especially useful here. The task for the investigator is to take the practice effect into account.

REGRESSION EQUATIONS. The client who obtains a given score on one test should obtain similar results on a quite different (criterion) measure if indicated by previously calculated regression equations. Performance outside the statistical confidence interval employed is suspicious because of the mathematical rarity. Scores on the Slossen Intelligence Test (SIT), for example, should approximate scores on the Stanford Binet even though there is a difference in standard deviations. The Shipley-Hartford can be used to predict Weschler Adult Intelligence Scale (WAIS) scores.

FAILURES ON ILLUSORILY DIFFICULT ITEMS. This involves tasks that are very easy for normal persons. Apparently some fakers believe mistakes are allowable on all tests and make a number of deliberate errors to suppress performance and perhaps to look consistent across the entire battery of tests. Various aphasic screening devices and simple memory tasks can be used for this (e.g., California Memory Test). One example is to present 1, 2, ; I, II, III; A, B, C; O, , ; a, b, c in rows of three on a single sheet of paper. The examinee is told that this task involves 15 different figures with a delayed starting time of 10 seconds. It is presented as a difficult task. Virtually all persons can perform this with at most several errors.

A variation of this is the use of a word recognition test in which a series of 15 simple words are read to the client at the rate of one per second. After a five-second delay, a sheet of paper containing 0 words is given with instructions to underline recalled words. After at least 10 minutes, an auditory-verbal learning task is administered, consisting of a list of 15 different words of comparable difficulty. The number of words recalled is then compared to the number of words recognized in the first test. If the number of recalled words exceeds the number of recognized words, then evaluator suspiciousness should increase since recognition is generally easier than recall.

EASY VERSUS DIFFICULT VERSIONS OF A SIMILAR TEST. The method here is to present the evaluation of a performance under easy-versus-difficult versions of a similar task, such as the task of counting dots in clusters of five versus massed in groups of 100. Not all fakers believe one task is easier than the other and therefore may perform in a similar manner on both tasks by slowing down clustered counting.

INTRASUBTEST SCATTER IN GRADUATED SCALES. Some persons make deliberate errors on measures graduated in difficulty, such as within various Weschler subscales. Many fakers do not perceive the graduated nature of the item difficulty and hence display errors throughout the test. Normal and even brain-impaired subjects may perform in a nonscattered manner, but psychotic subjects often display scatter. A variation of this error is intersubtest scatter. Fakers tend to show more variable test results where little would be expected.

LEARNING CURVES. Here, the test may require repeated trials in order to produce a typical learning curve with initial acceleration of correct responses until performance becomes more difficult and levels off. Fakers may show no learning curve, or even a decrease in performance, where none would be expected.

VALIDITY SCALE ANALYSIS ON OBJECTIVE PSYCHOLOGICAL TESTING. The most well known and most utilized validity scales are those on the MMPI. They include analyses of individual validity scales (i.e., L, F, K scales) and those in combination (e.g., F-K, F+K) for the detection of faking bad, faking good, degree of defensiveness, and random or otherwise invalidating response sets.

Other objective psychological tests, such as the California Personality Inventory (CPI), the 16 Personality Factor Questionnaire (16 PF) and the Bipolar Psychological Inventory (BPI) have built-in validity scales for analysis. A variation of this method is the comparison to results of studies using known fakers. Subjects instructed to fake on a neuropsychological test battery did poorly on math and sensory tests, for example, but well on measures tapping cognitive functions (e.g., see Heaton, et al., 1978).

TEST ITEM ANALYSIS. On the MMPI and other objective psychological tests, checks can be made for item consistency, number of questions unanswered, and differences in scores reflecting subtle-versus-obvious items endorsing psychopathology.

GOODNESS OF FIT BETWEEN PSYCHOLOGICAL TEST PROFILES AND COMMUNITY/INSTITUTION BEHAVIOR. Here, a patient may attempt to simulate or suppress a maladaptive condition on psychometric testing, yet have difficulty maintaining the chosen behavioral role once in the other, more unstructured settings. The attempt at distorting test outcome should also be reflected in validity-scale performance unless the examinee is psychologically sophisticated.

Assessment Considerations:
Decision Tree and Proposed Format

How does an evaluator make sense of the foregoing clinical guidelines, empirical indicators, and presented systems of distortion analysis, a number of which rest on different theoretical bases and investigative techniques? Perhaps a partial answer lies in not so much what to choose among the array of available signs but how the forensic distortion assessment should be conceptualized, implemented, and reported to the referral sources. This section discusses such clinical considerations, presents a rationally derived decision tree, and suggests that the report format should be linked to the decision path of the clinician.

General considerations include an evaluator's alertness to, but not an assumption of, misrepresentation in high-risk groups such as criminal defendants and personal-injury litigants. Resnick (1984) zealously stated in this regard, "Above all, malingering must be suspected." This includes possible distortion to achieve desired outcomes by those genuinely affected with maladaptive behavioral patterns such as borderline mental retardation and schizophrenia. Yet a determination of forensic distortion should be arrived at not by an assumption of its occurrence or by eliminating other factors (e.g., test score variance, stress responses) as DSM–IV suggests, since this may be impossible, but by a positive demonstration of its occurrence. Forensic distortion is "true" when it can be reproduced by accepted measurement procedures.

Evaluation Process

Prior to the evaluation, the clinician should have knowledge of the available data for relevant events (e.g., police reports, prior evaluations, school, job, military records) in order to link historical influences with specific acts, feelings, and thoughts that occurred before, during, and after alleged crime events. The evaluator should have as much information as possible in order to establish baseline responding to independently derived events. The first part of forensic evaluations by one of the writers, for example, involves a set of 10–20 questions to elicit answers already known from multiple other sources and that are prepared prior to the evaluation. This is an attempt to establish "ground truth" behaviors; nonverbal leakage, semantic style, affirmation, or denial of established behaviors and events can then be observed and compared to later interview responses associated with unknown answers regarding to what actually transpired.

Other considerations for the time prior to the evaluation include knowledge of the relevant forensic distortion literature; evaluating the assessee as soon after the relevant event as possible to reduce the time for the assessee to rehearse or modify a story, or to simply lose recall; and independence from attorneys on both sides of the adversary process; practically, this may mean that the clinician obtain a clear understanding from the referral source that the final report must be distributed to all relevant legal parties and be paid for prior to court appearance.

During the evaluation, the clinician should take the following steps:

- Insist that only the assessee and the evaluator are present so as not to violate standardization guidelines upon which assessment methods may be based. This is not always possible, but is clearly preferred.
- Orient the assessee as to the nature and purpose of the evaluation, lack of confidentiality, dissemination of the final report, and mechanisms for challenging report conclusions. Another forensic mental health evaluation, paid for by the assessee, is allowed in some jurisdictions as a supplement to court-ordered evaluations.
- Audio tape or video tape the procedures to include the orientation and post-assessment termination behaviors. Taping allows for a more detailed analysis than afforded by clinical notes, refreshes the memory in preparation for court or other relevant gatherings, and better allows for independent evaluation of the assessment if necessary or desired. For some procedures such as forensic hypnosis, audio/visual taping of the evaluation is considered a minimal standard of intervention. Taping runs the risk of being utilized by the opposing party for cross-examination and scrutiny by their expert, and this should be discussed with the referring attorney.
- Use multimodal methods in establishing possible distortion. This is based

on the notion that the state of the art in detection of distortion is primitive and no one discipline or assessment technique has the total answer to possible distortion. The argument that multimodal methods may not cumulatively contribute to accuracy may not be relevant for forensic settings because (a) no empirical studies have rigorously compared the relative combined effects of several distortion methods, (b) the stakes in legal settings are often much higher than in other evaluation settings, and (c) it communicates to the court or other relevant parties that much care may have been devoted to the assessment procedure, which potentially increases testimonial impact.

- Empathize with the assessee in order to obtain his or her view of relevant events. Empathy, as discussed, refers to the art of perceiving events from the perspective of the assessee. There is no need to seduce the assessee by artificially showing positive regard or genuine warmth in a manipulative attempt to extract data. The assessee often perceives this for what it is and responds to it with increased caution or counter manipulation–both potential sources of further forensic distortion. Assessees are offered the opportunity to present their side of what happened, and they have the opportunity to discontinue, if desired.
- Ask open-ended questions when interviewing after baseline questions are presented, encouraging the examinee to work out the details of the answers. Use visual recall methods if possible (e.g., "Tell me what happened as if I were looking through a video camera," or "If I had been present, what would I have seen?"). Proceed to specific questions after the flow of information stops or becomes irrelevant. The literature reveals that answers to open-ended questions are generally more accurate than responses to specific queries, and specific questions may modify the assessee's later evaluation behavior.
- Show flexibility of evaluator response. Modify the evaluation as needed if distortion is indicated in a particular area. The evaluation may be prolonged in order to tax defensive styles, questions can be inserted quickly to catch the defendant off guard, and tasks can be presented to give an opportunity to affirm unrealistic symptoms or behaviors.

Toward the end of the assessment, the assessee can be confronted with the evaluator's suspicions, giving every opportunity to change an earlier version of relevant events. The assessee may be asked to write down a list of his or her distortion behaviors in evaluative settings. This seems to disconcert the psychopath in particular, who may be investing much energy in presenting a consistent story. The affirmed distortion behaviors can be further used to test the limits of the crime account. Multiple interviews allow the assessee to be seen on "good days" and give the opportunity to repeat questions to assess consistency across time.

After the evaluation, the principal task is to present the clinical findings to the referral source in a standardized format. The post-hoc decision path of the examiner should be reflected in the proffered report. A rationally derived decision tree in this regard is presented in Figure 5. Such a model of forensic distortion (1) enables the examiner to better understand and present to the court or other relevant agencies the process as well as the data content that constituted the basis for proffered conclusions, (2) links a reporting format to the decision path, (3) generates hypotheses regarding examinee distortion leading to new areas of inquiry, and (4) provides a framework for eventual standardization of the forensic distortion concept.

The basic premise of the decision tree is that possible deliberate misrepresentation by the assessee must be considered in every forensic examination as a total or partial focus on the part of the examiner, depending upon referral questions. Proffered conclusions in forensic reports rest on an assumption that data used to validate those conclusions is known to represent either actual or misrepresented events. Totally or partially fabricated or denied events can be used as data if the examiner knows the nature and quality of the distortion or at least its measurable or noticeable aspects. The basis of drawn conclusions describes a cognitive process of the examiner acting upon the content of the gleaned but usually imperfect data. Each step in this decision process contains inclusionary criteria that, when not fulfilled, invalidate final conclusions.

All data and interpretations must therefore be clearly identified as relevant either to the time of the evaluation or for the crime (or other relevant event), or both. This is because all utilized information from the forensic database comes from particular people who gather information at particular temporal points. Hence, that input is subject to distortion errors for those times. Some information is cross-temporal in nature. Information drawn for the time of the evaluation may be relevant for the time of the relevant event in that some maladaptive conditions or behaviors are known to be chronic in nature (e.g., process schizophrenia, mental retardation, alcoholism, personality disorders).

Inclusionary criteria for the time of the evaluation would include knowledge of the assessee's and/or witness's mental status, current and anticipated stressors, competencies and limitations, and other relevant factors. For the time of the crime (or other relevant event), an accurate finding of distortion may or may not have relevance for evaluation behavior. The behavior may have constituted a habitual response linked together with similar historical patterns, or perhaps was a rare or unique event triggered by an unusual combination of environmental or internal circumstances. Inclusionary criteria include historical analysis of previous-versus-crime (or other relevant event) behavior, an analysis of how evaluation behavior may in part represent behavioral patterns at the time of the instant offense (or other relevant event), and analysis of crime (or other relevant event) occurrences in terms of assessee behaviors interacting with responses of others involved.

The strongest part of the forensic distortion analysis may be the database upon which the eventual conclusions rely. Hall (1985) discussed parameters to consider. One parameter is inclusionary criteria such as utilizing a multi-sourced, multidisciplinary approach that relies on information drawn from

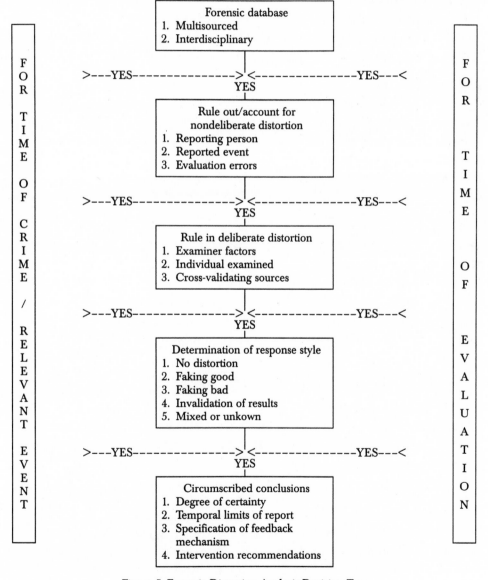

Figure 5. Forensic Distortion Analysis Decision Tree

sources other than the examinee for purposes of cross-validation. another parameter is exclusionary criteria such as deficits of the examiner, subjects, and assessment. Data should be gathered especially from sources the examinee wishes to conceal because of likely unfavorable information (e.g., juvenile records, school records, prison or hospital records, so-called expunged records that may be available in unmodified form at the government archives center, former spouses and mates, military performance reports, information in other states or countries). It is helpful for the credibility of the examiner to cite as many database sources as possible when subject to cross-examination in court on particular points. It is important to stress that for both mental illness and mental retardation, a documented prior history is imperative to rule out malingering.

The next step in the decision process consists of ruling out or accounting for nondeliberate distortion within the reporting person, the reported event, and evaluation error. Table XI presents circumstances associated with these three nondeliberate factors. It is possible to reconstruct the cumulative stress experiences of the assessee at the time of the crime (or other relevant event) by the use of any of several tests (e.g., Social Readjustment Rating Scale). Nondeliberate distortion may largely explain both evaluation and crime behavior and therefore should be considered first. Note here that a finding of nondeliberate distortion does not prevent the evaluator from proceeding in the decision analysis. It must be weighed with all other factors.

The exclusion of all sources of nondeliberate distortion may be impossible, as discussed earlier. The third step in the decision process is to rule in deliberate distortion by a positive and replicable demonstration of misrepresentation as shown in Tables XI to XVI. Deliberate distortion may be shown by the examiner, the examinee, and all cross-validating sources. Examiners can and do deliberately distort for various idiosyncratic and system-based reasons. It is not inappropriate to look at evaluators track records for particular types of forensic assessments (e.g., percentage of the time for which they testified for the defense versus the prosecution) and whether or not proffered findings can be replicated by equally competent examiners. You can be sure that the opposing side will be looking at *your* prior performance.

Although the natural evaluation target of distortion is the assessee, much more emphasis should be placed upon scrutinizing cross-validating sources for misrepresentation. Psychometric testing is highly appropriate for assessing distortion in victims and other cross-validating sources, assuming their willingness after a clear and open explanation of the limits of confidentiality. Data derived from the input of significant or knowledgeable others that indicate bias or a given motivational set (e.g., desire for revenge, to rejoin defendant) should be excluded from the data pool or placed into proper perspective by comparison with other known data.

The fourth step determines the type and magnitude of the basic distortion styles apparently used by the assessee, if measurable. Two of 25 response-style combinations may be chosen, corresponding to faking good, faking bad, no perceived distortion, invalidation of results for whatever reason(s), and mixed or unknown response styles under the two time conditions. It is appropriate to link mental conditions to each of the response styles if mental conditions affected behavior during the interview, or crime or other relevant event.

The last step in the decision tree consists of offering focal, time-limited conclusions in accordance with the spirit of scientific parsimony and psycholegal wisdom in hedging one's forensic bets. A statement that the forensic database and methods used to gather data were sufficient to draw relevant conclusions and that those conclusions were arrived at independently from the other current examiners in the case is appropriate. Degree of certainty should be reported, thus accounting for missing or conflicting data regarding distortion, but be careful to offer reasonable levels of certainty, given limits of the materials used. Some clinicians have been known to offer their opinions with "absolute" and even "100% certainty." Such unscientific and exaggerated statements will certainly be exploited upon cross-examination. The temporal limits of the report should be presented both for reassessment and liability purposes. Lastly, a feedback mechanism should be specified for subsequent reevaluation of opinions.

Phenomenological and Assessment Considerations

Results of the forensic distortion analysis inexorably lead to suggestions regarding case disposition. Considerations for assessment include two major points.

First, all persons have a history of misrepresenting events depending upon a host of factors such as stage of development, styles of adaptation to environmental events, perceived role in the assessment-and-crime process, peculiar characteristics of involved perpetrators, victims, contextual stimuli, and vested interests in given outcomes. Further, all database sources should be considered suspect in that since they are fundamentally derivable from what people have reported, they contain a degree of inaccuracy whether or not descriptive criteria, operationalized guidelines, or instrumentation are used in the process. Nondeliberate sources of distortion may account for much of the statistical variance of total distortion in reported events and thus should be differentially considered as a key focus of every forensic evaluation. For deliberate distortion, the assessment task is not to determine whether misrepresentation has occurred or whether the examined party possesses the trait of honesty. Rather, since even the most credible source presents but partial truths, the assessment attempts to determine possible response styles and crudely estimate the magnitude of distortion both for the time of the evaluation and particular previous events. The whole truth for a given event will probably never be known. Yet, it is important to remember that the world of the forensic clinician is very different from that of the courtroom, where ultimate questions are decided and truth is weighed.

Second, the forensic distortion analysis is necessarily based on limited methods and assumptions regarding human behavior, although it has one distinct advantage over other methods. This is based upon the notion that the truth stands by itself and deliberate distortion takes energy and thought and oftentimes reveals inconsistencies. Response styles of individuals with regard to specific situations appear highly resistant to extinction and hence are measurable and replicable.

The state of the art in forensic distortion analysis is nominal/ordinal; a crude taxonomy has emerged in terms of response styles representing various types of possible misrepresentation. Until a unified theory of distortion emerges, with the breakthrough probably occurring in instrumentation, psychometrics, and methodology, interval/ratio properties described by deductive mathematics will be beyond our reach. Until that time, the best advice is to use methods in combination, particularly at three levels–cognitive, affective, and behavioral–as each represents one of the three psychological pillars of understanding human behavior.

SUMMARY

The forensic distortion analysis is a first-generation set of procedures relevant to the reporting of deliberate and nondeliberate client misrepresentation as it relates to violence or other maladaptive behaviors. Contributions to the conceptualization of the forensic distortion analysis are discussed and include legal theory/statutes, nondeliberate stress factors, developmental studies of memory recall, use of psychological validity scales, nonverbal "leakage" behaviors, and semantic analysis to determine believability. A decision tree in regard to client response styles for the time of the evaluation and the time of the crime or other relevant event is presented with implications for the reporting of client believability.

Chapter 7

ACCURACY AND IMPACT LITERATURE REVIEW AND DEMONSTRATION STUDIES

Excerpt from Prediction Task #3: Ensley Takamura

ON NOVEMBER 24, 1975, AT 8:30 P.M., Doris Tanaka ran into the Criminal Investigation Unit of the Honolulu Police Department (HPD) and reported that she had been raped and sodomized by an individual, later identified as Ensley Hiroshi Takamura.

Ms. Tanaka provided a statement in which she related the following: Early in the afternoon, she left her home in the Palama section of Honolulu to catch a bus to the University of Hawaii where she was a first-year undergraduate student. As she waited at the bus stop, a yellow late-model Mercury Cougar pulled up alongside her, and the perpetrator, who was holding an unfolded map, called to her, asking for directions to a street in the area.

The perpetrator, feigning confusion as she explained the proper route, asked her to accompany him to show him the way. Inasmuch as he presented a clean-cut, young, perplexed appearance and it was broad daylight, she agreed to do so. The perpetrator had also told her that he would drop her off at school, thus actually saving her time. She then directed the perpetrator to the location he had asked about, which was an unpaved road leading to the rear of Koko Head Park.

The perpetrator stopped the car after it was hidden from view, reached down near his seat, and pulled out a large kitchen knife. He pointed it at her and in a soft voice said, "All right, take off your clothes." She initially refused, but removed her clothing when he brandished the knife viciously. The perpetrator ordered her into the back seat. While she was obeying, he removed his pants and shorts, leaving his shirt on.

He then said to her, "I want you to suck me first." At that point, he had an erection. She lay on the back seat and the perpetrator leaned over her, thrust his penis into her mouth, and again told her to perform oral sex. After

117

a few minutes he turned her over onto her stomach and attempted to enter her anus. Upon finding it difficult, he called her a "bitch." He persisted and managed to enter her anus, which was painful to her. They had intercourse in this manner for about one minute. Then the perpetrator told her to turn over onto her back, whereupon he had vaginal intercourse with her to ejaculation.

Following the culmination of the acts, the perpetrator pulled out a second knife and stared at her as if debating some course of action. A car passed and the perpetrator seemed to "snap out of it." Doris then asked him to take her to school and he replied, "I don't know, I don't have any gas." He subsequently dropped her off on a main street a few blocks away. He was quiet during the latter part of the abduction and did not volunteer any further information.

A vaginal examination conducted on Doris following her report was positive for the presence of spermatozoa.

On January 25, 1976, police were dispatched to the Red Hill area of Diamond Head Park, where they found a group of people gathered around the body of a young Asian female, later identified as 14-year-old Linda Asari, who showed no signs of life. A witness related that while riding his bicycle up the road, he observed the female lying face down on the road in a puddle of blood. He related that she had displayed a weak pulse, and he reportedly attempted to render aid. She had tried to speak but had only coughed blood. Another witness reported hearing the voice of an angry male, followed by "what sounded like a loud shriek" shortly before observing a yellow sedan speeding away from the area.

An examination of the deceased revealed the presence of spermatozoa in her vagina. An autopsy revealed that the victim had sustained five deep stab wounds anteriorly, three of which had passed completely through her heart, and one stab wound, posteriorly in the upper back. Her bloodstream was negative for alcohol and barbiturates.

During the ensuing investigation, a bloodstained knife with a five-inch blade was found near the scene of the crime. It was presented to Doris Tanaka, the previous rape and sodomy victim, who positively identified it as the one that had been used against her.

DEFENDANT'S STATEMENT. Primarily through the tracking efforts of the first victim, the defendant was arrested and formally charged with murder, two counts each of rape and sodomy. During the sexual assaults, Doris Tanaka noticed the number of the parking sticker issued by a local high school. Searching through the yearbooks, Doris identified the perpetrator. For several months, the police refused to act on this information, claiming that since they had contacted the school and the administration refused to reveal the student/owner of the sticker, the information might not be allowed in court. Only after noticing similarities between the rape/sodomy incident and the subsequent murder, did they pursue the investigation. When arrested, Ensley Takamura declined to make a statement, and he was subsequently placed in a youth detention center.

In a later written statement, the perpetrator addressed the question of motivate for the multiple acts of violence. He said he had no insight into his reasons for the crimes and added that he was sorry. He claimed no unusual stresses or state of mind due to ingestion of chemicals or alcohol on the days of the offenses. Indeed, later questioning of acquaintances and family revealed that no one had noticed Takamura acting in an atypical fashion. He had no history of significant violence before these acts.

Referring to the rape of Doris Tanaka, he wrote, "All I know is before all this started I would read the newspapers and read about sex. All my classmates were talking about sex. It seemed like the magazines were filled with sex. I was a virgin before the [Tanaka] rape. I felt a lot of pressure to have sex with someone, but I did not know how to do it. I was afraid and embarrassed to ask anybody."

Almost four years passed before the perpetrator successively plea bargained for reduced charges and came up for sentencing (see Appendix F). Maximum imprisonment for the reduced charges was ten years with the possibility of release after 48 months for good behavior. Assuming the four-year period after the instant crimes was violence free (he worked part time as a volunteer and lived at home), what would you tell the sentencing judge in terms of the defendant's future dangerousness? What factors from his history, nature of the crime, or behavior patterns could back up your violence prediction? A thorough reading of Appendix F, except for the Case Outcome Section, is suggested before an expert opinion is rendered.

Chapter 4 *Toward Decision Analysis*, discussed how the history of prediction of dangerousness has been, until recent years, dismal. For example, in 1978, a task force of the American Psychological Association concluded, "The validity of psychological predictions of dangerous behavior . . . is extremely poor, so poor that one could oppose their use on the strictly empirical grounds that psychologists are not professionally competent to make such judgments." (p. 1110) Similar comments came from the American Psychiatric Association about the ability of their membership to make predictions, as well as from critics of the scene, and from popular commentators. Despite these naysayers, courts continued to insist that mental health professionals conduct assessments of dangerousness, for society demanded that such assessments be completed before an individual could be involuntarily committed or otherwise lose basic rights.

Not until the ground-breaking MacArthur Foundation risk assessment studies of the 1990s has research been able to strengthen the hand of those professionals who must attempt to predict dangerous behaviors. Of course the MacArthur findings are limited to persons incarcerated in mental hospitals and thus represent only a very small proportion of those persons who come before the courts and the criminal justice system. Nevertheless, the success of these studies strongly argues that well-structured analysis and careful data gathering will increase the accuracy of our predictions.

Inherent in the argument that one cannot/should not predict dangerousness are two assumptions that are the empirical focus of this chapter. The first assumption is that previous follow-up studies on predicted dangerousness accurately reflect the low frequency with which violence is assumed to occur. It is commonly held that dangerousness predictions are inaccurate because of the assumed low base rate of violence. Stone (1975) summarized extant arguments when he stated that even if a psychological test could be developed that was 95 percent effective in predicting who was to be violent, out of 100,000 persons tested, several thousand would be falsely labeled as dangerous.

A second assumption holds that even if dangerousness prediction accuracy is high, the impact in court and other decision-making settings is minimal because its alleged key statistical correlates (e.g., sex, age, race, and socioeconomic status), are largely ignored for sociomoral reasons (Monahan, 1981a, b). Therefore, from two perspectives—low accuracy and low impact— dangerousness prediction has been seen as a hazardous and risky enterprise.

This chapter presents data suggesting that dangerous behavior can be predicted with both accuracy and impact. Further, it is argued that the factors in the decision-making prediction process may be quite different for long-term, short-term, and imminent dangerousness as the function of temporality, data availability, and other relevant issues are considered. This chapter questions the assumptions that earlier studies on dangerousness (e.g., Kozol, Boucher and Garofalo, 1972; Steadman and Cocozza, 1974; Cocozza and Steadman, 1976; Steadman, 1977; Thornberry and Jacoby, 1979), which use arrest, and to a much lesser extent, rehospitalization data to indicate dangerousness, have provided anything but extremely limited conclusions, primarily because of the truncated nature of the dependent variables employed and the nonrandom nature of the crimes reported. The focus typically is on serious criminal violence, which represents only a portion of total violence. Family and institutionally sanctioned violence is usually ignored, as is dangerousness to self or property. Finally, it is argued that dangerousness prediction by forensic mental health professionals does indeed have positive impact in the courtroom and is differentially influential depending on which specific prediction methods are utilized.

Violence Base Rates

Empirical literature supports the commonsense notion that much dangerousness is not reflected in available violence base rate data. The National Victimization Panel (U.S. Department of Justice, 1978) estimates, for example, that only about half (53%) of violent crimes are reported. Fear of involvement, unwillingness to subject oneself to official inquiry, and the threat of retaliation are among the often-stated reasons for nonreporting. Once reported, arrests are completed for about one-third of the violent crimes (Kelly, 1976; Webster, 1982). This works out to about 20 percent of violent crimes culminating in arrest, closely corresponding to yielded proportions found by other investigators (e.g., Petersilia, Greenwood & Lavin, 1977).

Conviction rates for those arrested represent an even lower figure with less than 2 percent of rape complaints, for example, resulting in conviction (Hotchkiss, 1978). Once convicted and released, recidivism rates for rapists within four years after parole is about 70 percent (Kelly, 1976). In a study by Abel, Blanchard, Becker and Djenderedjian (1978), rapists currently free in the community were found to have raped anywhere from five to one hundred times, a phenomenal rate that highlights the slim chance of aversive legal consequences for this type of predatory violence. Reporting of attempted rapes also reflects a low rate depending on whether or not resistance was shown by the victim. Block (1981) stated that only 27 percent of attempted rapes involving minimal resistance by victims ended in notification of the police. Even murder, with the best clearance rate ranging from 70 to 75 percent (Webster, 1982), results in about one out of four murderers not being apprehended and charged for their acts. Table XVII presents data on exhibited dangerousness not culminating in arrests.

Violence is defined as such by many victims only when serious actual or threatened bodily harm is involved (National Victimization Panel, 1978, 1983). Crimes likely not to be reported include family violence such as child, parent, elderly, sibling, and spouse abuse, and assaults perpetrated by acquaintances of the victim or those acts that did not involve medical treatment for sustained injuries. In the first study to be presented, for example, less than 2 percent of the nearly 100 acts of clearly arrestable violence actually resulted in arrest by policy authorities. These violent crimes included primarily family violence and assaults, as mentioned above, as well as robbery and arson. Contrary to findings by some (Shinnar and Shinnar, 1975; Wolfgang, Figlio and Sellin, 1972; Monahan, 1981a), the vast majority of these violent acts were not perpetrated by those whose prior violence resulted in notification of authorities. Perhaps the small core of repeat violent offenders, variously estimated at around 5 to 10 percent of offenders who cause the bulk of criminal violence in a given community, only applies to

TABLE XVII
VIOLENCE NOT RESULTING IN ARREST

Reporting population	Violent acts	Ratio acts/arrests	Empirical study
Incarcerated offenders	Robbery	10/1	Petersilia, Greenwood, & Lavin (1977)
Military personnel	Assault (including spouse and child abuse)	10+/1	Hall, Catlin, Boissevain, & Westgate (1984)
Juvenile offenders	Felonious violence	9.5/1	Wolfgang (1977)
Adult offenders (recidivists)	Injury offenses	7/1	Wolfgang (1978)
Incarcerated rapists	Rape	5.2/1	Groth, Longo, & McFadin (1982)
Incarcerated pedophiles	Sex assaults against children	4.7/1	Groth, et al. (1982)
Adult offenders	Felonious violence	4.5/1	Wolfgang (1977)
Adult offenders (nonrecidivists)	Injury offenses	3/1	Wolfgang (1978)

certain crime categories and circumstances.

Overall, most arrestable violence in this country probably does not result in notification of the authorities by the victim, arrests by police agencies, convictions by the court, or incarceration in penal institutions. Further, the rates for each level of governmental intervention may differ depending on crime category and other variables. The importance, therefore, of including measures to estimate true basal violence is essential in dangerousness evaluation since this is highly relevant to dangerousness prediction (Ziskin, 1981; Hall, 1982, 1984, 1986).

This suggests that the previously cited follow-up studies of dangerousness may not accurately reflect the accuracy of violence prediction. Perhaps violence is not as low a base-rate phenomenon as previously supposed. Finally, it would leave open the question as to whether forensic mental health professionals are accurate dangerousness predictors, since this may not have been adequately assessed by extant research.

TABLE XVIII
VIOLENCE PRE/POSTDICTION STUDIES

Code	Population	N	% True positives	% True negatives	Outcome measure	Time span	Prediction context	Author, year
A	Criminally insane	257	37	46	Arrest/hospitalization	3 yrs.	Community	Cocozza & Steadman (1976)
B	Military enlisted	120	75	75	Self-report, observation	3 mo.	Community	Hall, Catlin, Boissevain, & Westgate (1984)
C	Felony probationers	339	39	91	Conviction	32 mo.	Community	Holland, Holt, & Beckett (1982)
D	Sex offenders	435	35	92	Arrest	5 yrs.	Community	Kozol, Boucher, & Garofaro (1972)
E	Pretrial patients	158	28	25	Arrests/medical & other records	2 yrs.	Community/hospital/incarceration	Menzies, Webster, & Sepejak (1985)
F	Criminally insane	81	69	80	Institution records	≥12 mo.	Forensic hospital	Perkins (1980)
G	Psychiatric inpatients	118	41	92	Medical records	46 days	Hospital	Rofman, Askinazi, & Fant (1980)
H	Parolees	2,200	30	92	Arrest	14 mo.	Community	Michigan Corr. Dept. (1978)
I	Criminally insane	152	41	59	Arrest/hospitalization	3 yrs.	Community	Steadman (1977)
J	Criminally insane	98	70	30	Arrest/hospitalization	45 yrs.	Community	Steadman & Cocozza (1974)
K	Parolees	7,712	<1%	>99%	Conviction & incarceration	1 yr.	Community	Wenk, Robison, & Smith (1972)
L	Psychiatric inpatients	40	39	27	Medical records	1 wk.	Hospital	Werner, Rose & Yesavage (1983)

Does dangerousness prediction research show higher accuracy as a function of increasing state of the art knowledge relevant to violence? Indeed, a historical trend toward increased accuracy is observed. Table XVIII lists most of the original dangerousness research from a variety of settings. Overall accuracy, as measured by the average of true positives and true negatives, reveals that two-thirds of the six most-accurate dangerousness prediction studies occurred in the 1980s (studies coded B, C, D, F, G, H). Two-thirds of the six least accurate studies were reported in the 1970s (studies coded A, E, I, J, K, L). This suggests that a second generation of dangerousness prediction research in the 1980s that Monahan (1984) described is qualitatively different and superior to most of the earlier classic works. At least there is an acknowledgment, based upon second-generation studies, that violence can be predicted but with limitations. Problems of the first-generation research include:

- Restricted outcome measures. The massive study of Wenk, Robinson and Smith (1972), involving more than 700 offenders, demonstrated how sound predictor variables can be nullified by unreasonable criteria measures. The investigators used conviction and incarceration for violence as the criterion variables to be included for follow-up of dangerousness.
- Lack of knowledge in regard to how predictors made their dangerousness prognostication.
- Sole use of two abnormal population groups (i.e., offenders, mentally ill, or both).
- An apparent vested interest in stating that violence could not be predicted, particularly in those studies showing very low accuracy levels.

The recent research described in Chapter 4, Toward Decision Analysis and Violence Prediction: Second Generation and Beyond attempted to take these limitations into account by specifying criteria measures, utilizing control groups, defining terms and procedures, and proceeding in a thoroughly professional and unbiased fashion.

Once violence is defined and adequate outcome criteria selected, the question then turns to which predictor variable contributes most to overall accuracy. Table XIX addresses this question by asking which studies include history, especially frequency, severity, and recency of violence acts, opportunity variables that allow or expand the expression of violence, and triggering stimuli to aggression. History and triggers in a Hall et al. (1984) study, for example, accounted for more than 70 percent of the statistical variance. Opportunity factors were nicely accounted for by Perkins' (1980) institutional study, as he essentially had a captive audience, but he failed to build in for recency or triggers. Falling in dead last of the studies considered, Menzies, Webster and Sepejak (1985) went through an elaborate analysis of pretrial patients' personality traits as judged by two raters with bachelor degrees in

TABLE XIX
VIOLENCE PRE/POSTDICTION STUDY HIT RATES AND CRITICAL FACTORS (TP+TN/2)

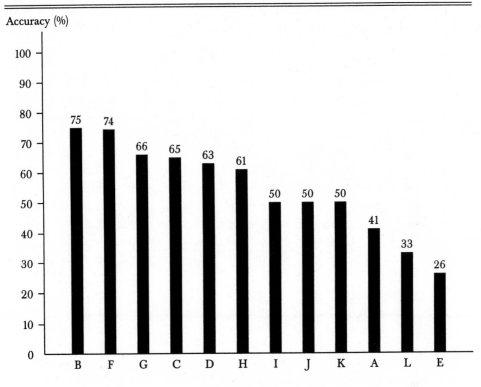

Accuracy (%)

(TABLE XVIII)

Critical Violence Factors:

	B	F	G	C	D	H	I	J	K	A	L	E
Severity	X	X		X	X				X			
Frequency	X	X	X	X	X				X			
Recency last act			X			X	X			X	X	
Current triggers	X		X	X	X		X	X	X	X	X	X
Current opportunity		X	X								X	

Investigation code

psychology and no prior clinical experience. This study would have probably still yielded poor accuracy rates as the investigators did not seem to be aware of the predictees' basal history of violence. They instead focused on assumed personality traits, already established in the literature to be a poor prediction of violence. In general, more use of history, triggers, and opportunity factors, increases the accuracy as reported in the violence literature.

Another salient fact derived from a review of the literature is that the base rate of the predictee is considered the most accurate measure of dangerousness (Steadman, 1980; Steadman, Vanderwyst and Ribner, 1978; Monahan, 1981). Basically, these studies are concerned with long-term prediction because base rates for short-term or imminent dangerousness are generally not available. An example of base rates is the Federal Bureau of Investigation finding that the chances of reoffending violently within four years after release from incarceration for murder, rape, robbery, or aggravated assault conviction generally exceed 70 percent (Kelly, 1976). Unless the forensic examiner is working with a highly select client pool over a protracted period of time (e.g., in prisons, jails, and probation offices) most assessed individuals would not fall into this base rate category.

Yet the base rate strategy reasoning persists. The base rate for perpetrating homicide, roughly paralleling the number of murder victims, is about 10 per 100,000 population unit per year (Webster, 1982), which means, for example, that even allowing for the warranted assumption that homicide is underreported by a factor of 10 and assuming the predictee was not a felon with a prior conviction (and subsequent release) for a serious violent act, the best long-range prediction accuracy would still occur simply by stating that most people will not engage in lethal violence. In essence then, base rates are held to be the best index of long-range dangerousness potential, especially since many circumstances of future events will not be known. A functional statement of long-range dangerousness prediction could be the following:

$$Dp = f \text{ (group violence rate)}$$

where the probability of dangerousness (Dp) to others within a long-term temporal period is a function of the base rate of violence exhibited by the group to which the predictee holds membership. For certain groups (e.g., the FBI four-year-recidivism group), a major proportion of the statistical variance may be accounted for by relevant group membership.

Unfortunately, the use of base rates may rest on limited outcome criteria representing only a fraction of exhibited violence, as discussed earlier in this chapter. Second, very few base rates are known, and those that are appear relevant only to long-term predictions. Third, base rates that are available, such as the PROMIS (1977) research project's finding that the probability of a violence-related arrest after five previous violence arrests approaches mathematical certainty, may be distorted by a labeling-and-selection process in which some persons are perceived by police authorities as dangerous and are arrested more frequently than others, independent of actual exhibited violence. Certainly easily identified minorities such as black, Latino, or Asian people can attest to increased stop, search, and arrest rates by local police. Among black urban dwellers, the phrase "D.W.B." refers to being stopped for "Driving While Black." Fourth, base rate strategies are always nomothetic in that the predictee is being compared to group performance in regard to violence and thus individual factors are not considered.

Another approach to the dangerousness literature deals with the variables associated with violence that are assumed to lower the threshold for its occurrence. This is primarily an idiosyncratic method in that individual behavior patterns, traits, and relevant events are compared against one another and the predictee's own history in predicting violence. This approach can be used in conjunction with "anchoring" methods of predicting violence, which rely on base rates as the first estimate of possible violence before individual factors are taken into consideration.

Four main clusters of such variables seem to emerge from the behavioral science literature over the last four decades.

1. Historical variables characterize the nature of past violence and have been linked to future violence. These include multiple incidents of past violence (Wolfgang, 1972); fatal or potentially fatal past violence (Steadman and Cocozza, 1974); immediate recency, for example, within the previous year (Michigan Corrections Department, 1978); and past violence being maintained or intensified by the pain cues from the victim (Dubonowsky, 1980). Relevant developmental events associated with later childhood or adult violence include a violent parental or sibling model (Bandura, 1973), victim child abuse status (Goldstein, 1974), and relevant school problems such as assaults on teachers, temper tantrums, fighting, and threats (Justice, Justice and Kraft, 1974).

2. Current operating variables are long-term events associated with violence or that are assumed to directly influence it, or short-term events that are assumed to be intense in impact and thus set violence into motion. Long-term events include demographic characteristics such as young adult male status (Webster, 1982), poor socioeconomic status (Monahan, 1981a), single or divorced marital status (Michigan Corrections Department, 1978), conditions or attitudes of the predictee such as a self-perception or image of dangerousness (Webster, et al., 1979), deficits in verbal skills (Toch, 1969), low frustration tolerance (Geen & Berkowitz, 1967), and a subcultural acceptance of violence to solve problems (Blumenthal, 1976). Short-term events include, as the two most frequently mentioned triggering events, substance abuse

(MacArthur, Wolfgang, 1972; Petersilia et al., 1977; Monahan, 1981), and breakup of the central love relationship (e.g., Bandura, 1973); other examples are insults to self-esteem (Toch, 1969), body space invasion (Kinzel, 1970), and instructions to aggress (Milgram, 1963, 1965).

3. Opportunity variables expand the possible severity of exhibited violence or allow its expression. Examples in the former category include availability of a firearm (Berkowitz and LaPage, 1967), presence of a physically weaker potential victim (Bandura, 1973), and elevation to positions of high authority where violence toward others is institutionally sanctioned (Fromm, 1973; Milgram, 1963). Variables that allow the expression of violence include release from incarceration into the community (Kelly, 1976) and cessation of taking tranquilizing medication (Stone, 1975).

4. Inhibitory variables operate to lower the probability that violence will occur; this type of variable falls into the lower range of frequency, intensity, duration, or recency of the previous three factors. A nonexistent basal history, for example, acts as an inhibitor by virtue of its absence (Kozol et al., 1972; Kelly, 1976). Current operating conditions associated with lower propensity to aggress include female sex, old age, high socioeconomic status, and high educational level (Kelly, 1976; Monahan, 1981); although these of course are changing with the times (e.g., females are catching up) and do not apply in certain crime categories (e.g., terrorism) whose group membership may be unique. Opportunity variables assume an inhibitory status when significant events eliminate or reduce the probability of aggression, (e.g., placement in solitary confinement, loss of means of transportation, or an invalid physical status).

From this behavioral science literature, a functional statement can be constructed relevant to the study of individual dangerousness prediction as follows:

$$Dp = f (H, C, O, I)$$

where the probability of short-term dangerousness, for example, up to several months after prediction, is a function of history (H), current operating conditions (C), opportunity (O), and inhibitions (I) as well as the availability of weapons. Where each variable is an operationalized expression of represented events, the entire functional statement becomes a testable hypothesis.

Yet problems remain even if this functional statement in operationalized form is later found to account for most of the statistical variance of the violent acts in groups of individuals or in the same individual over time. Most importantly, it may not predict imminently dangerous situations simply because essential information is lacking. As long-term prediction may be based on a different prediction strategy (i.e., idiosyncratic use of relevant factors), so imminent dangerousness prognostication strategy may be qualitatively different than both long-term and short-term predictions, especially when variables not available in more protracted temporal periods are scrutinized. These especially include contextual stimuli and victim traits. Contextual stimuli include such variables as location of the crime scene and the presence of third parties (Steadman, 1981), architectural features (Atlas, 1982), availability of a weapon (Boyanowsky & Griffith, 1982) and noxious environmental stimuli (Berkowitz, 1983; Horowitz and Willging, 1984).

Victim characteristics include acceptance of dominance from others and low self-esteem (Wetzel and Ross, 1983), similar socioeconomic status to that of the perpetrator (McClain, 1982), a proneness to group influence (Glezor, 1981), membership in some minority groups (Lightcap, Kurland and Burgess, 1982), and a tendency for acting out (Justice and Justice, 1982). Notice that victim traits sound similar to perpetrator traits, an observation that receives some support from a review of the victim literature (e.g., Block, 1981) and is worthy of further analysis.

A functional statement incorporating perpetrator, contextual stimuli, victim, and inhibitory factors for imminent dangerousness may be offered as follows:

$$Dp = f\,(P, C, V, I)$$

where the probability of imminent dangerousness up to several days after the prediction is a function of perpetrator variables (P), contextual stimuli (C), victim characteristics (V), and inhibitory factors (I). Inhibitory factors may be built into perpetrator, contextual, and victim factors, as in the contextual stimulus represented by the presence of a police officer inhibiting robbing responses, or the large body size or inappropriate gender diminishing chances a potential victim would be sexually assaulted. At this time we can only speculate due to a paucity of knowledge about imminent dangerousness prediction. It is interesting to note, however, that imminent dangerousness to others or self has emerged as the principal criterion for involuntary hospitalization in most jurisdictions, in the clear absence of sufficient normative data regarding the accuracy of such prognostications.

Demonstration Project #1: Dangerousness Prediction Accuracy

In an effort to investigate the feasibility of short-term dangerousness prediction, a prospective exploratory study involving approximately 700 volunteer male U.S. Army servicemen representing a cross-section of the military enlisted population was conducted over a three-month period (X age = 22.7 years; SD = 3.42 years). The purpose of the study was to investigate the following functional statement within a relatively controlled subject environment:

$$Dp = f (H, C, O, C, I)$$

where Dp was the probability of exhibiting of dangerousness within 90 days and H was basal historical violence, operationally defined; O were opportunity variables; C were conditions associated with violence; and I were inhibitions to aggress. A history of significant violence included penal code defined assault and aggravated assault; homicide; rape, sodomy, and other forced sex acts (not including statutory rape); robbery; kidnapping (to include hijacking); arson; and assisting other to commit suicide. A history of no significant violence included such antisocial behavior as animal cruelty, extortion, threats to assault, property damage (excluding arson), self-injury, and accidental infliction of harm on another person. A primary question of the research concerned how much of the statistical variation in the exhibited violent acts would be accounted for by the relevant factors.

A research team consisting of the chief investigator as project leader, a physician, an attorney, and several noncommissioned officers trained in mental health intervention explained to all Ss the purpose of the study from a research perspective with a detailed discussion of precautions against possible misuse of the results. Since research numbers were substituted for names after the second testing and the master list destroyed, Ss ran little actual risk of harm. A signed letter from the commanding officer guaranteeing no punitive action for revealed information was presented, and Ss were assured by the government attorney that no adverse legal consequences would occur.

Testing I consisted of a battery of evaluation devices with questions relevant to subject distortion (Bipolar Psychological Inventory validity and lie scales; Marlow-Crowne Social Desirability Scale), history of violent acts, attitudes toward violence (Buss-Durkee Hostility Scale), drug and alcohol abuse within the month preceding testing (questions were derived from Diagnostic and Statistical Manual III substance abuse criteria), breakup or difficulty within a central love relationship, and work difficulties. Total time for Testing I was two to three hours including the orientation on procedures and legal safeguards.

From the 700 Ss pool, 120 Ss were selected for Testing II (X age = 22.7 years, SD = 3.42 years, range = 18–38 years; X years education = 11.9, SD = .75). Whites represented 75% of the sample, followed by blacks (14%), and other minority groups (11%). These Ss represented individuals who chose to participate; signed their tests and waivers; passed all of the distortion and lie scales, psychometrically defined; and answered the questions on violence history, violence attitudes, chemical abuse, and other relevant areas. These

120 Ss were then divided into two groups Group A = 20 Ss, X age = 22.5; Group B = 100 Ss, X age = 22.7) with racial composition for each group similar to the selected sample of 120 Ss, in order to test the following hypotheses:

1. Those Ss with a prepotent history of violence and the operation of at least two stimulus triggers (i.e., intoxication, breakup, work problems) will show some form of significant violence toward others in the relevant time span. Prepotent in this context refers to a past history of multiple, varied, and severe exhibited violence.

2. All other Ss will show no significant violence toward others in the relevant time span.

   Testing II consisted of administering of the same battery of tests in Testing I; interviewing of the subject and his supervisor; and for the relevant time period, reviewing Provost Marshal records, troop medical clinic records, the hospital social work service child and spouse abuse log, emergency room reports, and department of psychiatry files. Several hundred person hours were expended in the data collection alone. Two cross-checks for reliability were performed as follows: the chief investigator randomly rechecked portions of those record sets previously examined by other research team personnel, and he also reinterviewed ten subjects from the selected pool. In only two cases did discrepancies appear, possibly due to the concrete format of the inquiry procedures with the revealed violent acts representing discrete yes/no events within a relatively short time period.

   Results revealed that a total of 94 acts of significant violence were perpetrated by Ss during the period of this research project. This included several aggravated assaults where weapons were involved, one rape, and one negligent homicide involving a vehicle. Assaults on others (other than spouse/child abuse) constituted the bulk of exhibited violence (32%), followed by spouse abuse (26%), low-grade robbery of fellow soldiers where small amounts were robbed and the perpetrator knew the victim (22%), and a deliberate fire setting (6%). Interestingly, only rarely was the violence reported to the police authorities even though it was clearly arrestable behavior. Likewise, the troop medical clinics, hospital emergency room, hospital social work service, and psychiatric records yielded very little data of value, and when documented, the data tended to be distorted by the perpetrating source, as revealed by later interview responses. Confirmation of violence was largely determined from S interview statements, S test responses, and in a few cases, eyewitness observation by interviewed others. Figure 6 is a histogram that displays exhibited violence in this study.

Dangerousness prediction accuracy was moderately high for both groups in the hypothesized directions. True positive accuracy rate was about 75 percent, meaning that of Ss predicted to be violent, 75 percent did show some sort of significant violence to others in the relevant time period. This leaves a false positive rate of 25 percent of Ss incorrectly identified as potentially violent. True negative accuracy was about 75 percent, leaving a false negative rate of 25 percent consisting of Ss incorrectly predicted to be nonviolent. The differences between the proportions were, as expected, highly significant, with $z = 2.49$ (p .006) for true positives/all positives versus false positives/all positives and $z = 6.30$ (p .001) for true negatives/all negatives versus false negatives/all negatives. Figure 7 presents a histogram of violence prediction accuracy.

Violent base rates yielded information relevant to the original hypotheses tested. Of Ss with no history of serious violence, 13 percent showed violence during the study. Of Ss with a history of serious violence, 47 percent

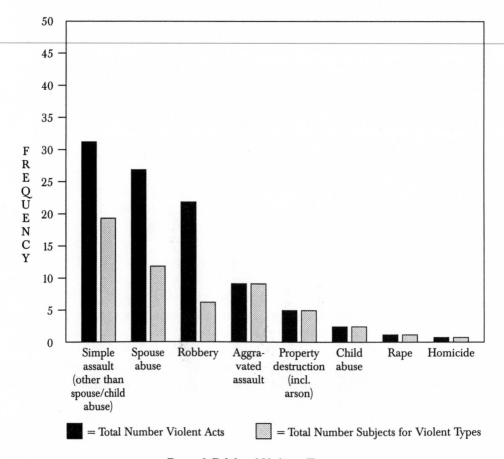

Figure 6. Exhibited Violence Types

showed some kind of violence during the relevant period, with 55 percent displaying violence for Ss with both a history of violence and with current triggers. Of those Ss with both a prepotent history of serious violence and the operation of several triggers, 75 percent showed violence.

Proportion testing showed significant differences between history and no history ($z = 3.36$, p .0005) and no history versus history with triggers ($z = 4.50$, p .0001) but not between history alone and history with triggers. However, all triggers were associated with a previous violence history, so the comparison of triggers alone versus history could not be determined. Possible inhibitions (greater age, higher education) yielded nonsignificant values. Opportunity variables could not be assessed as the military units would not release, for classified reasons, the exact movements of Ss within the prospective period. Figure 8 presents information on exhibited violence for historical and triggering variables.

The principal finding of this demonstration project was that short-term violence potential toward others can be predicted with a promising degree

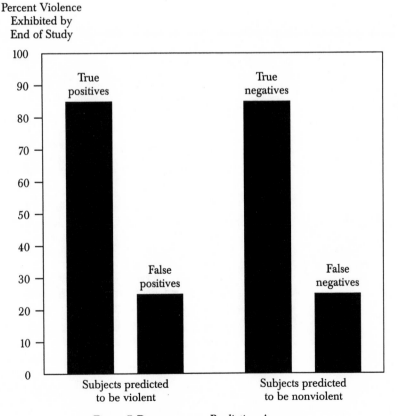

Figure 7. Dangerousness Prediction Accuracy

of accuracy. The obtained accuracy rates of around 75 percent are not remarkable and certainly not sufficiently high enough for legal purposes. However, the obtained accuracy rates are about twice the rate reported in the behavioral science literature for true positives and about the same for true negatives.

The remaining 25 percent of the variance for both positives and negatives may have been due to unknown historical influences, triggering stimuli, or opportunity factors, which for practical reasons were not adequately assessed in this pilot effort. Recency of the last violent act was not controlled, for example. The true positive rate of 75 percent seems to have been accounted for largely by historical factors, a finding important in itself. Violence frequency and severity up to the threshold for a determination of prepotent basal violence was considered. Two factors may account for this result. First, much attention was given to measuring historical violence since it was thought to be the best predictor variable; second, an unusual feature

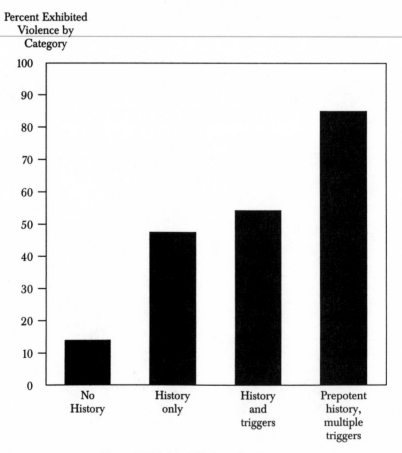

Figure 8. Exhibited Violence by Category

of the present study involved vigorous efforts to uncover actual exhibited violence in lieu of relying on official records.

Another important finding is that the traditional means of measuring outcome violence reported in the literature, usually arrest information and hospital/clinic data were essentially useless in determining amount and type of violence exhibited, even within a relatively controlled stimulus environment. Out of approximately one hundred acts of clearly arrestable violence, only two incidents were even reported (one negligent homicide and one aggravated assault), both culminating in arrest. In addition to observations by others, it may be necessary to carefully interview and test Ss directly, as many persons will admit in writing what they will not volunteer verbally and vice versa. It is clear that direct contact can yield more-complete data than can be obtained from records and institutional sources.

Demonstration Project #2: Violence Severity and Acceleration

This section explains a new standardized system of calculating crime severity and discusses how it can be applied individually to show the acceleration of violence over time. The system stems from the U.S. Department of Justice's National Survey of Crime Severity (June 1985), which is a radical departure from the Standard Classification of Offenses (SCO) system used by the Federal Bureau of Investigation (FBI) in their Uniform Crime Reports. The SCO system breaks serious offenses into Part I offenses (i.e., non-negligent homicide, rape, robbery, aggravated assault, burglary, larceny, auto theft) and Part II offenses (all others). Flaws in the SCO system include

• Not providing for multiple offenses within the same arrest, with the most-serious crime the only one counted. An incident that involved the brutal assault of a victim, rape, and robbery of her money will only be recorded as rape, for example.

• Not recognizing that each crime category consists of a range of offenses that should not be equated. A robbery, for example, may involve the armed hold-up of a bank or the taking of a child's lunch by a schoolmate.

• Treating attempted crimes the same as consummated offenses when the actual harm to the community may differ considerably.

• Failure to provide a weighting system. Thus, two grand thefts are allowed to contribute as much to the overall crime picture as two homicides.

The present system solves these problems by providing for six categories of crimes that consider victim injury, forced sex acts, intimidation, forcible entry into premises, auto theft, and property theft/damage. Each component within a category is assessed for the number of victims affected multiplied by a weighted value. The classification system derived from responses of more

TABLE XX
SERIOUSNESS SCORING SYSTEM

Score sheet

Identification number(s):_____

Effects of event:　I　T　D　(circle all that apply)

Column 1	Column 2	Columns 3	Column 4
Component scored	Number of victims　x	Scale weight　=	Total
I. Injury			
(a) Minor harm	_____	1.47	_____
(b) Treated and discharged	_____	1.47	_____
(c) Hospitalized	_____	1.47	_____
(d) Killed	_____	1.47	_____
II. Intimidation			
(a) Verbal or physical	_____	1.47	_____
(b) Weapon	_____	1.47	_____
IV. Premises forcibly entered	_____	1.47	_____
V. Motor vehicle stolen			
(a) Recovered	_____	1.47	_____
(b) Not recovered	_____	1.47	_____
VI. Property theft/damage	_____	1.47	_____
		Total score	_____

$\log 10Y = .26776656 \log 10X$
where Y = crime severity weight
X = total dollar value of theft or damage

than 60,000 (see Table VII on page 62). A verbatim explanation of the system by the U.S. Department of Justice (1985, pp. 130–133) follows.

Determining the Effects of the Event

1. NUMBER OF PERSONS INJURED. Each victim receiving some bodily injury during an event must be accounted for. Physical injuries usually occur as a direct result of assaultive events, but they may be a byproduct of other events as well. The four levels of bodily injury are

（a）Minor harm—An injury that requires or receives no professional medical attention. The victim may, for instance, be pushed, shoved, kicked, knocked down, and receive a minor wound—cut, bruise, etc.

（b）Treated and discharged—The victim receives professional medical treatment but is not detained for further medical care.

（c）Hospitalized—The victim requires inpatient care in a medical facility, regardless of its duration, or outpatient care for three or more clinical visits.

(d) Killed–The victim dies as a result of the injuries, regardless of the circumstances in which they were inflicted (e.g., accidental vs. purposeful).

2. SEXUAL INTERCOURSE BY FORCE. This event occurs when a person is intimidated and forced against his or her will to engage in a sexual act–rape, incest, or sodomy, for instance. Such an event may have more than one victim, and the score depends on the number of such victims. A continuous relationship such as that which may occur in forced incest is to be counted as one event.

A forced sex act is always accomplished by intimidation. Thus, the event must also be scored for the type of intimidation involved as discussed in the next section. Intimidation is scored for all victims in a forced sex act, unlike for other events.

The victim of one or more forced sex acts during the event is always assumed to have suffered at least minor harm. Even when medical examination may not reveal any injuries, the event must be scored for minor harm. This level of injury rather than treated and discharged, should also be scored when the victim is examined by a physician *only* in order to ascertain if venereal infection has occurred or to collect evidence that the sex act was completed.

3. INTIMIDATION. This is an element in all events in which one or more offenders threaten one or more victims with bodily harm or some other serious consequences for the purpose of forcing them to obey demands to give up something of value or to assist in a criminal event that leads to someone's bodily injury and/or to property theft or damage. In addition to rape, robbery is a classic example. Ordinary assault and battery, aggravated assault and battery, or homicide are *not* to be scored for intimidation merely because someone was assaulted or injured. The event must also have included the threat of force for intimidation to have been present. With the exception of forced sex acts, criminal events involving intimidation are scored only once, regardless of the number of victims who are intimidated. The types of intimidation are

(a) Physical or verbal–Physical intimidation means the use of strong-arm tactics such as threats with fists, menacing gestures, etc. Verbal intimidation means spoken threats only, not supported by the overt display of a weapon.

(b) Intimidation by weapon–Display of a weapon, involves showing an item such as a firearm, cutting or stabbing instrument, or blunt instrument capable of inflicting serious bodily injury.

4. NUMBER OF PREMISES FORCIBLY ENTERED. As used here, forcible entry means unlawful entry, even when not by "breaking," into a premise of a pri-

vate character to which the public does not have free access or the breaking and entering into a premises to which the public ordinarily has free access. Such an entry is, in itself, an event to be scored if it causes some degree of damage to property—a broken lock, window, or door, for instance—even though it is not followed necessarily by an injury to a person or by theft of and damage to property inside the premises.

Usually, only one distinct premise will be entered, such as a family dwelling, an apartment, or a suite of offices, although some events may embrace several such entries. The scoring depends on the number of premises forcibly entered during the event and occupied by or belonging to different owners, tenants, or lessees. Contrary to the "hotel rule" used in the Uniform Crime Reports, each hotel, motel, or lodginghouse room broken into and occupied by different tenants should be scored. If a building was forcibly entered and further entries made inside, the total number of entries scored should include the forcible entry of the building even when the building belongs to someone who is victimized by a further entry inside.

5. NUMBER OF MOTOR VEHICLES STOLEN. As used here, motor vehicle means any self-propelled vehicle—automobile, truck, motorcycle, tractor, airplane. Disregard self-propelled lawnmowers and similar domestic instruments in this section; the value of such items is accounted for in the "value of property" section. Because motor vehicles may be either stolen and recovered, or stolen and never returned to the legal owner, the number of vehicles in each category must be accounted for separately and will receive a different score value.

6. VALUE OF PROPERTY STOLEN OR DAMAGED. Regardless of the kind of event scored and the number of victims, the total value of all property stolen or damaged must be determined, whether it is wholly or partially recovered and whether or not the loss was covered by insurance.

Motor vehicle thefts require special handling. Because the score of the event does not depend on the value of the vehicle stolen, the dollar value of the vehicle is ignored. However, if the vehicle is recovered damaged and/or property has been taken from it, the loss of the sum of the cost of the damage and the value of the stolen articles should be tallied.

The Seriousness Scoring System

The offense components discussed in the previous section constitute the scale items in an index to determine the gravity of crime. The scoring system used to evaluate the seriousness of crime can best be presented by first describing the elements of the system and then illustrating the scoring procedure with hypothetical offenses.

The elements of the system may be defined as follows. The first item that must be collected is the *identification number*. This is the number given to a particular criminal event. It may be a central complaint number, a district number, or some similar designation. If the same event is represented by more than one such number, all numbers should be recorded so that the event can be scored as a whole. In most cases, an event will be described in complaint or investigation reports carrying but one identifying number. In some cases, however, one event may become the subject of reports with two or more such reports and numbers for the same event. For instance, in a rape event with two victims, each victim may file a separate complaint and necessitate coordination of the separate reports before the event could be scored.

To classify the event, the presence of I (injury), T (theft), and D (damage) components must be determined. Because the construction of subindices is often necessary, as many of the components as apply should be circled. From this procedure, it is possible to arrive at seven classifications of an event–I, T, D, IT, ID, TD, and ITD. This classification scheme can be used as a solution to the problem of dealing with the complex criminal event.

After determinating of the class to which the event belongs, score the event for seriousness. Column 1 in Table XX lists the various offense components and the possible levels of each. Column 2 refers to the number of victims who experienced each level of the offense components. The exceptions to the rule of accounting for the number of times each component occurs involve nonrape event intimidations where this component is scored once regardless of the number of victims, and the value of property loss, which is summed across all victims. Column 3 lists the scale weight assigned to each element of the offense. Multiply the figure in Column 2 (where applicable) by the weight listed in Column 3 to determine the score for each component. Add all the figures in Column 4, to find the total event score.

The following examples illustrate how the proposed scoring system works. For the purpose of showing how it differs from that of the UCR system, the problems have been copied from the Uniform Crime Reporting Handbook (Federal Bureau of Investigation). The problems as originally listed there generally do not contain all the necessary information. Therefore, hypothetical data have been supplied in the parentheses.

PROBLEM 1. "A hold up man forces a husband and his wife to get out of the automobile. He shoots the husband, gun whips and rapes the wife (hospitalized), and leaves in the automobile (recovered later) after taking money ($100) from the husband. The husband dies as a result of the shooting."

Solution: UCR-1 nonnegligent homicide.

Proposed Scoring
Effects of event: I T D

Component scored	Number of Victims x	Scale Weight =	Total
I(c) Injury–hospitalized	1	11.98	11.98
I(d) Injury–killed	1	35.67	35.67
II Forcible sex acts	1	25.92	25.92
III(b) Intimidation–weapon	1	5.60	5.60
V(a) Motor vehicle stolen-recovered	1	4.46	4.46
VI($100) Property theft	NA	3.43	3.43
		Total Score	87.06

In this event, the husband was killed (35.67); the wife was raped (25.92), threatened with a gun (5.60), and she sustained injuries requiring hospitalization (11.98). The car was stolen and recovered (4.46). The total value of the property loss was $100 (3.43). In comparison to the UCR solution of one, nonnegligent criminal homicide, we arrive at an injury-theft event with a total score of 87.06.

PROBLEM 2. "Two thieves break into a warehouse (damage $20) and have loaded considerable merchandise (worth $3,500) on a truck. The night watchman is knocked unconscious with some blunt instrument (treated and discharged). The thieves drive away in the stolen truck (not recovered)."

Solution: UCR-1 robbery

Proposed Scoring
Effects of Event: I T D

Component scored	Number of Victims x	Scale Weight =	Total
I(b) Injury–treated and discharged	1	8.53	8.53
IV Premises forcibly entered	1	1.50	1.50
V(b) Motor vehicle stolen–not recovered	1	4.46	4.46
VI ($3,520)	NA	8.91	8.91
		Total Score	23.40

This offense involves the forcible entry of a building (1.50), injury to the night watchman requiring treatment (8.53), theft of an unrecovered motor vehicle (4.46), and property loss of $3,520 (8.91). The UCR would classify this event as one robbery, whereas our system demonstrates the complexity of one event that combines three primary effects of crime (injury, theft, and damage) and has a total seriousness score of 23.40. Note the prior problem involving a homicide received a seriousness score more than 60 points higher.

PROBLEM 3. "Three men break into a public garage (damage $20) after closing hours. They steal cash from the garage office ($50) and two automobiles from the lot. One vehicle was recovered undamaged; the other was not found."

Solution: UCR-1 burglary.

Proposed Scoring
Effects of Event: I T D

Component scored	Number of Victims	x	Scale Weight	=	Total
IV Premises forcibly entered	1		1.50		1.50
V(a) Motor vehicle stolen-recovered	1		4.46		4.46
V(b) Motor vehicle stolen–not recovered	1			8.07	8.07
VI ($70) Property theft/damage	NA		3.12		3.12
				Total Score	17.15

The UCR solution to this problem would be the reporting of a burglary. We classify the event as a theft-damage crime that involves forcible entry (1.50); two motor vehicles stolen with one recovered (4.46), the other not found (8.07); and property loss totalling $70 (3.12). The total score for the event is 17.15.

PROBLEM 4. "An automobile containing clothing and luggage valued at $375 is stolen. The car is recovered (undamaged) but the clothing and luggage are missing."

Solution: UCR-1 auto theft.

Proposed Scoring
Effects of Event: I T D

Component scored	Number of Victims	x	Scale Weight	=	Total
V(a) Motor vehicle stolen–recovered	1		4.46		4.46
VI($375) Property theft	NA		4.89		4.89
				Total Score	9.35

In this example, the two scoring systems are close because the UCR would record one auto theft while our classification would also record theft. However, our scale further signifies that the vehicle was recovered (4.46) and there was a loss of property in the amount of $375 (4.89), which produces a final score of 9.35.

PROBLEM 5. "Answering an armed robbery in progress broadcast, police become engaged in a gun battle with three armed robbers; one of the bandits is killed and the other two captured. (Presumably no one was injured except the offenders.)"

Solution: If no one was injured except the offenders, this would be a theft event if theft had actually occurred before the police arrived. If so, the event would be scored for intimidation by weapon (5.60) plus the score for the value of property taken, for instance $100 (3.43), which totals 9.03 for the event. If the robbers failed to carry out the offense because the police came before any property was taken, the event would be considered an attempt and not scored at all within the index of crime severity. Despite all these considerations, the UCR would still record this event as one robbery.

PROBLEM 6. "Answering a riot call, police find that seven persons were in a fight. A variety of weapons are strewn about. None of the participants is particularly cooperative. Each one claims innocence but is vague regarding who is responsible for the assault. Three of the seven are severely wounded (all were hospitalized) while the remaining four receive only minor cuts and bruises (no medical treatment)."

Solution: UCR-3 aggravated assaults.

Proposed Scoring
Effects of Event: I T D

Component scored	Number of Victims	x	Scale Weight	=	Total
I(a) Injury–minor harm	4		1.47		5.88
I(c) Injury–hospitalized	3		11.98		35.94
				Total Score	41.82

The UCR procedure for enumeration of the event calls for the designation of three aggravated assaults. Our scoring process accounts for these same effects (35.94) as well as the four minor injuries (5.88). Taken together, these consequences produce a combined score of 41.82 for this injury event.

PROBLEM 7. "Ten persons are present in a nightclub when it and the ten persons are held up by armed bandits. Two of the victims resist the robbery and are seriously injured (hospitalization). (The combined property loss is $1,800.)"

Solution: UCR-1 robbery.

Proposed Scoring
Effects of Event: I T D

Component scored	Number of Victims	x	Scale Weight	=	Total
I(c) Injury–hospitalized	2		11.98		23.96
III(b) Intimidation– weapon	NA		5.60		5.60
VI($1,800) Property theft	NA		7.44		7.44
				Total Score	37.00

The UCR classification of the event as one robbery clearly hides several important ingredients. Namely, we arrive at a combined injury-theft event that involves two hospitalized victims (23.96), intimidation by a dangerous weapon (5.60), and dollar loss of $1,800 (7.44). The overall score of 37.00 indicates that the mere recording of one robbery could be very misleading.

PROBLEM 8. "Six rooms in a hotel are broken into (damage $60) by two sneak thieves on one occasion. (The total value of property stolen from the rooms, occupied by different tenants, amounted to $1,200.)"

Solution: UCR-1 burglary.

Proposed Scoring
Effects of Event: I T D

Component scored	Number of Victims	x	Scale Weight	=	Total
IV Premises forcibly entered	6		1.50		9.00
VI($1,260) Property theft/damage	NA		6.76		6.76
				Total Score	15.76

Utility of the System

The Department of Justice crime-severity system begins with individual criminal events and clearly makes the case that other systems that do not take into account quantitative degrees of severity within different offense categories may be of limited value. The crime-severity system also suggests that the use of a rap sheet or criminal history of arrests, charges, and dispositions to construct total seriousness of crime for an individual is not sufficient. These labels only give a vague idea of severity.

Improved case selection is presented as another possible benefit of the system. Cases with high seriousness scores can be attended to first, keeping the cases reflecting low seriousness for later program intervention. Allocation of personnel resources to cases, work shifts, or areas of high seriousness can be evaluated. Focal application to career criminal identification and prosecution can be considered. Sentencing practices could be positively affected because the cumulative seriousness of harm that an accused has perpetrated can be built into the judicial decision process.

How can the severity system be used in violence prediction? First, it is statistically permissible to classify or score only threatened or consummated violence to others if the predictor is only interested in these acts. The scaled scores stay the same, and you have simply narrowed the band of serious acts considered. The overall gravity of the act or net harm may be lost, however.

Second, individual crime analysis fits nicely into the severity system. Victim impact and other qualitative variables can yield information about how the perpetrator behaved. Did pain cues from the victim increase or decrease aggression? Did bystanders act as an inhibitory stimulus to violence? What were the verbal and nonverbal interactions with the victim before, during, and after the crime? Individual crime analysis can be strengthened by examining possible unreported violence or contributing conditions of the perpetrator. Crimes of high seriousness where no money was taken or obvious gain achieved, for example, are often associated with one of two types of triggering stimuli–substance intoxication and threatened/actual break-up in the central love relationship–superimposed upon previous violence. Thus, seriousness scores and the individual crime analysis upon which they are based may lead to other areas of inquiry.

Finally, forensic professionals may want to determine if *known* violence appears to be escalating over time. This approach calls for calculating total seriousness scores for different historical periods and comparing noted differences. Basically, this is a judgment call as no extant statistical technique (including analysis of Markov chains or other specialized analysis of trends) has yet been developed that will tell with any degree of certainty whether an *individual* will act out. The strategy and limitations of the base-rate approach have already been discussed. Further, base rates for accelerating violence are not available for most crime categories. Until statistical techniques and base rates have been developed for individual variation over time, it will be impossible to determine with full confidence whether previously violent individuals will aggress again or whether their most-recent act of violence represented the last gasp of a dying proclivity.

This does not mean that individual basal violence cannot be assessed for severity, placed on a graph, and lead to general conclusions in regard to future violence. A declining slope suggests violence is dying out as much as an escalating slope suggests more violence may take place, simply because remoteness acts as an inhibitor and recency of violence often acts as a stimulus to more violence. Even a strong history of violence that is remote may not mean violence will reoccur; this merely allows you to render a violence prediction, whereas with no previous violence, a negative prediction (or no prediction) must be rendered. In cases where prepotent recent violence is present, triggering stimuli and opportunity factors should be present in order to reasonably render a prediction that violence will occur. In no case should plotting severity over time yield a dangerousness prediction unless other factors are taken into account that make it possible and set it into motion.

For purposes of exercise, chart the violence severity of John Brown (Dangerousness Prediction Task #2, Appendix E). Assume that his rap sheet includes all known acts of violence as you have determined by conducting a forensic distortion examination, helped a great deal by talking to his family and friends, and by examining school and medical records.

Demonstration Project #3: Dangerousness Prediction Impact

Once it is established that dangerousness predictions can be proffered with reasonable degrees of certainty and charted in quantitative form, attention then turns to how much impact violence prognostications have upon the civil and criminal courts, as well as in other decision-making agencies. A serious claim is that the courts tend to ignore the most promising dangerousness prediction methods, in particular actuarial or statistical approaches, in favor of clinical judgment and intuition (Wenk, Robison & Smith, 1972; Monahan, 1981a). But do courts actually behave in this manner? Although forensic mental health professionals generally do not know the global impact of courtroom violence prognostications (Perlin, 1977), there is evidence that courtroom testimony by psychologists does have significant impact on court decisions. Psychologists are increasingly accepted in the courtroom, and the side on which they testify wins a favorable judgment the majority of the time (Bobbit & Hock, 1961; Schwitzgebel & Schwitzgebel, 1980). Studies of impact address a critical issue, yet have not typically been a research factor in the mental health-law interface.

In one of the few extant studies on impact, Hall and McLaughlin (1981) presented data suggesting that courtroom dangerousness predictions by psychologists may have considerable influence on key criminal justice system actors. The study investigated questionnaire responses involving various courtroom dangerousness prediction vignettes from 31 forensic professionals (16 judges and 15 probation officers) of the State of Hawaii district, circuit, and family courts. The five hypothetical situations involved a different rationale for a psychologist's prediction of dangerousness, and included psychological testing, retesting, recitation of relevant recidivism statistics, the use of a standardized dangerousness prediction scale, clinical judgment and intuition, and single administration of psychological testing. On a seven point Likert-type scale, Ss first were asked to rate and then rank the perceived usefulness of the dangerousness prediction methods. Then they were asked questions concerning the validity of psychologists' courtroom testimony in regard to dangerousness.

Results showed that judges and probation officers responded in generally the same fashion, confirming earlier reports of a high concordance of rate of agreement between these two sets of forensic professionals (e.g., Fujioka, Iha, Wong and Wong, 1978). There were no significantly different Pearson r and Spearman correlation coefficients for professional membership, age, sex, years of legal experience, or ratings and rankings of testimony methods. Nor were there any significant differences among ethnic groups or occupational groups using nonparametric ANOVAs.

Courtroom prediction methods did show significant differences among ratings and rankings, with psychological testing-retesting considered the most useful but not significantly more useful than a specific violence test or recidivism statistics. For the ratings, a Friedman two-way ANOVA showed x (chi)(4) = 31.3, p .001. Moreover, there was a high and significant correlation between mean scores of the ratings and rankings, with r = .999, p .05. A global statement of results is that psychological testing and retesting, a specific violence test, and recidivism statistics pertaining to the case at hand are looked on as more useful than either one-time psychological testing or clinical observation and intuition.

Are psychologists' testimonial statements believable in the court? Two open-ended questions were asked; the responses to them could be categorized and rank ordered. They were: "What is your overall opinion concerning the predictability of dangerous behavior?" and "Are any other professionals more believable?" The judges and probation officers looked favorably upon psychologists' testimony (61.5%) with only 15.4 percent clearly negative. Both professional groups (62.5%) considered other professionals no more believable than psychologists, with only 12.5 percent stating that psychiatrists were more believable. Although historically the impact of the psychologist has been considered to be inferior to that of psychiatrists (Perlin, 1977), this study suggests a change in this second-class status, at least for the circumscribed setting of the present investigation. Parity between these two sets of mental health professionals may finally have been achieved in terms of courtroom violence prognostications.

Psychological Testing and Retesting

A psychological test demonstration of no personality or behavioral trait change over time, as reflective of continued dangerousness, is apprently convincing to forensic mental health professionals. An important distinction here is that the psychological testing per se was not as impressive, as how it was implemented (i.e., at several distinct temporal points). In light of these findings, routine testing and retesting, maligned in literature as unless at best and an unconstitutional invasion of privacy at worst , should be reexamined as a viable assessment strategy. Psychodiagnostic testing could be administered at several times during criminal justice system involvement (e.g., shortly after arrest, during post-trial proceedings, while incarcerated). Similarity of personality profiles as, for example, on the MMPI, clearly communicate little state/trait change for the relevant personality dimensions measured. To the extent that dangerousness is a function of personality characteristics, the test-retest findings are pertinent to the question of violence potential. This type of data is also helpful in establishing whether recent prosocial behaviors (e.g., those displayed in hospital or prison) have internalized to the extent of affecting core psychological attitudes.

For repeat measures, examiners should consider standardized, objective personality tests with built-in validity scales, since the target population may have a vested interest in faking bad or faking good. This would suggest scales like the Minnesota Multiphasic Personality Inventory, California Personality

Inventory, Edwards Personality Preference Scale, and the Bipolar Psychological Inventory.

Recidivism Statistics

The basic assumption here, apparently endorsed by the respondents, is that one of the best predictors of future dangerousness is past dangerousness, and baseline violence may by its quantity and quality suggest a numerical probability for reoccurrence. Combining recidivism statistics relevant to subjects' instant offense and history with data from test-retest and other violence assessment procedures could also be considered.

Dangerousness Test

Unfortunately, although respondents would be favorably influenced by a violence measure, no psychometric device or procedure has yet been developed that will by itself accurately predict or even postdict dangerousness to others (Megargee, 1970; Horowitz and Willging, 1984). Development of a test to measure the likelihood of inflicting harm on others should be of high priority to professionals within the criminal justice system since dangerousness is such a controversial, high-concern phenomenon and because indications are that such a standardized, objective measure would be favorably received.

Clinical Intuition and Judgment

Testimony based on clinical intuition and judgment seems to have minimal impact on forensic professionals, conforming to research reports over the last quarter of a century that demonstrate statistical/actuarial superiority over clinical judgment (e.g., Meehl, 1954; Wenk, 1972). Use of this assessment procedure should be reexamined in light of the largely negative literature and the findings of the more-recent study. Factors that clearly distort accuracy of clinical judgment include (a) masking influences of the subject's present circumstances (Kahneman and Tversky, 1973), (b) clinicians' demonstrated inability to detect faking good and faking bad in forensic subjects (Ziskin, 1981), (c) heavy use of "illusory correlations" or unsubstantiated associations of subject interview/test behavior with specific psychopathology (Chapman and Chapman, 1967, 1969), and (d) biases of the examiner (Sweetland, 1972). Recent results suggest that assessment methods not involving examination of historical data of the subject or a comparison group in a systematized way are unlikely to influence judges and probation officers. The literature also suggests that dangerousness predictions based on such assessments are unlikely to be accurate.

Psychological Testing

A single battery of psychological tests administered once is not likely to impress forensic professionals favorably. Comments included the fact that the testing responses have not been replicated and further, may be irrelevant to the issue of dangerousness. Indeed, the question of reliability and validity is a serious concern. Even the most accepted objective test (MMPI) has a general reliability that clusters in the area of the 0.70s, barely adequate for test stability purposes, with about a 60% accuracy in clinical settings and possibly lower in forensic applications (Ziskin, 1981). In contrast, the convincing aspect of similar test-retest results lies in its demonstrated reliability. Even if those results are somewhat irrelevant to dangerousness, they may not be irrelevant to the personality states/traits measured. It is conceptually difficult to separate individuals' general personality characteristics from their future acts of aggression.

SUMMARY

Dangerousness predictions are presently in disfavor because dangerousness cannot be predicted with accuracy and even if it could, the courtroom impact is minimal. Results from a study of prospective violence prognostications and an investigation relative to courtroom testimony by psychologists suggest conclusions drawn from these assumptions may be premature.

The argument that dangerousness predictions are not accurate because they are based on a low-base-rate phenomenon falls apart on a number of scores. (a) Prediction studies finding low base rates for violence may use dependent measures reflecting on a small portion of consummated violence. (b) Even low-base-rate phenomena can and have been predicted in spite of their temporal rarity. Death, for example, only occurs once, yet can and has been predicted for *groups* within close limits for a number of events. These include the chances of being murdered as a function of age and race, traveling on U.S. highways, and exposure to various surgical interventions. Although for *individuals* an idiosyncratic method is suggested, that method can be used in combination with available base rates. Furthermore, it should be remembered that future dangerousness should never be predicted in the absence of a significant violence history, which then increases the chances of accurate prediction considerably. (c) Some groups and individuals having certain characteristics *do* exhibit high-base-rate violence for certain crimes. These include criminal violence such as rape, robbery, and aggravated assault; family violence such as spouse and child abuse; and sexual assault, especially against children. These crimes have been identified in the literature as highly recidivistic. These high base rates can legitimately be used for dangerousness predictions as a first estimate of predictee dangerousness.

The argument that courts have little faith in dangerousness predictions based on statistical or actuarial approaches, or a combination of nomothetic-idiosyncratic methods, is also suspect. A careful reading of the literature, relevant court decisions, and results from recent research, suggests that courts and other decision-making legal agencies may have more faith in these predictions than the primary organizations to which the forensic mental health professionals belong. Results of the impact demonstration studies (Hall and McLaughlin, 1981) also support the view that the influence of psychologists and psychiatrists rendering dangerousness predictions may be reaching parity.

New directions are suggested by a review of the dangerousness literature and the 1981 Hall and McLaughlin studies. Development of an operationalized taxonomy is a critical first step in order to facilitate communication among forensic professionals. Three dimensions were suggested in the first chapter, to include (a) dangerousness to self, property, and others; (b) severity of various degrees according to NIJ criteria, which can also be utilized to demonstrate violence trends for individual predictees; and (c) family, acquaintance, and stranger violence. Each combination may turn out, as the literature suggests, to have different probabilities of occurring and reoccurring, and to incorporate differential strategies for intervention. A new direction will be represented by the development of a valid and reliable dangerousness prediction battery. It is a sad commentary on the state of the art that no test exists to measure what many consider the principal issue in the mental health-law interface.

Chapter 8

THE CLINICAL INTERVIEW

Most Violent Event: (22-year-old married black male)

"THIS PARTICULAR INCIDENT HAPPENED ABOUT FOUR YEARS AGO. I was about 19 years old then, and until this day I remember it as if it were yesterday. I guess[sic] it was about 8:30 p.m. on a Thursday night. I was working a cash register, in a grocery store of my cousin, and being very busy I wasn't paying any particular attention to the customers that night, but this one customer got my attention without any questions being asked. I looked at him and he was standing there holding a gun; it was covered a little by his hand. I was so surprised and shocked to see this, and not to mention scared, and I didn't know weather [sic] to run, shout for help, or just simply faint. I thought I would do them all at the same time, but the man holding the gun nodded his head telling me not to make a sound. So I looked at the gun and he looked at the cash register and the gun looked at me, so I opened the cash register and pulled out all of the bills that I have and gave them to him. The man nodded again for me not to make a sound, so I looked back at the gun again and even it seemed to be nodding. The man walked out of the door slowly, and me not knowing that the people in the main office were being robbed, I told them simply that I had been robbed.

But the funny thing about this experience was doing [sic]the entire incident, the people in the store never new [sic] what was going on until it was all over with."

In order to predict violent behavior accurately, a thorough appreciation for the individual, his/her environment and history, life stressors and weapon availability, as well as degree of deception and personal motivation must be assessed. Numerous tools and strategies have been described to aid in this process, but without a careful and thoughtful clinical interview the answers will be sterile. This is not to minimize the value of assessment instruments with demonstrated reliability and validity. Nicholson and Norwood

151

(2000) discuss "forensic assessment instruments (FAIs)" as "a significant contribution of psychological science to forensic assessments." Borum and Grisso (1995) surveyed forensic clinicians to determine their use of psychological tests during forensic evaluations. The forensic instruments most frequently used in competency assessments were the Competency Assessment Instrument and the Competency Screening Test (Lipsett, Lelos, and McGarry, 1971), with objective personality tests (MMPI-2) and intelligence tests (especially the WAIS-R) used as well. In assessments of criminal responsibility the MMPI–2 and WAIS–R were most frequently cited. Of those who used FAIs in performing such assessments, the Rogers Criminal Responsibility Assessment Scales (R–CRAS); (Rogers, 1984) was by far the preferred instrument. In addition to the use of FAIs, instrumentation to assess deception or malingering is often utilized as adjunct to the clinical assessment. The Structured Interview of Reported Symptoms (SIRS) developed by Rogers (1992) is recognized as a well-validated instrument for this purpose. This structured-interview format folds nicely into a clinical assessment and produces scores that range from "honest responding" through intermediate steps to "definite malingering".

The clinical interview enables the examiner to pursue areas of investigation highlighted by the use of instrumentation; it also provides the opportunity to probe for material ignored or distorted over time or lost as the result of a lengthy legal process. Finally, the structured clinical interview aids in flushing out details that will assist in moving toward an understanding of the dynamics and motivation that may have led to previous violent episodes. Combined with the results of psychological testing, FAIs, record reviews and collateral interviews, the clinician is positioned to develop predictive risk statements upon as solid a database as possible.

It is important to remember that the forensic clinician is frequently expected to assist the court and by extension society to understand the reasons why a violent action has been taken. It is not at all unusual for the forensic clinician to see the jury, the judge, and the entire court sitting on the edges of their seats waiting for the explanation that will help them to understand better the reasoning behind an episode of violence that has stunned a community. It is this public role, perhaps more than any other, that requires the forensic clinician to pursue clinical interview as thoughtfully and in as much detail as possible.

The ideal clinical assessment should cover numerous interviews over an extended period of time. The strategy behind this process depends in part upon the mental state of the interviewee. If the person is disorganized or agitated, repeated interviews give the clinician the opportunity to observe the person during different mental states and enable the person to acclimate to the process, hopefully enabling him/her to gradually work to a position of trust and greater openness. Additionally, multiple interviews provide the opportunity to assess malingering or deception by repeating questions, comparing answers, and checking responses against objective data, such as that provided through eye-witness statements and interviews with collateral sources. Frequently, the interviewer will have contact with collateral sources and obtain records prior to a final interview, so that the opportunity is available to question and if necessary, confront.

In general, the interview should cover at least the following areas:
• Developmental history including family dynamics,
• Schooling,
• Relationships and marital history,
• Involvement with the juvenile and adult criminal justice system,
• Prior aggressive/violent behaviors,
• Substance-abuse history,
• Medical/health history,
• Mental health history and treatments,
• Sexual history, and
• Current mental status examination.

The remainder of the assessment will be determined by questions posed to the forensic examiner. Areas of interest may include an assessment stemming from the person's current violence potential, such as in which individuals are being assessed to determine whether they need continued hospitalization or treatment or questions of the individual's mental state at the time of a violent offense, as in criminal responsibility evaluations. The examiner may also be asked to evaluate competency to stand trial, competency to appreciate a Miranda warning, an individual's need for further treatment, or the person's sexual dangerousness. Each of these questions should be posed prior to the interview process and must be within the examiner's sphere of expertise. Standards against which to measure the data gathered must also be clarified. This information may be provided at the time that the interview is requested, or it may be necessary for the interviewer to obtain that information from the requesting source, such as the court or attorney.

When assessing an individual's current dangerousness, interviewers must analyze violent incidents. While some information should be available through police reports, grand jury records, and records of trials, a clinical interview will help to obtain detailed descriptors that are not usually contained in such material. Collateral interviews are often very helpful in supplementing such material. Interviews with prior victims, for example, can be a valuable means of gathering data that may not have come to the attention of police or courts previously. Arresting police officers, hospital staff, and prior therapists are often valuable sources. Questions concerning criminal responsibility require a post analysis of the perpetrator's mental state in the weeks, days, and minutes prior to the event and, particularly, in the moments during the event. Again, such information is best gathered by direct clinical interview but should be supplemented by police reports, victim statements, and eye witness interviews, if available. The only eye witness remaining is frequently the perpetrator, thus mandating a detailed clinical interview. Of course the assessment of deception becomes critical during such interviews because perpetrators will frequently distort in order to place the victim in a more culpable position or to escape the aversive consequences of their acts. Individuals might wish to blame their violence on cognitive impairment, psychosis, substance abuse, or some other condition to obtain exculpation or mitigation. It has been conservatively estimated that about 20 percent of criminal defendants assessed for insanity show suspected or definite malingering while another 5 percent demonstrate nondeliberate distortion in their self-report (Hall and Poirier, 2000).

The Interview

Begin all clinical interviews of a forensic nature by clearly explaining the purpose of the interview, the role of the clinician, and the limits of confidentiality. It is crucial that such a clear explanation be offered and documented, because without informed consent, a court may choose to discard any information the clinician obtains. Some clinicians have interviewees read and sign a document that provides the above information, and this can be addended to a report to the court, or held until requested for trial. The authors prefer to provide a detailed verbal explanation that is tailored to the individual's ability to understand. When examining an individual with mental retardation, it is often necessary to modify language so that the person can appreciate the information being to do. For example, it is reasonable to substitute the word "private" for "confidential" when helping the person understand that the information they provide will be shared and not held confidential. When the individual's presentation suggests that he or she may not be attending or understanding the information, it is good clinical practice to ask the interviewee to paraphrase the warning in order to assess more accurately their ability to comprehend. It is not at all unusual for someone to respond in the affirmative when asked if they understand and then be quite unable to paraphrase the information given them. At such times, providing the material slowly and carefully with frequent requests for feedback may help the interviewee understand the limits of confidentiality. Once such an understanding is obtained, the interview can begin. Should the interviewee be quite unable to understand the lack of confidentiality of the interview and their rights to not participate, it may be necessary to terminate the interview. Most interviewees are willing to participate in the interview even when they have limited appreciation of the limits of confidentiality. At such times, it is good practice to note their lack of understanding despite their willingness to participate and to include that information in a report to an attorney or to the court. It then becomes the responsibility of the court to decide whether or not to accept the information that was provided under such circumstances.

Where multiple interviews are possible, the recommended practice is to begin data gathering by dealing with information that is removed from the issue of dangerousness. This enables the interviewer to assess response style, memory for detail, and mental state in a nonstressed situation. Additionally, this should provide the interviewer an opportunity to develop a rapport with the interviewee, thus easing the process of data gathering. Generally, the initial topics to be covered should include developmental history, schooling history, and history of relationships and marriage, if any.

Developmental History

In addition to date and place of birth, developmental history should include any knowledge of birth-related problems, early medical or psychological issues, and family structure and dynamics. Questions of particular importance concern childhood abuse or neglect, early crises including accidents and illnesses, and early acting-out behaviors.

Schooling

Interweave with developmental history those detailed questioning about schooling, particularly in terms of success in academic areas, and behavioral issues. The question of relationship becomes important in the school years, and questions should be addressed to friendships, their closeness, and intensity. Early psychological and behavioral problems are often indicated by the experience of being teased and rejected by age mates.

Address questions concerning suspension, school counseling, and other interventions at each academic stage. Listing names of counselors and dates of treatment will facilitate record retrieval. Questions should progress chronologically with similar information gathered concerning elementary school, junior high school, high school, and any further academic experiences.

As information is gathered about academics, pose questions concerning evidence and/or diagnosis of ADHD, learning disabilities, and emotional or intellectual disabilities. It should be noted that most interviewees perceive the terms "mental illness" or "mental retardation" to be derogatory and often will not use them in reference to themselves. Therefore, be sensitive to these issues and should ask questions about "emotional problems" and "learning problems." When positive information is offered, then ask about special programs, tutoring, or other interventions that suggest atypical development.

Relationship/Marriage

Question them initially about childhood friendships, as noted. As the developmental history progresses, ask about interpersonal relationships, their intensity, duration, and reasons for termination. It is often necessary to probe for more more detail than is generally offered in order to better understand the individual's ability to form mutually satisfying relationships and to deal with interpersonal stress and conflict. Importantly, in the general forensic population, difficulties in relationships often show up in mid to late teens and continue throughout life.

If the individual has married, it is important to question in some detail how that relationship developed, the decisions for getting married, and the nature of the marital relationship, including a particular focus on arguments, psychological and physical struggles, and abuse, if any. If the marriage terminated, in-depth questioning is required to understand motivations for ending the marriage and the process that was followed. Again, aggressive individuals will often have difficulty terminating relationships, and such terminations are frequently painful and difficult.

Criminal-Justice Involvement

Early arrests and difficulties with the law may have come up while discussing the developmental history. If not, ask specific questions begining with the simple question "have you ever been arrested?" It is important to know the specific charges, the outcome of each case, and the punishment, if any. It is equally important, and perhaps more so, to obtain the details of each event. Information concerning motivation, mental state of the aggressor and victim, and degree of aggression are vital for predicting future dangerousness. If the examiner begins to observe a pattern either in violent behavior, or in choice of victim, questions need to be focused around these issues to clarify them. Since most juvenile records are sealed upon the age of maturity, the interview may be the first opportunity to obtain such historical information. By asking questions in this area, the examiner often begins to assess guilt and remorse, as well as motivation for aggressive behaviors. This can lead to a preliminary diagnosis of character disorder such as sociopathy at this stage in the interview. Other personal characteristics such as impulsivity, quickness to anger, and the use of substances and weapons will be open to examination at this point.

Prior Aggressive/Violent Behaviors

Since many criminal behaviors are neither brought to the attention of the police nor prosecuted, a discussion of prior arrests or interactions with the criminal justice system is usually insufficient to provide a detailed history of violent acts. Therefore, focus additional questioning on these areas. It may be necessary to begin collecting such history by targeting different areas of his or her life such as gang involvement, familial disputes, and relationship or marital difficulties. Again, be sensitive to the fact that most people do not label themselves as "violent" or "dangerous." Rather, a focus on "fighting" or "arguments that get physical" can help in obtaining the requested information.

As in questioning about episodes that lead to arrests, examine in detail each incident that is highlighted in order to understand motivation as perceived by the examinee; his or her mental status, including the use of substances; and the choice of victim. This is the point to gather detailed information about the actual violent behavior. Questions should focus not only on degree and outcome of the violence, but on intention. It matters significantly if the person's wish was to kill or maim, rather than to just "get even."

Substance Abuse

As previously noted, substance abuse plays a significant facilitating role in the expression of violent behavior. Therefore, a detailed history of use and abuse of all substances is very important. Ask at what age the interviewee began using substances, determine a detailed list of the substances, and learn the frequency and intensity of that use to the present day. When questioning about a particular violent episode, a well-detailed history of substance abuse at the time of the incident is critical. Explore relationship between substance abuse and violent behavior during this part of the interview, asking for example, "are you an angry drunk?" Document attempts at rehabilitation and note periods of abstinence. Names of treaters and treating settings, as well as dates will be important for later collateral interviews.

Medical/Health History

Multiple medical and health factors have been implicated in violent and disorganized behaviors. In addition to neurologically based disorders, reactions to medications such as steroids have been alleged to play a significant role in producing violent behavior. Additionally, the assessment of an individual's mental status at the time of a crime should include his or her health status emphasizing a reporting of chronic pain, altered states, or mental confusion. The tendency for many people to somatize emotional states means that a medical history may illuminate such problems far better than a history of mental health contacts. Obtain a full report of medical illnesses and treatments with more detailed analysis of those that suggest neurological or other mind-altering sequelae. Obtain names of relevant treaters, dates, and institutions with an eye toward possible data gathering. It is useful to provide prepared releases to the interviewee during such data gathering in order to facilitate contact with treaters.

Illnesses and injuries that result in chronic pain can often lead to depression and chronic substance abuse in order to alleviate that pain. Awareness of the link between these factors helps the examiner to obtain thorough data during the clinical evaluation.

The report of somatic conditions is frequently a doorway into confused and disorganized thinking. An individual's insistence that they have a serious illness such as cancer but that "doctors don't believe me" is more than a subtle clue to the existence of delusional states.

Mental Health History and Treatment

Because of a generalized resistance to acknowledging mental health problems, this area is usually reserved for later in the initial data gathering, although observation throughout the interview usually illuminates evidence of thought or mood disorders. It is often enough to ask if the individuals have ever been in counseling or in hospitals to elicit a description of treaters, both outpatient and inpatient. If the individual is able and willing to share this information, a careful history gathering is recommended, including dates, names of treaters and institutions, diagnoses, and medications. Questions concerning compliance with treatment are also very important, especially where the possibility of noncompliance may be connected to aggressive behaviors. The most detailed questions should be reserved for those treatments closest in time to the commission of a violent act so that a posthoc analysis of the individual's mental state can be better assessed. Questions concerning medication, treatment compliance, and substance abuse should also focus on this time period.

Sexual History

Much information may have already been gathered during the developmental, school, and marital history, but if information is lacking, it is appropriate to focus on this topic, with particular reference to aggressive and coercive behaviors. If the individual is charged with sexual violence, it will be especially important to conduct a thorough evaluation of the individual's sexual history. In such a detailed evaluation, explore early sexual experiences, including abuse, and an understanding of how the individual learned about his or her sexuality. Gather history about each of the individual's sexual partners and relationships, with a particular focus on traumatic or abusive experiences or behaviors. In detailed sexual evaluations, questions concerning fantasy life and unusual sexual practices is appropriate. Awareness of "safe" sex is important, particularly when questioning persons of limited intelligence.

As in all clinical interviews, it is important to respect an individual's privacy when questioning about highly personal matters. Questions should not be addressed in such detail unless they are directly relevant to the area under study.

Current Mental Status Evaluation

All forensic clinical interviews should include a comprehensive current mental status evaluation. Some of this data will be gathered as part of the questioning process, such as ability to concentrate, goal-directed thinking, and awareness of loose or tangential thoughts. However, specific questions that assess orientation, awareness of environment, memory, cognitive functioning, and social awareness are imperative as part of a standard clinical interview. Not only is this important in order to understand the person's current ability to function, but this can stand as a contrast to behaviors observed and described at the time of a prior violent offense, thus offering data that may help explain and perhaps impact upon culpability.

Specific forensic assessments such as competency and criminal responsibility are usually delayed until after the interview data has been collected. If questions of competency are raised by the attorney or court, questions and instruments for this purpose should be introduced. Sources such as Grisso, *Evaluating Competencies* (1986), or Melton, Petrila, Poythress and Slobogin, *Evaluations for the Courts*, second edition (1997) include for guidelines in these areas. Assessments of criminal responsibility, or lack thereof require a prospective analysis of the individual's mental state at the time of the alleged crime. This requires a detailed data gathering by clinical interview from the point of view of the interviewee. Particular focus on emotional state, mental health treatment and compliance or noncompliance, health status, life stressors including relationship and work-related concerns, and relationship with the victim are important aspects of such an interview. The individual's own description of the incident and his or her awareness and understanding of motivation becomes a critical factor here. In addition to assessment of deception at this point, the forensic examiner will want to interview collateral sources who are able to offer an eye-witness description of the interviewee's behavior and mental state at the time of the event. An awareness of the veracity and motivation of each individual is, of course, critical in judging the value of their observations.

The advantage to obtaining this information before the final interview is the obvious opportunity to question the interviewee about conflicting statements or information that has not already been shared. Not only is this a useful strategy in assessing veracity of the interviewee, it can sometimes lead to clarification and expanded descriptions of behavior.

In those circumstances where the examiner is asked to offer a prediction concerning future violence, such as in dangerousness assessments or in need for treatment determinations, examiners will want to review their data to be assured that information has been gathered on the primary risk factors known to be predictive of future dangerousness. Following the elements identified in the MacArthur Risk Assessment Project, Grisso (1999) recommends focusing on:

- *Personal Factors*
  - A. Demographic
  - B. Personality (impulsiveness, anger, psychopathy, personality style)
  - C. Cognitive (neurological, intelligence level)

- *Historical Factors*
  - A. Social history (family, educational, work, physical and sexual abuse)
  - B. Mental health history (hospitalizations)
  - C. Crime and violence history (arrests, incarcerations, self-reported violence to self and others)

- *Contextual Factors*
  - A. Perceived stress
  - B. Social supports (living arrangements, social networks)
  - C. Means of violence (access to weapons)

- *Clinical Factors*
  - A. Symptoms (delusions, hallucinations, severity, violent fantasies)
  - B. Diagnosis
  - C. Daily functioning (global assessment of functioning)
  - D. Substance abuse (alcohol, drugs)
  - E. Treatment (type, compliance, resistance)

Much of the data collected during the clinical interview, the review of materials, and interviews of collateral sources enable the forensic examiner to prepare a dangerousness prediction decision analysis, as previously described. Appendix B offers a worksheet prepared by the senior author for such a detailed analysis. Complete the form during the interlude between interviews so that necessary information can be gathered during the final stage of the interview process.

Chapter 9

THE DOZEN DANGEROUSNESS PREDICTION PITFALLS: DECISION TREE AND SYNTHESIS

Dangerousness Prediction Task #4: James Leed

A 34-YEAR-OLD POLICE SERGEANT, James Leed, of the Honolulu Police Department (HPD) was referred for a mental health evaluation due to complaints of recurrent nightmares, irritability, difficulty sleeping, poor concentration, and anxiety regarding his present job functioning. The nightmares were about an incident that occurred while he was on police patrol in 1968 in which a rioter killed his partner who was attempting to stop an assault on innocent bystanders. The nightmares were also about his job as an undercover vice officer where he was the target of several near-lethal attacks. He lost his second partner in 1973 during a mishandled police raid in a heroin operation.

Sergeant Leed did not relate any significant guilt about the deaths of his partners, but revealed a fear of being placed in similar situations again. At the time of the evaluation, the sergeant was assigned to undercover vice operations as a team leader. He worked mixed shifts. He reported distress symptoms to be most severe during mandatory target practice and field exercises, and described increasing difficulty in concentrating while working at his regular job. He also reported having occasional flashbacks while engaged in undercover operations.

The nightmares did not start until 1973, after the sergeant's partner, his close friend, was killed. Approximately one week after this incident, he started having the nightmares about both the riot and drug operation experiences. During the past few months, the nightmares increased to two to three times per week.

The sergeant reported being raised in a stable family, with no history of violence within the family. He graduated from high school without any problems. He was drafted into the U.S. Marine Corps and was sent to Vietnam for his first duty assignment, where he was involved in conflict military. He had an excellent military record and was well decorated for his performance in Vietnam. In 1967, he received his discharge and joined the police force. He married in 1974 and divorced in 1976, reporting no common interests with his wife. He was generally described as a friendly, outgoing, hard-working individual; however, he remained detached from other members of the police force, except for one or two "drinking buddies."

The sergeant stated that he had a very positive self-image and wanted to confront the issues in his nightmares directly because he believed his functioning was deteriorating. He was afraid that he would cause a problem because of his lack of concentration and irritability toward his undercover team over minor errors. He stated that "mistakes cost lives" and that he could not afford to make errors in either personal judgment or job responsibility.

A previous consultation with the police psychologist resulted in a diagnosis of delayed stress reaction. Recommendations included reality therapy and stress management, in group settings, if possible, and a transfer to undercover work. The sergeant's division chief agreed to the transfer until he felt able to return. Upon being transferred, the sergeant's anxiety level *increased.* He began feeling guilty about his failure to function at his job and became very hostile and suspicious of the other police officers. He believed they felt he was trying to "get away with something" by being transferred. These feelings intensified over time.

The police officer's fiancée reported that he talked about killing himself or others if the situation did not improve. His consumption of alcohol increased and their relationship became strained. There was no illicit drug abuse.

During the last two days of the annual police field training, the sergeant took a knife with him "for protection." This was the same knife that he had used in Vietnam to kill several enemy soldiers. He and his team had two minor mishaps during the training exercises, with one officer sustaining a broken leg when the undercover team unsuccessfully attempted to scout out a target area. The sergeant was unable to sleep for four days following that incident. He felt he was at the end of his ability to cope and was transferred to an assignment in the police department arms room. Upon returning to the police administration headquarters from the field exercise, the sergeant found that someone had urinated on his duffel bag. He then started to search for the responsible party, with the stated intention of killing the person.

At that point, the mental health evaluator reviewed with the sergeant his responsibility for his actions and his alternatives. The likelihood of a medical recommendation for an early retirement or transfer out of line of duty was not seen as high. Sergeant Leed was presented with the options of working on resolving his problems or leaving the police force at the end of the year.

The sergeant was irritated about the lack of assistance he had received. He reported having flashbacks during work hours of the incidents in which his partners had died. He agreed to contact the evaluator on a biweekly basis and made a contract not to attempt suicide. He refused to contract for *not* engaging in homicidal behavior. His division chief agreed to, and actually sat in on, several of the counseling sessions.

Predict whether violence to others, self, or property will occur within six months, the period of time for which follow-up data is available. Assume that the present data includes all of Sergeant Leed's basal violence (see Appendix G).

Violence Prediction Decision Tree

This chapter consolidates all previous materials, presents a formal decision tree, and enumerates 12 cardinal errors to avoid in predicting dangerousness to others.

Common errors in the clinical-forensic prediction of dangerousness to others have been discussed previously and reported in the behavioral science literature, 1978; Monahan, 1981a; Grisso and Applebaum, 1992, Steadman et al., 1994). These same errors and others have been observed by colleagues in a variety of service and research settings (e.g., Megargee, 1970; Bandura, 1973; Hall, 1982, 1984, 1985, 1986; Hall et al., 1984). The notions that each common error contains both inclusionary and exclusionary criteria that can be tied to a decision process regarding dangerousness prediction, and that the decision process itself can mirror a dangerousness prediction report format, has received scant, if any, attention. This chapter presents a fully developed dangerousness prediction decision tree, followed by the examination of errors reported in the empirical and clinical literature and observed by other clinicians. Scrutiny of this material suggests, further areas of inquiry and the need for a reporting format. Positive byproducts from such an endeavor may include

- Increasing the violence prediction accuracy rate among forensic mental health professionals by reducing errors that will someday positively affect both the level of community safety and the predictee's right not to be a "false positive,"
- Increasing report and/or courtroom impact in presenting relevant data and conclusions, and
- Lowering the risk of legal and other liability from rendering violence predictions given the current climate of fear and avoidance in regard to this type of prognostication.

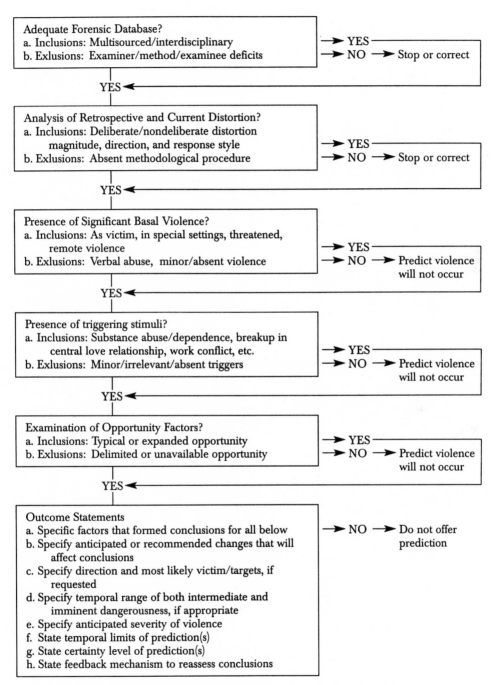

Figure 9. Dangerousness Prediction Decision Tree

The basic implied premise of the dangerousness prediction decision tree presented in Figure 9 is that the relevance of violence prediction must be considered in a significant proportion of forensic examinations as an implied or direct focus of inquiry, depending on referral questions and other factors. The basis for drawn conclusions describes a post-hoc cognitive process of the clinician acting upon the utilized forensic data base. Each step in the decision process contains both inclusionary and exclusionary criteria, which are sequentially delimiting in the amount of relevant information considered. When either criterion of any step of the decision path is not fulfilled, final conclusions cannot be proffered or a prediction of nondangerousness must be rendered. Analysis of data must be clearly identified as relevant either to the time of the evaluation or for historical events, as defendants and others differentially portray psychopathology and dangerousness depending on vested interests in given legal outcomes and other factors such as temporality (e.g., see Heaton et al., 1978; Ziskin, 1981; Resnick, 1984; Sierles, 1984).

Once the relevance of the dangerousness prediction is considered and an adequate database employed, as will be discussed in this chapter, the ensuing task in the decision process is to account for the predictee's retrospective and current distortion. The next step consists of attempting to uncover previous significant violence, if indeed it is present, based upon the notion that the false-negative error rate will be too high if predictions do not account for actual but unknown basal violence. The examiner engaging in this and the following steps must be alert to avoid illusory associations of various sorts with dangerousness and to recognize that other factors, while they may significantly correlate with violence, are symptomatic but not causitive of violence. These symptoms or "reflectors" change between predictors and situations with remarkable ease and even within the same person over time. Reflectors include such factors as certain psychological test "signs," assumed personality traits, and clinical diagnosis. The next step in the decision process is to determine possible triggering stimuli, short term in duration, intense in impact, which may set violence into motion and which almost always are historically precedented within the individual's behavioral repertoire. The next step in the decision process is to examine which factors— termed opportunity variables—make possible or expand the nature and quality of violence that has been or could be exhibited. As with each step, this involves the study of inhibitory factors that *lower* the chances for violence to occur. These are contained in the preceding factors. For example, an absent history of violence will act to prevent or diminish future violence. The last step in the decision process is to present circumscribed and replicable conclusions, taking into account the base rates that are available and relevant for the predictee, and outcome measures that reflect violence from a variety of criterion parameters including violence direction, severity, and acceleration/deceleration.

Dangerousness Prediction Pitfalls

The dozen common errors to predicting violence that are relevant to the presented decision tree are listed in this section.

(1) FAILURE TO SEE THE RELEVANCE OF DANGEROUSNESS PREDICTION AS A PERVASIVE, BINDING, AND KEY CONCEPT IN THE MENTAL HEALTH-LAW INTERFACE. Dangerousness prediction is often overlooked as a primary issue in clinical-forensic settings. Extending Shah's (1978) partial list, a more comprehensive list of situations or settings in which dangerousness predictions or post-dictions are important include but are not limited to the following:

- Tarasoff duty-to-protect assessments;
- Witness-protection programs;
- Grand jury investigations of problematic government workers (e.g., police officers, guards);
- Presentence evaluations of defendants;
- Furlough and work release from correctional programs;
- Release from state hospitals;
- Potentially violent clients in therapy;
- Mentally ill individuals applying for or in possession of firearms;
- Criminal profiling of suspects in violent crimes;
- Bail granting hearings;
- Decisions involving waiver of juveniles to adult court;
- Parole board determinations;
- Fitness-to-proceed examinations;
- Mental capacity examinations of cognitive and volitional impairments;
- Transfer of disruptive inmates from one institution to another;
- Involuntary commitment to outpatient treatment;
- Involuntary emergency commitment;
- Involuntary commitment of defendants found not guilty by reason of insanity;
- Sentencing as a habitual or dangerous offender as a function of accelerating or chronic violence;
- Child custody assessments involving previous or suspected child abuse;
- Pretrial investigation of defendants;
- Psychological autopsies in cases involving victim-precipitated violence;
- Selection for special programs (e.g., career criminal units, SWAT teams) involving frequent contact with violent offenders;

- Program planning for certain types of substance abusers who commit violent crimes to support their habit;
- Decisions regarding forced sterilization and castration;
- Intervention planning for significant others of violent offenders;
- Participation in research projects involving risk of violence from or to subjects.

Police Sergeant Leed is a good example of the special need of certain occupational subgroups to undergo violence assessment at times of crisis.

In terms of liability, the trend appears to involve an extension of settings and circumstances under which individual dangerousness prediction should be made. A therapist's duty to protect intended victims of violence is a clear example of the twin assumptions that dangerousness prediction is both possible and necessary as a preliminary step in risk intervention or prevention (e.g., *Tarasoff v. Regents of the University of California*, 1976; *McIntosh v. Milano*, 1979; Beck, 1985; Monahan, 1993). Should Sergeant Leed's potential violence, for example, be reported to other employees? Recent court decisions seem to have rejected the notion that violence cannot be predicted and now include as persons to warn those who stand in a "close relationship" to potential violence victims (e.g., *Hedlund v. Orange County*, 1983; *Jablonski v. U.S.*, 1983). Mental health professionals can now be liable for damages not only for failure to warn intended victims based upon a prediction of dangerousness, as in Tarasoff and McIntosh, but also for predicting nonviolence when, in fact, violence later occurs, a false-negative error (e.g., *Peck v. Counseling Services of Addison County, Inc.*, 1985). In this case, the Vermont Supreme Court ruled that the therapist was negligent because her prediction of nonviolence was "based on inadequate information and consultation." These decisions have significantly extended therapists' liability in that a dangerousness prediction process must be engaged in by the therapist at some level, and if a personal injury suit results, a dangerousness *post*-diction process is made by the civil court in an attempt to assess damages. In general, the traditional argument that the state of the art in dangerousness prediction is rudimentary and contradictory has not significantly swayed the courts.

The inclusionary criterion for the relevance of dangerousness prediction includes consideration of most clinical-forensic situations in which possible future violence is an issue, as listed in this subsection. The exclusionary criterion would include situations in which ethical or procedural principles may be compromised (e.g., death-penalty cases, job selection for routine positions, inadequate information available). Dangerousness predictions can and have been made in the absence of firsthand examination of the predictee, as with the use of base rates and "anchoring" strategies, but the forensic database should be sufficiently large to provide information on possible individual variation from group characteristics, if that is a focus of referral. At best, the forensic clinician can speak only to issues of base rate and *must* clarify that no individual prediction can be made without firsthand examination of the predictee. The forensic examiner should attempt to avoid situations in which firsthand examination is not allowed or is not possible. In those rare circumstances when it becomes necessary to offer a clinical opinion concerning prediction without first examining the individual, conclusions should be limited to group data, with the clear explanation that individual variation is the rule rather than the exception. The forensic clinician should avoid being placed in the position of "Dr. Death" in *Barefoot v. Estelle* (1983), where a psychiatrist testified that the defendant was "100% certain" to commit violent acts again, although the individual had not bee interviewed. This testimony was given in support of the death penalty and has subsequently been held out as a prime example of unethical and inappropriate professional behavior.

(2) LACK OF AN ADEQUATE FORENSIC DATABASE. The typical forensic evaluation of dangerousness stands in low esteem in the mental health-law interface. This occurred primarily because the dismal results of first-generation follow-up research, allegedly showing low accuracy and a tendency to overpredict dangerousness, are now well disseminated and believed. Predictor variables reported in the literature for first-generation research have usually been a review of *violence history*, examination of *current institutional* or *community adjustment*, and a consideration of various *demographic variables* such as gender, age, and socioeconomic status. Second-generation research involving promising degrees of accuracy is less well known or seen as exceptions to the general trend. Predictor variables from second-generation research accounting for the increased accuracy involve a wider selection of database measuring procedures to include all of the above plus specific tests for basal violence history, triggers to aggression (e.g., stress and substance abuse inventories) and distortion of maladaptive and violent histories (e.g., social desirability scales to tap response sets, use of objective psychological tests with validity scales to measure deception), in addition to increased use of base rate statistics, as will be discussed later.

More recent research, which we have labeled third generation, is even less well known publicly and focuses upon actuarial prediction. As previously described, the MacArthur Risk Assessment Study (Steadman, et al., 1994) has chosen four domains for analysis of risk factors. The first domain concerns dispositional variables involving demographic factors, personality variables, and neurological factors. A second domain includes historical variables such as family history, work history, hospitalization and treatment history, criminal history, and history of violence. Contextual variables make up the third domain, referring here to social supports and networks as well as physical environmental factors such as access to weapons, homelessness, etc.

Clinical variables make up the final and fourth domain, and these include traditional DSM–IV categorizations.

In general, inclusionary criteria for an adequate forensic database for dangerousness predictions involve the necessity of multisourced, multidisciplinary data sources. This is based upon the notions that drawing conclusions primarily from one source, such as the interview, leads to generalization problems and that no professional discipline has the total answer to knowing whether future violent behavior will occur. Examiners should always keep in mind that the fundamental strength of their conclusions regarding dangerousness may rest on the diversity and depth of database sources upon which rendered conclusions rely. A partial list of database sources includes observations and findings from the following assessment procedures or circumstances:

- Clinical interviewing of the predictee;
- Interview and/or testing of previous victims and significant/knowledgeable others;
- Behavioral observations of the predictee in social and nonsocial contexts;
- Behavioral observations of the predictee in structured and nonstructured situations;
- Behavioral observations in both stress/intoxicated (e.g., alcohol, EEG, standardized stress field tests) and tranquil/nonintoxicated circumstances;
- A functional analysis of previous violence-related responses;
- Environmental assessment to include culture-bound stimulus factors;
- Psychological and neuropsychological assessment;
- Developmental assessment;
- Competence assessment;
- Description of probable but unknown behavioral traits from actual demographic traits;
- Other relevant violence-base-rate data;
- Medical, neurological, and laboratory examination;
- "Cognitive" interviewing to include recall of the events in different orders and changing perspectives;
- "Body leakage" analysis in terms of behavioral clues to deceit and distortions;
- Records produced by the predictee (diaries, letters, etc.);
- Records produced by others (e.g., military, school, job);
- "Expunged" records usually available to sanity or other mental examiners;
- Operant reinforcement and other intervention paradigms designed to assess behavior by changing it;

- Relevant psychological-mathematical inductive models, which are then used as a basis for further inquiry;
- Computer simulation of predictee's profile and future behavior based on a deductive analysis of binary input source combinations.

Additional database sources that have been identified as problematic because of problems with validity, acceptability in court, and intrusiveness include the following:

- Forensic hypnosis;
- Various intrusive medical deception analysis procedures (e.g., sodium amytal, sodium pentothal);
- Somatic and transcript analysis;
- Handwriting analysis;
- Guided imagery and other methods to attempt reconstruction of past events;
- Instrumentation such as polygraph, plethysmograph, and the voice stress analyzer;
- Stress interviews.

Exclusionary criteria fall into one of three categories as follows: (1) *examiner deficits* (e.g., unfamiliarity with the predictee's culture, untrained); (2) *assessment deficits* (e.g., failure to assess over several temporal points, use of invalid measuring devices); and (3) *subject deficits* (e.g., noncooperation, successful masking attempts).

(3) FAILURE TO ACCOUNT FOR RETROSPECTIVE AND CURRENT DISTORTION. Forensic databases, unfortunately, are often distorted by predictees who often have a vested interest in faking good (i.e., denying or minimizing true psychopathology or dangerousness) or faking bad (e.g., exaggerating or fabricating psychopathology or dangerousness), depending on their perceived desired legal outcomes and other factors. Assuming that predictees only fake good to hide violence or present no distortion can and does lead to serious data misinterpretation. Invalidating evaluation results, faking bad, and combinations of styles are also possibilities (Rogers, 1984; Hall, 1982, 1985, 1986).

The predictee may employ these strategies differentially for data relevant to basal history and the evaluation. This means that as many as 25 distinct distortion tactics can be presented, corresponding to five strategies (faking good, faking bad, no distortion, invalidating results, mixed styles) under two time conditions. The point is that the predictee's evaluation stance should be taken into consideration in interpreting data in all forensic evaluations of dangerousness. Identification of the strategy combination employed breaks down initially into utilizing methods that validly reflect present or past representation of events, whether distorted or not, and then determining the probable type, direction, and magnitude of distortion. Hall (1986) presented a list of nine quantitative methods to assess deliberate faking, gleaned from the neuropsychological and clinical testing literature, to include use of parallel forms, regression equations, and forensic "booby traps."

Differential strategies of faking bad and faking good for the present and the past are instructive to examine. A client may attempt to portray past dangerousness but deny current dangerousness, for example. He or she may be saying that they were dangerous in the past but have been rehabilitated, have changed, and are not now at risk. The message they communicate may be that it is appropriate to trust this individual, or at least to perceive change in a positive direction. The implication for a lower sentence, such as release from a state hospital, or placement on a witness protection program, etc. may represent the desired outcome. It is desirable to know the motive of the predictee for assuming a particular response style, but it is not essential if the direction and relative magnitude of the distortion has been noted. Faking good for both the past and present may occur when the crime was minor and the defendant does not desire to have psychological intervention. The assessment situation may also encourage the natural desire to appear normal. If it serves the interests of clients, or if they are honest even though it is to their disadvantage, presenting no distortion is occasionally revealed, as evidenced by verification from independent facts and sources, and other factors. Faking bad for the present with faking good for the past may be associated with a plea for help, as when the individual has been typically harmless, but is now dangerous due to unusual and highly stressful outside events. It is not unusual for people to present to emergency rooms with the complaint that they are afraid of losing control, hurting themselves or others.

A schematic of the distortion style concept is presented in Table XXI along with some methods used to assess for distortion.

(4) PREDICTING DANGEROUSNESS IN THE ABSENCE OF PAST VIOLENT BEHAVIOR. Assuming that the database is adequate and that one has corrected for client distortion, both yielding a negative finding for basal violence, the chances of producing a true positive may be equal to base rates for violence for the general population (i.e., about 250 violent acts per 100,000 population per year; 5–10 per 100,000 for homicide, etc.–all less than 1%). This observation is so primary, it assumes the status of a rule: Never predict violence in the absence of a history of previous significant violent behavior.

Does this mean that clinicians will invariably predict false negatives for first acts of significant violence? Not necessarily. Clinicians can always refuse to predict in individual situations. Questions will emerge. "What about command hallucinations in psychotic individuals with the availability of weapons and hate toward a given person or group?" "What about a substance-intoxicated teenager in a stolen car?" Generally, the false-positive rate will be too high, unless previous violence can be demonstrated. Further, in most indi-

TABLE XXI
FORENSIC DISTORTION ANALYSIS

Past behavior	Current behavior (time of evaluation)				
	Fake good	Fake bad	No distortion	Invalidating results	Mixed styles
Fake good	1	2	3	4	5
Fake bad	6	7	8	9	10
No distortion	11	12	13	14	15
Invalidating results	16	17	18	19	20
Mixed Styles	21	22	23	24	25

Method:	Will detect faking good?	Will detect faking bad?	Possible other alternatives:
Observation of clinical behavior	X	X	Genuine strength or pathology in subject
Parallel forms, significant difference		X	Actual work decrement
Learning curves		X	Performance or procedural problem
Regression equations		X	Statistical anomaly
Illusory difficult tasks			
• Dot counting		X	Visual problems
• Memory of clustered items		X	Organic problems
• Auditory discrimination test		X	Auditory problems
Easy-versus-difficult versions of the same test		X	Memory problems
Underreporting of significant verfiable events			
• Criminal record	X	X	Lack of recall
• Events of instant offense	X	X	Natural tendency to accentuate positive
• Activity with peers or family	X	X	Distorted information
• Stated alcohol consumption versus BAC reading	X	X	Blackout or pathological intoxication
Goodness of fit between psychological test profiles and community/institution behavior	X	X	Faulty sampling of observed behavior

viduals who do turn out violent, the data support the notion that there may be some significant violent past of which the examiner was unaware. A variety of this error is to downplay a violence history in favor of recent events. The best predictor of future violence remains past violence; in the study by Hall, et al. (1984), basal violence accounted for more than 70 percent of later exhibited violence, compared to about 5 percent of the statistical variance for stimulus triggers, as will be discussed later. The MacArthur studies (Steadman, Mulvey, Monahan, Robbins, Applebaum, Grisson, Roth and Silver, 1998) emphasize the value of thorough research on specific populations to refine predictive accuracy. Here, evidence strongly supports that the best predictor for violence among hospitalized mental patients is the interaction among major mental illness, substance abuse, and other characterological diagnoses, such as psychopathy. Note, of course, that a diagnosis of psychopathy supposes a prior history of aggression.

Inclusionary criteria would emcompass all relevant historical events of the predictee such as exposure to war and violence while a teenager or child, which although involving violence in special circumstances, demonstrate that violence is now part of the predictee's behavioral repertoire. *Threatened* violence is considered violence in the sense that serious harm could occur from noncompliance, as in robbery and rape. The consequences for the victim of threatened violence in terms of post-traumatic-stress-disorder symptoms and other conditions can be significant. Threatened violence often precedes physical violence, and tends to escalate and generalize when reinforced by the behavior of the victim or onlookers. Attempted violence is likewise considered violence in that the chain of behaviors leading to physical violence has been initiated. The difference between murder and attempted murder is often due to lack of opportunity, unexpected occurrences and disruptions, and other "dumb-luck" factors.

Exclusionary criteria for historical violence would be "minor" violence (e.g., sibling squabbles, a school fist fight), and illegal but nondangerous behavior such as theft and some other property and victimless crimes.

(5) FALLING PREY TO ILLUSORY CORRELATIONS BETWEEN EVALUATION. It was long thought, as a standard example, that obtaining a high color-to-human movement ratio on the Rorschach reflected dangerousness, when there was and is little empirical support for this claim. Another false association on this test was the belief that reporting eyes or white space responses suggested of paranoia or oppositional tendencies, respectively, when no such empirical link had been demonstrated. The psychological lore on test responses falsely associated with dangerousness has been thoroughly reviewed by Megargee (1970), who stated that there is no test when used alone that will postdict, let alone predict, dangerousness. Tests he reviewed included the Rorschach test, the Rosenzweig Picture-Frustration Technique,

the Hand Test, and the Minnesota Multiphasic Personality Inventory. His observations remain valid as of the date of this writing and are supported by later work, such as that of Rogers (1988).

(6) PREDICTING FROM CLINICAL DIAGNOSIS. In general, no diagnosis signifies past, current, or future dangerousness to others, and therefore, no psychiatric diagnosis alone should be the rationale for predicting dangerousness to others. This includes the following diagnoses from the American Psychiatric Association Diagnostic and Statistical Manual–IV (1994) (DSM–IV) diagnoses:

- *Conduct disorder* (disorders of infancy, childhood, adolescence) 312.8– a persistent pattern of behavior in which the rights of others are violated, as manifested by three or more instances of relevant signs in the past year: (e.g., aggression to people and animals including bullying or threatening, physical violence, and purse snatching);
- *Phencyclidine (PCP) intoxication* 292.89–demonstrated by clinically significant maladaptive behavioral changes such as belligerence, assaultiveness, and unpredictability;
- *Cocaine intoxication* 292.89–again, with clinically significant maladaptive behavior such as anxiety, tension, or anger;
- *Sexual sadism* 302.84–involving psychological or physical suffering (including humiliation) of a victim. It should be noted that this behavior can occur with a consenting partner and in such cases, victim status may not be appropriately defined;
- *Antisocial personality disorder* 301.7–requires evidence of conduct disorder before age 15 as well as maladaptive behaviors after age 18. The earlier behaviors must include either aggression to people or animals or destruction of property, but may also involve nonviolent violations of rules such as staying out late at night, running away from home, or being truant from school. Post age 15, three additional maladaptive behaviors are required for a diagnosis. Such behaviors can include failure to conform to social norms to the point of being susceptible to arrest, deceitfulness, impulsivity, irritability and aggressiveness, reckless disregard for the safety of self or others, consistent irresponsibility (poor work history), and lack of remorse. The person must be at least 18 years of age to receive this diagnosis;
- *Schizophrenia, paranoid type* 295.30–many of the delusional beliefs or sensory aberrations may have nothing at all to do with violence either through cause or effect. Even when command hallucinations are reported, the predictee can exhibit a great deal of control and may be able to disregard or ignore the instructions. However, Borum, Swartz and Swanson (1996) review research that supports high rates of reported violence in patient groups when psychotic symptoms are evident.

They note, "The presence that active psychotic symptoms (particularly those involving perceived threat or overriding of internal controls) and/or comorbid substance abuse appear to be more important risk factors than the mere presence of a diagnosable disorder." As has been substantiated by the MacArthur Risk studies (Steadman et al., 1998), the combination of mental illness and substance abuse presents a very high risk for violent behavior. The interaction of paranoid delusional symptoms such as command hallucinations with substance abuse should be considered a potent indicator;

- *Post-traumatic stress disorder* 309.81—a diagnosis unfortunately often encountered in persons who are recipients of violent attacks and who later are victims of delayed stress (e.g., Vietnam veterans). PTSD can and often does occur with noncombatents such as victims of rape or of auto accidents or of other civilian catastrophes. In these situations, individuals may relive the trauma to the point of believing that they need once again to defend or protect themselves against imagined assailants.

In the DSM–IV (1994) decision tree for acting out or oppositional defiant disorder (313.81), there is *no* option for having no mental disorder. At the end of the decision tree, a person is placed in a category that resembles the old professional criminal category (dissocial personality). All antisocial, aggressive, violent, defiant, or oppositional behavior in DSM–IV is seen by the American Psychiatric Association as resulting from mental illness or other maladaptive behavior patterns. Appropriate violence is not a choice (e.g., police, institutionally sanctioned violence, aggression in defense of one's family, to prevent a crime). The framers of future DSMs need to build in a cultural relativism factor to avoid this unreasonable and unrealistic conclusion.

The DSM–IV (1994) decision tree (p. 345, 689) is instructive. If you show violence, aggression, or oppositional behavior as the prominent clinical features, the following decision path is followed:

First, rule out *brain damage* or *substance abuse.*
Second, rule out *mental retardation.*
Third, rule out *psychosis.*
Fourth, rule out *explosive disorder.*
Fifth, rule out *antisocial personality disorder.*
Sixth, rule out *conduct disorder.*
Seventh, rule out *oppositional disorder.*
Eighth, rule out *adjustment disorder with disturbance of conduct.*

You are left at the end of the decision tree with childhood, adolescent, or adult antisocial behaviors. The diagnosis of adult antisocial behavior is given when the focus of attention for treatment is antisocial behavior that is not due to a mental disorder. Examples include professional thieves, racketeers, and drug dealers.

In general, DSM–IV is not helpful in either identifying past violence or predicting dangerousness unless the problem is obvious. Those with these diagnoses may have a higher base rate of violence than "normals," possibly because exhibited violence was seen as evidence of an assumed mental condition. Further, labeling a predictee as mentally ill and potentially violent has the essence of a self-fulfilling prophecy and hence involves more than the "right" not to be a false positive.

The inclusionary criteria for consideration in this error would include all DSM–IV criteria plus all diagnoses from the International Classification of Diseases. Exclusionary criteria would emcompass conditions that are not formally thought of as mental disorders, such as chronic rapists, serial murderers, and the violent cyclothymic crises reported in the early forensic literature.

(7) FAILURE TO TAKE INTO ACCOUNT TRIGGERING STIMULI. Triggering stimuli involve events associated with the subject's behavioral repertoire that are precipitating causes, short term in duration, intense in impact and that set violence into motion. Factors in this cluster primarily include substance intoxication of various sorts and interpersonal stress. Breakup of the central love relationship for adults or gross disruption in the primary family unit for minors seem to be primary stress triggers. As with the earlier cluster, the potential for triggering events must be established within the subject's existing behavior patterns and environmental opportunity.

Inclusionary events for triggering stimuli would include any events in the predictee's past that appeared to set violence into motion. Triggers may vary over time, combine during one violence episode as in intoxication and stress caused by a breakup with a mate, are short term in the sense of lasting only days or weeks at most, and are assumed to be intense in impact upon the individual's typical mode of adjustment. There are usually only a few prime triggers, upon historical analysis of an individual's previous violence. Exclusionary events are long-term factors, low grade in correlation with violence, that may be associated with violence such as poverty, subcultural "acceptance" of violence as a solution to problems, and crowded living conditions. What were possible triggering stimuli to violence for Police Sergeant Leed?

(8) FAILURE TO TAKE INTO ACCOUNT OPPORTUNITY VARIABLES. Opportunity variables include the availability of a firearm (Berkowitz and Lapage, 1967; Monahan, 1981), presence of a physically weaker potential victim (Bandura, 1973), and elevation to positions of authority where violence towards others is institutionally sanctioned (Fromm, 1973; Milgram, 1963, 1965). Opportunity variables, which allow the expression of violence

include release into the community from incarceration (Kelly, 1976) and cessation of taking tranquilizing medication (Stone, 1975). The importance of the opportunity variable represented by firearms and other potentially lethal weapons is highlighted by the fact that 37 percent of all violent victimizations are perpetrated by armed offenders (Rand, DeBerry, Klaus and Taylor, 1986). This includes half of all robberies, a third of all assaults, and a fourth of all rapes. Use of weapons is associated with a high crime-completion rate, greater possibility of victimizing multiple persons at the same time, and chances of the victim(s) requiring medical attention or hospitalization.

Mispredicting from one setting to another may be caused by not taking into account the opportunity variable. A movement from one setting to another changes the context of validation as well as the opportunity for acquiring weapons, transportation, and victims. Therefore, it should not be surprising if a highly violent individual who is nonviolent in prison, given its structured setting and strong sanctions against certain kinds of exhibited violence, then returns to the community to aggress once more. Perhaps more obvious is the pedophile or rapist who is held for treatment in a special setting for sexually dangerous individuals. Upon appeal for release, the individual's attorney will often highlight the fact that he has had no observed victims or misbehavior for the years of his incarceration. Although it should be obvious that opportunities for victimization against children or females are significantly decreased during a period of incarceration, this argument has won over juries and even, on occasion, judges. It should be no surprise when the released sexual offender reoffends within a very short time. The circumstances of one setting should not be applied to another setting unless a functional equivalence exists in terms of the relevant opportunity variables. If no such equivalence is operative, behavior in other settings in the individual's past similar to future settings should be used as the basis for prediction rather than what has been observed in the most recent but artificial and controlled environment.

(9) FAILURE TO TAKE INTO ACCOUNT INHIBITORY FACTORS. Inhibitory variables operate to lower the probability for violence; this type of variable falls into the lower range of frequency, intensity, duration, or recency of the above three factors. A nonexistent basal history, for example, acts as an inhibitor by virtue of its absence (Kozol et al., 1972; Kelly, 1976). Current operating conditions associated with a lower propensity to aggress include female sex, old age, high socioeconomic status, and high educational level (Kelly, 1976; Monahan, 1981a). Opportunity variables assume an inhibitory status when significant events eliminate or reduce the probability of aggression, for example, placement in solitary confinement, loss of means of transportation, or an invalid physical status. Triggers assume inhibitory qualities when their presence suppresses or delays violence such as the sudden arrival

of police officers, motionless victim behavior, bright illumination, house alarms, and other circumstances.

Inclusionary events would include any factors that are assumed to lower violence in the past or can be expected to operate in the future and are usually found in the extreme ends of historical, opportunity, or triggering variables idiosyncratic for each individual. These factors may vary over time. For example, a possible perpetrator may not engage in violence or may stop when onlookers are present, and at other times, because the victim pleads for mercy or shows unexpected resistance. Exclusionary criteria would include events that are associated in time with lowered aggression but that are incidental or irrelevant to its diminution such as when a perpetrator stops assaulting due to exhaustion or distraction.

(10) IGNORING RELEVANT BASE RATES. The FBI's recidivism data from 1972, for example, showed that individuals convicted and released from incarceration for particular violent crimes, that recidivate within four years with homicide (64%), robbery (77%), rape (73%), or aggravated assault (70%). The PROMIS research data (1977) showed that with five or more arrests for violent crimes, the probability of similar future arrests approaches certainty. Wolfgang (1977) found that the probability of future arrest varied directly with number of previous arrests (e.g., 80% with four priors). Guze (1976) found that of male felons released from incarceration 72 percent were rearrested and 41 percent were reimprisoned if they had been diagnosed as sociopathic (three year follow-up); 90 percent were rearrested and 67 percent were reimprisoned over an 8–9-year period after release if they had been "flat-timers" (no early release or parole for "good time"). Over a three-year period after release, 81 percent were rearrested and 56 percent were reimprisoned, pointing to the time soon after release as the critical period where most recidivism occurs; 90 percent were rearrested and 50 percent were reimprisoned if they had a drug dependence diagnosis (three-year follow-up); 74 percent were rearrested and 45 percent were reimprisoned if they were primarily alcohol abusers (3-year follow-up). Compare to these statistics a relatively low 33 percent rearrest rate and 21 percent reconviction rate for released females and a 57 percent rearrest rate and 28 percent reimprisonment rate for some types of male parolees, both over three years. High rates for reoffending are thus found for some types of individuals (e.g., flat-timers, substance abusers with previous drug dependence, especially high sociopaths) and much lower for others (e.g., females, some types of parolees).

Violence within criminal recidivism has also been measured. Holland, Holt, Levi and Beckett (1983) found that in their population of 339 male adult felony probationers followed over 32 months, 74 to 81 percent were rearrested with 19 to 64 percent exhibiting robbery, aggravated assault, forcible rape, and homicide, depending upon assignment to one of four categories. Assignment was based on a "silent factor score" derived from information collected through psychological testing and interviewing, institutional conduct, and the presentence report. Thus, outcome discrimination was possible depending on known factors before later violence occurred. Compare to this a 2 percent rate of violence within an overall 20 percent recidivism rate shown by rearrest and/or rehospitalization for released mentally ill offenders in the Baxstrom studies (i.e., Steadman & Cocozza, 1974). Their findings have recently come under methodological attack, however.

In general, there should be stated reasons for ignoring or disagreeing with the relevant base rates that do exist, assuming that the predictor is aware of them. The use of "anchoring" (Shapiro, 1977), that is using the base rate of a condition as the first estimate of the probability of dangerousness in an individual, should be considered before adding client-specific data to individualize the prediction. The initial use of baselines also helps to avoid the error of overplaying current events and downplaying the violence history.

(11) USING ARREST, CONVICTION, OR INCARCERATION FOR A VIOLENT CRIME, ALONE OR IN COMBINATION WITH PSYCHIATRIC HOSPITALIZATION, AS THE ONLY OUTCOME MEASURES TO VIOLENCE. As mentioned, violence predictions are often based on dependent variables such as rearrest rate or, much less frequently, rehospitalization) that reflect only about 20 percent of known serious violence (Hall, 1982). The National Victimization Panel (1978) and National Crime Survey (1985) found that only about one-half of criminal violence is reported. Once brought to the attention of the police, about one-third of the serious violence is cleared, where the perpetrator is identified and brought into custody (Kelly, 1976; U.S. Department of Justice, 1985).

Other outcome measures can be used to include several factors. The predictee reporting verbally during the interview the occurrence of previous violence. Various investigators have noted the close correspondence between reported and actual previous violence (e.g., Petersilia, et al., 1977);

- Reporting in writing the occurrence of previous violence. A checklist of violent acts can be presented to the predictee and who is asked to indicate the occurrence and frequency of previously exhibited violence. Given proper protection and orientation, many predictees will affirm in writing what they will not relate verbally, and vice versa, which can be used as a basis for further inquiry;
- Input from witnesses/observers directly or from reports;
- Circumstances of violence-related sequelae. This data can be used to demonstrate that violence did occur whether the accused admits to it or not, and whether or not witnesses corroborate the findings of violence by their first-hand observation;
- Results from distortion measures. Distortion detection procedures, dis-

TABLE XXII
VIOLENCE PREDICTION: SUGGESTED DEGREES OF CERTAINTY

Risk category	Description	Probability range	Legal description	Possible associated factors
• Substantial	Very high likelihood of	91 to 100%	Beyond a reasonable doubt	Recent[1], prepotent[2] violence history, multiple triggers[3], opportunity
• Considerable	Strong likelihood of	76 to 90%	Clear and convincing	Prepotent violence history, trigger, opportunity
• Moderate	Violence more likely than not	51 to 75%	A preponderance of evidence	Violence history, trigger, opportunity
• Mild	Fair likelihood of violence	26 to 50%	Nondangerous	Violence history or not, trigger, opportunity
• Minimal	Low likelihood of violence	11 to 25%	Nondangerous	Violence history or not, trigger, opportunity
• Negligible	Very low likelihood of	0 to 10%	Nondangerous	Violence history or not, trigger and opportunity or not

[1] Recency can be linked to basal violence when anchoring strategies are utilized. The degree to which violence was shown within a three-month period prior to the evaluation can be examined and associated with a three-month base rate involving similar characteristics as the predictee. A three-month temporal period of prediction can then be presented in the report as the prediction time under consideration.

[2] Prepotent means at least two previous serious acts of violence, as defined by the penal code (Hall et al., 1984).

[3] Multiple triggers means at least two out of three of the following from Hall et al. (1984): (a) Substance abuse within the previous month (DSM–III criteria); (b) Actual or threatened breakup in the predictee's central love relationship; (c) Work problems with colleagues and/or supervisors causing disciplinary action, attempts at intervention, or termination.

cussed earlier, can be used in combination to estimate the direction and magnitude of misrepresentation. See also the list of possible assessment procedures presented earlier.

(12) FAILURE TO LIMIT AND OPERATIONALIZE PROFFERED CONCLUSIONS. A prime example of this is offering yes/no and noncontingent conclusions instead of a probability or risk statement based on available baselines and client-specific data. Once the degree of dangerousness is specified, there are often failures to specify the direction of dangerousness, the factors that formed the conclusions, the feedback mechanism that should be included to evaluate the predictions, the temporal limits of the prediction, and other important factors. A scheme to present suggested degrees of certainty is provided in Table XXII.

Report Formatting

A dangerousness prediction report format follows directly from the decision tree and discussion of avoidable errors, and is available upon request. This report format in concrete detail sequentially (1) presents the referral questions and concerns; (2) reveals the forensic database and measures upon which the conclusions rely; (3) analyzes possible client and significant/knowledgeable other's deliberate and nondeliberate deception and distortion; (4) scrutinizes extant basal violence of the predictee; (5) highlights triggering stimuli to violence; (6) examines opportunity variables to violence; and (7) presents circumscribed and operationalized conclusions, utilizing base rate and "anchoring" strategies. Further investigation of the dangerousness prediction concept along the lines of the MacArthur Study is urgently needed for groups beyond mental patients.

SUMMARY

This chapter presents the dozen most-common errors in predicting dangerousness to others by forensic mental health professionals as suggested by the behavioral science literature and observation of colleagues. A proposed decision tree leads into a discussion of errors as a prelude to the eventual standardization and measurement of the dangerousness prediction concept. These errors include the following: (1) Failure to perceive the relevance of dangerousness prediction as a specific focus of inquiry; (2) Lack of an adequate forensic database; (3) Failure to account for retrospective and current distortion; (4) Predicting dangerousness in the absence of previous dangerousness; (5) Falling prey to illusory correlations; (6) Predicting from clinical diagnosis; (7) Failure to take into account triggering stimuli; (8) Failure to take into account opportunity variables; (9) Failure to take into account inhibitory factors; (10) Ignoring relevant base rates; (11) Use of limited outcome measures; (12) Failure to offer circumscribed conclusions. The view that individual dangerousness prediction is a ubiquitous, significant forensic enterprise that can be engaged in with accuracy, report/courtroom impact, and relatively limited liability is discussed and supported.

Chapter 10

ETHICAL CONSIDERATIONS IN FORENSICS AND THE ASSESSMENT OF DANGEROUSNESS

T HE MAJORITY OF THIS TEXT has been focused upon an understanding of the process through which forensic clinicians may arrive at reliable predictions of dangerousness. At least as important, and perhaps even more important, is consideration of the standard by which such conduct is carried out. All applications of mental health practice have a direct impact upon the individual being studied, treated, or assessed. Nowhere in the field of mental health practice is this perhaps more critical, however, than in the forensic arena, for here issues of loss of freedom, restriction of liberty, and perhaps even loss of life hinge upon the professional's conduct of work.

Discussions and arguments have ranged widely around ethical considerations for clinicians in the courtroom. Alan Stone argued in 1984 that psychiatrists did not have clear ethical guidelines concerning their forensic practice, and thus he advised that they should stay out of the courtroom. Others, notably Paul S. Appelbaum, more recently (1997) has offered a theory of ethics for psychiatrists that focuses upon what he considers to be the primary value of forensic psychiatry, that is advancing the interest of justice. He clarifies the schism between the traditional doctor-patient relationship, supported by general medical ethics, and the forensic relationship that does not hold to these principles. Perhaps his writings will provide comfort to those made uncomfortable by Alan Stone's dire warnings.

The American Psychological Association took a pragmatic approach and issued their Ethical Principles of Psychologists and Code of Conduct in 1992, including specific ethical codes concerning forensic activities. It is a set of standards crafted uniquely for the forensic clinician and designed to provide a code of behavior by which the highest ethical standards can be carried out.

The objective of this chapter is to review these standards in some detail, offering commentary where appropriate and assisting the reader in carrying out work that will meet these standards. It should be stressed that individual clinicians at all times are responsible for evaluating their own behavior against professional standards, current law, and community practice. Psychologists who are members of the American Psychological Association must adhere to the American Psychological Association ethics code. Those psychologists who are not members of the APA or are students should be aware that this code can very well be applied to them by state boards and parties as well as by local courts. Professionals who are not psychologists should be aware of their own ethical codes of conduct, particularly where such codes make specific reference to forensic activities. Where such codes are not available, the reader is advised to consider the American Psychological Association's code for guidance and direction.

Professionalism

In Standard 7.01 (APA, 1992) the code specifies that "Psychologists who perform forensic functions, such as assessments, interviews, consultations, reports, or expert testimony, must comply with all other provisions of this ethics code to the extent that they apply to such activities. In addition, psychologists base their forensic work on appropriate knowledge of and competency in the areas underlying such work, including specialized knowledge concerning special populations."

Clearly, this initial forensic standard indicates that psychologists who work in the forensic arena are psychologists first, and thus are required to be in full compliance with the general ethics code. As Stronberg, Lindberg, and Schneider (1995) noted, there is no exception granted to forensic psychologists from ethical conduct expected of all psychologists. Additionally, this standard suggests that individuals cannot call themselves forensic psychologists without "appropriate knowledge of and competence in the areas underlying such work." Thus, formal education, attendance at workshops and conferences, and ongoing review of professional literature should be thought of as minimum criteria for such specialized work. Some states such as Massachusetts offer structured training and certification in court-related aspects of forensic work, and this is increasingly viewed by members of the court as an accepted standard. Experienced forensic psychologists are urged to apply for Diplomate status through the American Board of Professional Psychology. This imposing credential is obtained only after rigorous training and examination and assures all parties the diplomates have "knowledge of and competence in" the forensic arena.

Forensic Assessments

In Standard 7.02 (APA, 1992), the code says, "(a) Psychologists' forensic assessments, recommendations, and reports are based on information and techniques (including personal interviews of the individual, when appropriate) sufficient to provide appropriate substantiation for their findings."

This standard, when carefully met, assures that the clinician in court is serving to provide an objective and professionally competent data set for utilization by the finder of fact.

Fischer (1997) writes about the "hired gun" who attempts to present dishonest opinions in the guise of scientific analysis. The clinician who follows 7.02(a) is an objective professional who provides documented findings to the reader of their reports. When Judge Bazelon of the Federal District Court addressed the American Psychological Association's annual meeting, he began by noting that he had eagerly invited clinicians into the courtroom to assist in the fact-finding process (e.g. *Jenkins v. U.S.*, 1961), but he then criticized the clinicians in the audience for attempting to usurp the role of the judge once they got inside the hallowed halls. He clearly, and not so gently, reminded his audience of their role in the courtroom—as providers of objective data that can be utilized in the service of justice.

Standard 7.02 (APA, 1992) also states, "(b) Except as noted in (c), below, psychologists provide written or oral forensic reports or testimony of the psychological characteristics of an individual only after they have conducted an examination of the individual adequate to support their statements or conclusions."

With an exception to be noted below, the forensic clinician must not just examine an individual, but do so with enough care and attention to obtain the data necessary to form conclusions. This may mean repeated and extensive interviews as well as the use of various tools such as psychological testing. While the clinician must take care not to exceed reasonable time and budget, it is not reasonable to have only cursory and fleeting contact, or to have no contact at all. Few professionals would like to find themselves in the position of the psychiatrist in *Barefoot v. Estelle* (1983), who offered a clinical opinion that claimed the certainty of dangerousness in support of a death sentence without having interviewed the defendant.

Also from 7.02 (APA, 1992) comes the following: "(c)" When, despite reasonable efforts, such an examination is not feasible, psychologists clarify the impact of their limited information on the reliability and validity of their reports and testimony, and they appropriately limit the nature and extent of their conclusions and recommendations."

Forensic clinicians will occasionally come upon circumstances in which individuals refuse to be interviewed after they receive consent-related information or they may find themselves unable to interview someone because of the severity of that person's illness or aggression. In such circumstances, where an opinion has been requested, it is incumbent upon the clinician to indicate clearly the limited sources of information and the impact of those limitations upon the value of their conclusions. It is very important in such cases that any conclusions and recommendations be couched in language that clarifies the limitations of such an examination. At best, the clinician should reference base rates and risk factors, and also qualify the limits of prediction without an assessment of individual characteristics.

In a recent experience of one writer, a court required that an opinion concerning custody be offered in a circumstance where the father in a case refused to meet with the clinician. An initial attempt was made by the clinician to inform the court of the reluctance of the parent and to suggest to the court that the request for an opinion be voided. The court, in its wisdom, ordered the clinician to proceed to an opinion, but to offer clear information concerning the sources of data and the impact of any limitations of data upon the clinician's conclusions. This guidance enabled the clinician to provide information to the court based upon limited information and in keeping with this aspect of the ethical principles.

Clarification of Role

The APA (1992) writes in Standard 7.03, "In most circumstances, psychologists avoid performing multiple and potentially conflicting roles in forensic matters. One psychologist may be called on to serve in more than one role in a legal proceeding–for example, as consultant or expert for one party or for the court and as a fact witness–they clarify role expectations and the extent of confidentiality in advance to the extent feasible, and thereafter as changes occur, in order to avoid compromising their professional judgment and objectivity and in order to avoid misleading others regarding their role."

It is this issue, role conflict, that has produced more problems for forensic clinicians than any other, in the opinion of these writers. It is not unusual for a clinician working in a hospital to be asked to offer testimony concerning commitment or dangerousness about individuals whom they continue to treat. Similarly, clinicians in private practice report being asked to appear in court in matters of custody or even criminal action on behalf of individuals who are their patients. Much has been written (Greenberg et al., 1997; Strasburger et al., 1997; Shuman et al., 1998) about such role conflict and writers have invariably argued for role separation. For those who are in a therapeutic relationship with a client, playing a forensic role is bound to impact future treatment negatively and to confuse issues of confidentiality.

Problems of objectivity arise in such circumstances as well. In institutionalized settings, particularly in those designed for forensic patients, problems of forced compliance in treatment and informed consent cloud the picture.

This standard also speaks to the need to clarify roles in confidentiality in advance of an evaluation. This certainly is a critical aspect of the initiation of an examination. Some states actually provide case law guidance in such matters. In Massachusetts, clinicians are required to give a "Lamb" warning to persons who are being interviewed for purposes of forensic assessment. This requirement grows out of state case law that found that a certain Mr. Lamb was not properly informed about the purpose of a psychiatric evaluation when being examined as a Sexually Dangerous Person. As a consequence of the lack of informed consent, the psychiatrist's opinion was not allowed in court. Important in such preliminary clarifications should be at least the following:

- Name and title of examiner
- Purpose of evaluation (assessment, mental status, competency to stand trial, or determination of dangerousness)
- Who has employed the examiner in this matter (client's own attorney, prosecution, court)
- Limitations to confidentiality
- Right of the individual to avoid/limit participation due to the limitations of confidentiality.

As has been previously discussed, it is important not only to document that the clinician has provided this information to the individual, but the degree to which the interveiwee understands this information. It is usually not advisable merely to ask whether the person understood and then accept the "yes" or "no" as an accurate measure. It is preferable to ask for a paraphrase of significant parts of the information. Where individuals are unable to offer an accurate paraphrase, it is recommended that at least one training trial be attempted before a determination is made that the individual is unable to process this information. Should this be the case and the person be willing to continue with the examination, it is extremely important that the clinician document both the individual's inability to appreciate the interviewer's role and the extent of confidentiality as well as the individual's willingness to participate. It then becomes possible for the decision maker to determine whether information obtained can be used in court.

Despite the clear stricture to avoid conflicting roles, there are certainly times when this is not possible. In the current atmosphere of cost containment and lean staffing, it is not unusual for clinicians to be required to take on a forensic role in a commitment hearing for individuals they have been treating. Similarly, given limitations on mental health insurance, clinicians may find themselves in a position of being asked to provide a letter to the court (and perhaps subsequent testimony) concerning an individual they are currently treating. In such circumstances, it is imperative that the clinician carefully explain to the parties the difficulties inherent in such a circumstance and the ethical obligation to provide truthful and factual data to the court.

Truthfulness and Candor

Standard 7.04 (APA, 1992) states, "(a) In forensic testimony and reports, psychologists testify truthfully, honestly, and candidly and, consistent with applicable legal procedures, describe fairly the basis for the testimony and the conclusions."

These authors have frequently experienced that truthful and candid reports result in a decision by a defense attorney not to proceed with the use of the expert at trial. This is entirely appropriate within the eyes of the law and should be understood in the context of the need for the attorney to represent the best interest of his or her client. It is critically important for the forensic clinician not to succumb to the role of the "hired gun" who offers opinions that are not truthful, honest, or candid. It is far better, in the author's opinions, to gain a reputation for candor than a reputation for a willingness to prostitute oneself.

Suggested in this standard is the need to appreciate "applicable legal procedures" so that a basis for testimony and conclusions can be offered. Consultation with attorneys is invaluable in forensic work, but particularly so when preparing testimony. Clinicians must be aware of the legal standard against which to measure their data and be able to provide a clear and coherent description of that data in the context of the standard.

The least-useful testimony in a courtroom from an expert witness is the conclusary opinion that "Mr. Smith is a paranoid schizophrenic" without providing a basis for that opinion. It is hard to tell whether it is simply arrogance or just anxiety that can lead a clinician to provide a clinical opinion without substantiating data, but it is, frankly, of little value to the Court. Rather, a careful description of the assessment process and the results of that process, including specific attention to symptomatology are required before any conclusion should be offered.

Standard 7.04 (APA, 1992) further advises, "(b) Whenever necessary to avoid misleading, psychologists acknowledge the limits of their data or conclusions."

Here, the clinician is expected to consider issues of malingering and deception, as well as available data sources. Additionally, in assessments of dangerousness, awareness of both actuarial and predictive literature is crucial. Degree of certainty must be included in all reports and should also be provided during testimony.

Prior Relationships

In Standard 7.05m, APA (1992) says, "A prior professional relationship with a party does not preclude psychologists from testifying as fact witnesses or from testifying to their services to the extent permitted by applicable law. Psychologists appropriately take into account ways in which the prior relationship might affect their professional objectivity or opinions and disclose the potential conflict to the relevant parties."

As opposed to expert witnesses, any clinician may be called as a fact witness during a trial. A prior client, for example, may choose to call her past therapist to testify as to the impact of a mental illness on her ability to parent. Remembering that the client continues to own the confidentiality of the treatment, the clinician will want a written release from the client. There are, of course, situations in which courts can override confidentiality, as in cases involving child abuse; again, it is important for the clinician to seek legal counsel to make sure that confidentialities are not violated. When called upon to testify as a fact witness, this standard is a reminder that professional objectivity can be tainted by a prior relationship. It is important to reflect on one's objectivity in such circumstances and reveal this to the client's attorney early in the process. One of the authors was recently asked to testify as a fact witness in a case concerning a prior client who alleged religious persecution by a landlord. Upon reviewing his files, it became clear that his many years of work with the client indicated that he suffered from delusions of persecution, with a hyperreligious overtone. This information provided to the client's attorney resulted in the fairly predictable decision not to call him as a fact witness.

Compliance with Law and Roles

APA (1992), in Standard 7.06, writes, "In performing forensic roles, psychologists are reasonably familiar with the rules governing their roles. Psychologists are aware of the occasionally competing demands placed upon them by these principles and the requirements of the Court system, and attempt to resolve these conflicts by making known their commitment to this ethics code and taking steps to resolve the conflict in a responsible manner."

Any clinicians entering into the hallowed halls of the judicial system have quickly become aware that they are in a strange land where foreign languages are spoken and unusual behaviors practiced. Depending upon their level of anxiety, it is not uncommon for them to flash back to their first days at high school or some other traumatizing setting. Adherence to Standard 7.06 should help the anxious clinician considerably in this regard. The legal system requires many different standards and behaviors from the mental health clinician, and those unlucky enough to enter unprepared will find themselves embarrassed and humiliated, if not verbally assaulted. Preparation for the forensic role is crucial and carries with it the responsibility to learn about the legal system, legal standards, and expectations of the forensic clinician. Training and supervision are crucial ingredients in adequate preparation.

This may be a good place to note that the practice of forensics, unlike the majority of mental health work, is a public action. Nowhere else in this field is a clinician called upon to stand in front of a group of strangers, present an opinion and conclusions, and provide the basis for such opinion and conclusions. Most often, clinicians operate behind closed doors and certainly discuss cases only with our colleagues. Questioning is usually gentle and, as is the nature of mental health professionals, supportive. Cross-examination is a very public process and is usually neither gentle nor supportive.

A nervous forensic clinician would do well to observe judicial proceedings during the time of study. To imagine placing yourself in the role of the expert on the stand and thinking about how you would have answered a question is a marvelous strategy for learning. Having the opportunity to weigh competing experts in the matter of criminal responsibility and imagining how you could have done differently or even better will stimulate the novice to read and study in preparation for your day in the spotlight.

After many years of forensic practice, the authors can unequivocally state that strict adherence to a set of ethical guidelines similar to those developed by the American Psychological Association in 1992 is not only comforting but assures the highest quality of professional conduct in the often strange and stressful world of the courtroom.

Appendix A

DANGEROUSNESS PREDICTION TASK #1
SERGEANT STRYKER

The Instant Offense: Murder. At exactly 11:47 p.m. on April 15, 1982, Sergeant First Class Robert Stryker, in front of more than 20 witnesses, killed a man by shooting him in the back.

Witnesses reported on events as follows: At about 10:30 p.m., Sergeant Stryker entered the Noncomissioned Officer's (NCO) Club in Erlangen, West Germany, and ordered a beer. At a table about ten meters from the bar, Staff Sergeant Ralph Dolbert, the victim, was sitting with the perpetrator's wife, Hilda, and a battalion executive officer. Shortly afterward, Sergeant Dolbert started slow dancing with Hilda; Sergeant Stryker danced with another woman. At a point about halfway through the musical score, the perpetrator left his partner standing on the dance floor and returned to the bar. He then threw a small object, later identified as a pocket dictionary, at the victim, hitting him on the shoulder. In recation, Sergeant Dolbert made a motion as if to attack Sergeant Stryker but was restrained by observers. Minutes later, he joined the perpetrator at the bar in what appeared to be intense conversation.

Throwing up his hands as if ending the discussion, Sergeant Dolbert laughed loudly and walked in the direction of his table. The perpetrator then yelled for the victim to stop, but the latter continued, his face set in a wide smile. From the back of his waistband, Sergeant Stryker pulled out a pistol, a nine-millimeter German Luger, and fired in the direction of the victim. The bullet went low and to the right, ricocheting into a jukebox. Sergeant Dolbert, still smiling, did not slow his pace. The perpetrator then assumed a "competition stance"–legs spread apart with both hands gripping the pistol– and fired twice more in rapid succession. It was never determined which bullet was fired first, the one that entered slightly above the right knee, or the bullet that entered the back and tore through the heart, but the victim lurched forward with his right leg crumpling noticeably before he fell on his face.

After Sergeant Stryker set the pistol on the bar counter, a witness grabbed him and asked, "Are you crazy, you just killed a man." Sergeant Stryker responded, "I told you I'd get him and I got him. Turn me loose; I'm not going anywhere." Taken to a military police jeep, he stated, "My God, what have I done? I love my wife, I love my kids. I've always been a day late and a dollar short." He then started to bang his head against the side of the vehicle interior. During this behavior, he told the military police officer to shoot him if he tried to escape. He then asked that the door be opened so he could run out. In a later search of the area and the perpetrator's vehicle, investigators found another pistol, a .22 caliber semi-automatic and extra ammunition for both that firearm and the murder weapon.

After the Criminal Investigation Division (CID) completed its investigation, the Judge Advocate General (JAG) took over the case and charged Sergeant Stryker with premeditated murder. He was to await trial at the Mannheim High Security Confinement Center.

Referral: The prosecution and defense asked the senior author to assess Sergeant Stryker's fitness to proceed, degree of criminal responsibility, and later, dangerousness. The examination consisted of three interview-and-testing sessions (July 15, 20, and 21, 1982) for a total of approximately eight hours of evaluation. All sessions were conducted at the Outpatient Clinic, Department of Psychiatry, U.S. Army Hospital, Ansbach, Germany. The defendant was transported under armed guard from Mannheim for the evaluations. In addition to several clinical interviews, the following tests were administered: Minnesota Multiphasic Personality Inventory (MMPI, Form R); Sacks Sentence Completion Test (SSCT); Bipolar Psychological Inventory (BPI) Lie Scale; Social Readjustment Rating Scale (SRRS, administered once to assess current functioning; and for early April 1982); Self Description; and the MMPI Critical Items List. The defendant was also referred to the Medical Specialty Clinic of the hospital for an electroencephalograph and neurological examination.

In addition, the following persons were interviewed: Dr. Black, pathologist who performed the autopsy on the victim; Mr. Tom Smith, defense attorney (twice); Colonel Raymond Bergstrom, sanity board member; Mr. Lane Paul, American Elementary School counselor, Erlangen; Captain Donald Mack, commanding officer of the accused; and Mrs. Hilda Stryker, the defendant's wife. Mr. Paul was the counselor of Sergeant Stryker's eldest son. Dr. Margot's report to the defense attorney, as a retained psychiatrist, was reviewed along with all CID witnesses' statements, investigator reports, and the defendant's personnel and medical files.

Concerning assessment validity, both the defendant and prison staff stated that he ingested no prescribed or unprescribed drugs or alcohol prior to the evaluation sessions. A standardized stress test indicated that Sergeant Stryker was under high cumulative stress at the time of the evaluation, and had experienced severe traumata within the past year and a massive disruption of his support system. Lie scales revealed distortion attempts and supported the interpretation of a mild-to-moderate tendency to minimize or deny psychological problems, and/or unfavorable features of his everyday behavior. This finding was seen as important because it was in the vested interest of the defendant to appear psychopathological, given his insanity defense. Symptoms noted by corrections staff at this time included insomnia, crying spells, and some suicidal ideation.

Some other noteworthy behavior was reported. For one thing, he reported amnesia for the shooting after the first bullet. Second, he seemed deluded in that he rigidly clung to the belief that his wife loved him and that they would reconcile. Sergeant Stryker was aware that his wife not only had a new boyfriend, a sergeant from another Erlangen unit, but was also willing to testify for the prosecution that the killing was premeditated by her husband. He spent most of his free time during confinement writing love letters and composing poems to his wife, reminiscing about their presumably happier past and planning for their future.

While incarcerated after the shooting, Sergeant Stryker showed frequent crying spells, insomnia, irritability, and rumination and related activities during most of his waking hours. Occupational and social functioning were seriously disrupted due to confinement but were also seen as impaired before incarceration. Suicide potential was seen as mild to moderate, which could increase to substantial given further strong stressors (e.g., a negative legal outcome, the finalization of divorce proceedings). Testing affirmed moderate depression and anxiety, distrust of others, and a tendency to avoid responsibility for the negative outcome of events. His intelligence was seen as above average but somewhat rigid in application. There were no indications of an organic or thought disorder. Positive and basically conservative attitudes were expressed toward family, people, and work.

Relevant Background: Born and raised in North Carolina, Robert J. Stryker was the eldest of three children. His two sisters were two and twelve years his junior. The home was described as middle class and conservatively religious (Southern Baptist), although the subject attended church infrequently. His mother, a housewife, was seen as extremely bright, supportive and nonconfrontive. It was she with whom Robert felt emotionally close during childhood and adolescence. Robert perceived his father, an accountant and later a manager for a large textile company, as stern and distant, although they sporadically hunted and fished together. Evidently, for the most part, his father spent early evenings and many weekends on the job. He was remembered for having frequent and severe migraine headaches, occasionally followed by outbursts of rage. The relationship with the older of his sisters was described as distant. In fact, Robert resented her attempts to intrude into his activities. Speaking of his younger sister, he stated, "I was her hero. I was seen by her as the kind of person I wanted to be."

Robert was self-described as introverted and shy during adolescence. His typical free-time play was to prowl nearby woods with his rifle and dog. Other times, he would read during most of his waking hours for days on end, having few friends with whom to socialize. He dated few women and married the woman with whom he first had intercourse. They had two daughters; after seven years of marriage, he was divorced by his wife.

Robert had joined the army and then the Special Forces after high school graduation. He quickly became proficient in light weapons and guerrilla warfare; at that time his military records listed awards for expert medals in the .45 caliber pistol, all rifles used by the Army infantry, and the grenade launcher. Like all Green Berets, he was jump qualified for day and night combat conditions. He did not receive a Good Conduct Medal because he was court martialed for assault on a fellow soldier. During the fight, records stated, Robert severely bit the victim on the face near the eyebrow, necessitating medical attention and several sutures. Sergeant Stryker stated that he did not remember the event too clearly as he was allegedly intoxicated. He did recall, however, that the victim had started the fight.

Most of Sergeant Stryker's assignments appear to have been in counterinsurgency activities in foreign nations, ostensibly traveling as an "advisor" to the local population. Duty in Panama was followed by stints in Uraguay and Peru as part of a "mobile training team." In 1968, he was sent to Vietnam for 12 months, during which time he did not kill any enemy soldiers to his direct knowledge. "You couldn't see them in the bush." For his performance he was awarded the Bronze Star, Combat Infantryman Badge, Air Medal, Vietnam Campaign Medal, Combat Jump Wings, and the Good Conduct Medal. In his words, "I was not a hero; I just did my job as a soldier."

Robert was divorced by his wife in 1969. Shortly afterwards, he was arrested for attacking a policeman with a hammer. He stated that he was on his motorboat, very intoxicated, and that he did not know that the person who approached him was a policeman, as the latter was in plain clothes. Records revealed a simultaneous arrest for reckless driving of a powered vehicle.

In 1973, Sergeant Stryker was assigned to West Berlin in counterespionage activities. During this tour, he met his current wife, a (health) card carrying German prostitute 13 years his junior, whom he married four months later. She gave birth to a boy several months after the wedding, and a second son was born in 1976.

In 1978, the subject was reassigned to Fort Benning, Georgia. His wife reportedly had several short-term affairs with soldiers about whom Sergeant Stryker eventually became aware. In the spring of 1981, he was promoted to sergeant first class and was sent back to Germany. His wife and two children joined him several months later. The killing of Sergeant Dolbert occurred about six months after arrival on post.

Findings: The writer's diagnosis of the defendant at the time of the instant offense was Major Depression (DSM–III, 296.2), evidenced in part by prolonged and severe feelings of sadness and discouragement that permeated most of the defendant's daily life. Other symptoms included a 20-pound weight loss, severe insomnia, psychomotor agitation, sexual impotence, marked irritability, difficulty in thought concentration, vocational and social impairment, and serious thoughts of suicide. Many of these symptoms appeared at least six months to a year before the crime. Triggering stressors may have included the following: (1) Severe marital discord to include a separation; (2) Multiple instances of spousal infidelity before the separation. Moreover, the defendant's friends, acquaintances, and work superiors were aware of or assumed the infidelity, according to CID reports, thus adding the stress of public humiliation; (3) Recent death of his father from metastatic cancer. During the interview, Sergeant Stryker cried at length when he related that he never told his father that he loved him, despite many opportunities during the long illness; (4) Job reassignment at Fort Benning for substandard performance just prior to the move to Germany, accompanied by a marginal efficiency report. Records suggested that Sergeant Stryker was elevated to sergeant first class because the promotion was in process before he was relieved of his post. The drop in duty performance occurred at a time when his wife was allegedly engaged in an extramarital affair; (5) Related to the last stressor, were difficulties with his supervisors at both Ft. Benning and Erlangen; (6) Several geographic relocations; (7) Significant loss of sleep, which was seen both as a symptom of depression and a cause of further stress. The defendant reportedly was averaging about three hours of sleep nightly for several months before the crime.

For several weeks before the killing, he suffered from severe headaches, insomnia, and lack of concentration, and he experienced vivid images and thoughts of suicide. Shortly afterward, he increased his life insurance policy substantially, with his wife remaining the principle beneficiary.

On March 2, 1982, approximately six weeks before the homicide, Sergeant Stryker's combat engineer unit was out on field maneuvers when he called his residence in Erlangen. His six-year-old son reported that his mother could not come to the telephone as she and a man were in the master bedroom with the door locked. From that temporal point on, Sergeant Stryker's colleagues noticed a dramatic shift in his behavior which persisted until the instant offense. He became preoccupied, irritable, seemingly tense, and in general, marginally competent in his job as the company first sergeant.

On March 4, upon returning from the field, Sergeant Stryker found his wife in Sergeant Dolbert's Bachelor Enlisted Quarters (BEQ). Robert shouted to the victim that he would "blow his head off" if the relationship continued. Sergeant Dolbert showed him a pistol with ammunition and said, "Go ahead."

For the next several weeks, Hilda left her residence in the late afternoon, just before her husband was due home from work, and did not return until the early morning hours. At one point, Sergeant Dolbert and Hilda met Robert in the Stryker home. Hilda informed Sergeant Stryker that she and the victim were in love, considering marriage, and had no intentions of stopping social or sexual contact. About that time, witnesses reported seeing the couple at public entertainment places almost nightly.

At the NCO club on March 15, Hilda screamed at her husband in front of her boyfriend and other patrons. Her words were, "Shut the fuck up, you old man. You're an old man and a dried up prune."

Battalion leaders became aware of the severe marital problems and decided to intervene. Their solution was to transfer the victim to the perpetrator's unit. The logic was that Sergeant Dolbert's marriage-disrupting behaviors could then be more directly under command control in that the same commander could observe the behaviors of both sergeants' in interaction and intervene appropriately. Around this time, Sergeant Stryker confided to his company commander that he was thinking of killing or crippling the victim by shooting off his kneecaps, but that he realized that this was "no way to win Hilda back."

On March 25, Sergeants Stryker and Dolbert were seen shooting skeet together at the Erlangen Rod and Gun Club. On at least two other occasions, the same conjoint behavior was observed.

A marital separation was signed by Robert and Hilda Stryker one week later. The same day, Robert moved into the BEQ. JAG presented Sergeant Dolbert with a restraining order to stay away from Hilda.

Hilda and Sergeant Dolbert continued to see one another daily. Sergeant Stryker voiced more threats to kill the victim; he now expanded his verbal scenario to homicide and then suicide by purposefully getting shot. He reported that his insurance company would not pay off for self-inflicted death. These comments were made primarily to unit members, who upon later reflection, did not really believe Sergeant Stryker would commit the violent acts.

On the day of the instant offense, the victim and Hilda had been locked in the latter's residence master bedroom for more than 11 hours. At the BEQ, Sergeant Stryker was throwing a "housewarming" party. He acted as the bartender and reportedly consumed large amounts of a medium-priced Greek wine. At about ten o'clock in the evening, he left alone for the NCO club. His blood alcohol concentration (BAC) on the morning after the crime indicated mild intoxication; calculating temporally backward, a pathologist reported to CID that a BAC indicative of moderate intoxication was reasonable for the time of the shooting.

On a standardized stress test, reconstructed for the days just prior to the killing, Sergeant Stryker obtained a score reflective of extremely high cumulative stress seen in a very small minority of people at any given time.

A secondary diagnosis at the time of the instant offense was Alcohol Intoxication (DSM–III, 313.00). This was based on the retrospective BAC analysis; the self-report of the defendant, corroborated by witnesses, that he consumed a large amount of alcohol prior to going to the NCO club; and associated symptoms of impulsivity, aggressiveness, and poor social judgment. The substance intoxication acted as a trigger. It was interesting to note that the defendant had previous opportunities to kill the victim "accidentally" (e.g., during skeet shooting). This highlights the idea that opportunity factors, although necessary for violence to occur, are rarely sufficient by themselves to create that outcome. Publicly flaunting an adulterous relationship superimposed on a depressed, stressed, and intoxicated individual with a history of serious violence may have made the choice of assault relatively easy.

During a final, brief conversation with Sergeant Stryker several weeks after the trial, he made the following facts clear: (1) It was not immoral to kill the victim, as the latter really caused his own death. If the defendant could say anything to the victim it would be, "See you S.O.B., see what you did to me?" (2) It is not immoral to kill people; society decides that is wrong or right. There are no moral absolutes. (3) There was no chance of violence to reoccur personally as fear of imprisonment will act as a deterrent.

Case Outcome: A four-year follow-up with the defendant and unit records, to the extent that arrest data was available, indicated no instances of serious violence toward others. Several fist fights were reported with unknown males, associated with drinking, but no other violence. The accused's wife eventually entered into another adulterous relationship and finally sued SFC Stryker for divorce. The subject was tempted to kill his wife but made no threats or attempts, stating, "She just wasn't worth the rest of my life in prison."

Appendix B

CHECKLIST OF FACTORS ASSOCIATED WITH VIOLENCE

I. Historical Data and Establishing the Violence Baseline

As differential responses to stress and other provoking stimuli are common, past violence must have occurred in order to reasonably predict future violence. These historical events pave the way for future dangerousness to others.

A. Past Violent Behavior   YES   NO   UNKNOWN

    1. Incidence of violence
       is single (if multiple incidents,
       rate each act on the factors
       that follow)   ____   ____   ____

    2. Severity is fatal
       Injurious with hospitalization
       Injurious with medical care
       but no hospitalization
       Minor harm   ____   ____   ____

    3. Recency is immediate   ____   ____   ____
       (<1 month)
       intermediate (1 to 12 months)
       remote (>1 year)   ____   ____   ____

    4. Violence maintained/ intensified
       by pain cues from victim   ____   ____   ____

5. Firearms or potentially lethal
weapons used   ____   ____   ____

6. History of reinforcing results
for violence (e.g., money, no
convictions, dominance)   ____   ____   ____

7. Serious institutional misconduct
including violence   ____   ____   ____

B. Other Helpful Historical Information; Developmental Events

1. Physical or sexual abuse as a
child   ____   ____   ____

2. Violent parental or sibling
model (especially same sex)   ____   ____   ____

3. Pathological triad (pyromania,
cruelty to animals, enuresis)   ____   ____   ____

4. Emotional abandonment as
child   ____   ____   ____

5. Hostile/assaultive feelings
toward parent(s), sibling(s),
and/or significant others   ____   ____   ____

6. Self-reinforcement or self-
praise for aggression   ____   ____   ____

7. Juvenile record (nonviolent,
staus offenses)   ____   ____   ____

8. Preference for violent films   ____   ____   ____

9. Spontaneous or concussion-
related loss of consciousness
before age 10   ____   ____   ____

10. School problems
(temper tantrums, truancy,
threats, fights)   ____   ____   ____

II. a. Possible Triggering Stimuli Associated with Predictee's Behavioral
Repertoire

These are precipitating causes, short-term in duration, intense in
impact, which set violence into motion. The potential for each of
these possible future events must be established within the individual's existing behavior patterns. Triggering stimuli are a mildly
influential predictor of dangerous behavior when superimposed on
a history of violence and when opportunity variables are operative.

A. Chemicals Associated with Violence

1. Alcohol intoxication, alone
or in combination with
other chemicals   ____   ____   ____

2. Nonprescribed substances
(especially PCP, LSD,
cocaine, amphetamines)   ____   ____   ____

3. Abuse of relevant prescribed
medication   ____   ____   ____

B. Stressors, Intense and Recent or Soon to Occur

1. Fired or laid off from work   ____   ____   ____

2. Central love relationship
break-up   ____   ____   ____

3. Sudden worsening of
financial state   ____   ____   ____

4. Sudden pain   ____   ____   ____

5. Body space invasion   ____   ____   ____

6. Peer pressure to join or
initiate violence (e.g., gang
rape, bar fight) ____ ____ ____

7. Status threat in group
context; insults ____ ____ ____

8. Unfavorable change in
reward structure (e.g.,
demotions, reduction
of pay) ____ ____ ____

II. b. Present Operating Conditions or Traits that Lower Threshold for Violent Behavior

These are reinforcing causes of violence that tend to maintain behaviors which may lead to acting out. Long term in duration, they may define the form (topography) of violence. These reinforcing causes are neither necessary nor sufficient to predict violence but are helpful to know.

A. General Current Variables

1. Age <30 years ____ ____ ____

2. Male sex ____ ____ ____

3. Subcultural acceptance of
violence ____ ____ ____

4. Belief that certain types of
violence will go unpunished
(e.g., child or spouse abuse) ____ ____ ____

5. Relevant principal diagnosis
(Especially antisocial,
paranoid, or explosive
disorders; disorders that
involve prefrontal lobe
damage or paranoid
schizophrenic type) ____ ____ ____

B. Behaviors That Suggest Any of the Following Chronic Traits

1. Obsessive thoughts of
   revenge or violence   ____   ____   ____

2. Low frustration tolerance   ____   ____   ____

3. Low control wanted
   from others   ____   ____   ____

4. Low need for affection   ____   ____   ____

5. Tendency to act out stress   ____   ____   ____

6. High suspiciousness   ____   ____   ____

7. High hostility   ____   ____   ____

8. Hypersensitivity to self-
   esteem attacks   ____   ____   ____

9. Strong feelings of
   helplessness   ____   ____   ____

10. Frequent use of projection
    and denial   ____   ____   ____

11. Deficits in verbal skills and
    expression   ____   ____   ____

C. Social Environmental Conditions

1. Violent peers   ____   ____   ____

2. Trouble at work   ____   ____   ____

3. Prolonged conflict in central
   love relationship   ____   ____   ____

4. Other continued stressors;
   specify   ____   ____   ____

     5. Weak community
       support base   ____   ____   ____

     6. Nightmares with
       violent themes   ____   ____   ____

III. Opportunity Variables

These are events or behaviors that make violence possible or that expand the type or severity of its expression.

A. Interpersonal situation presents
   opportunity for instrumental
   aggression (e.g., beating up drunk
   for his money)   ____   ____   ____

B. Violent behavior motivated by
   perceiving no peaceful option
   (e.g., aggression when cornered
   by mugger or rapist)   ____   ____   ____

C. Recent purchase of potentially
   lethal weapon   ____   ____   ____

D. Ownership of firearms   ____   ____   ____

E. Availability of weaker victim   ____   ____   ____

F. Availability of transportation   ____   ____   ____

G. Release from incarceration into
   the community   ____   ____   ____

H. Cessation of regular psychotropic
   medication   ____   ____   ____

Appendix C

DANGEROUSNESS PREDICTION REPORT FORMAT

PSYCHOLOGICAL CONSULTANTS, INC.
A Professional Practice and Approved
Training Organization

Century Square • 1188 Bishop Street, Suite 2608 • Honolulu, Hawaii 96813
Mailing: Post Office Box 3798 • Honolulu, Hawaii 96812
Telephone (808) 538-3003

SAMPLE REPORT FORMAT FOR DANGEROUSNESS
Date of Report

Honorable William Smith
First Circuit Court
State Capitol Building
Anytown, Anystate 00001

Presentence Evaluation
RE: DOE, JOHN NMI
SS#:   000-00-0000
DOB: Month, Day, Year
Count 1:   Murder in the Second Degree
Count 2:   Robbery in the First Degree
Count 3:   Felon in Possession of a Firearm
Count 4:   Unregistered Firearm

Dear Judge Smith:

This is the report of the forensic psychologist (requested/appointed) by (you/the court/sanity board, etc.) to examine and report upon the dangerousness potential of the defendant, John NMI Doe, SS# 000-00-0000, who is currently (assigned/residing/incarcerated, etc.) at (location–name and address including zip code).

Mr. Doe was convicted of the murder of Jane Albrey, DOB July 5, 1962, on the night of June 25, 1993, in Anytown, Anystate, by shooting her with a firearm during the commission of a robbery. The last two counts refer to the possession and use of a firearm.

FORENSIC DATA BASE: The nature of the examination consisted of (clinical interviewing/psychological testing/neuropsychological testing/interview of significant others/ward observation/records review/naturalistic observation/behavioral assessment with a functional analysis of violence-related responses/ social environmental assessment/review of medical findings/developmental assessment/competence assessment) for a total of approximately (N) hours of evaluation. In addition to (one/two/N) clinical interviews, he was administered the following psychometric instruments: (list all tests including multiple administrations and unsuccessful attempts). Mr. Doe was examined both at the (place, date) and, the (place, date) where he was on (pretrial confinement status/in community on bail, etc.).

The following individuals were interviewed and/or rendered written statements to the undersigned: (list all persons and their relationship to accused or investigation process; indicate number of interviews and location, if significant). The following written materials were reviewed: (list source and type, include "nonofficial" materials, such as diaries, notes from accused to his attorney, etc.).

ASSESSMENT BEHAVIOR AND DATABASE VALIDITY: (Cooperative/uncooperative) and of (normal/disheveled./abnormal) appearance, this (single/,separated/divorced/widowed/married), (white/black, etc.), (N)-year-old (vocation and rank or status within vocation) exhibited a logical and coherent stream of (thought/a fragmented/tangential/ circumstantial/ blocked stream of thought, etc.). Affect was (appropriate/ inapproriate as in laughter or rage, blandness, labile). A trend toward (somatic preoccupation/paranoid suspiciousness/rumination about past injustices, etc.) was observed. Orientation was apparent for (time/place/person/circumstances).

Memory for (short/intermediate/remote) events was (intact/impaired) as evidenced by (performance on presented sequences of numbers short term/inquiries by examiner as to earlier evaluation events intermediate term/recollection of independently verified, historical events long term), (with/without) a tendency to confabulate. Judgment was (marginal,/adequate, etc.) as shown by (appropriate/inappropriate) responses to standardized comprehension questions (give examples–response to finding envelope, discovering theater fire). Abstraction ability as reflected by responses to proverbs (give example–glass houses, striking while iron is hot) was (appropriate/concrete–if so, give response). Associational lability as reflected by responses to similarity items was (concrete/abstract/appropriate) as shown by (give example–orange banana/chair/ table). Reading and writing skills are (normally developed/impaired, specify). Computationally, he had (no difficulty/difficulty) counting backward from 20 (but/and) had (difficulty/no difficulty) in (serial 7's/3's/adding/subtracting multiplying). Fund of information was (adequate/inadequate–if so, give responses to four presidents, population of USA, senators in U.S. Senate). Overall, his intelligence appeared (normal/ below normal, etc.), which is (congruent/incongruent) with his education (specify years, focus and grade performance). Insight into emotional basis of present condition was (minimal/ apparent, etc.). No (other, if applicable) pathognomonic features of his clinical appearance were noted (if features such as tattoos are present, state "for identification purposes . . .).

Distortion analysis of Mr. Doe's evaluation responses revealed for the time of the interview an attempt to (fake good/fake bad/invalidate results/present himself in an accurate manner–explain terms). This is based on (validity scale results/goodness of fit between test profile and clinical behavior/ performance on scales or test procedures specifically designed to assess attempts to misrepresent/discrepancy between responses and established events). Distortion analysis for the time of reported past violence revealed an attempt to (fake good/fake bad/confuse the violence picture/represent his basal history in an accurate manner–explain terms if not done previously). This is based on assessment of claimed violent behavior conditions when compared to known the likelihood of (claimed dangerous acts with DSM–IV diagnostic criteria/comparing similarity of current distortion to claimed past violence).

Interviews of others and written materials were also scrutinized for distortion. Statements by significant others may have been influenced by (a desire to assist the accused since they wish to be rejoined/a sincere desire to represent the fact honestly/the lengthy period between reported past violence and the written recollection of such). Statements by the victim may have been influenced by (a desire for revenge/stress at the time of the instant offense(s)/a state of intoxication/the lengthy time between the alleged violence and investigation results, etc.).

Generally, evaluation results of Mr. Doe are considered an accurate portrayal of the accused, taking into consideration mental status, test-taking attitudes, (psychological/intellectual/neuropsychological/etc.) limitations and competencies, and (witnesses'/investigators') input.

RELEVANT DEVELOPMENTAL AND HISTORICAL EVENTS: The (accused/client/etc.) was born and raised in (location) the (ordinal position) oldest of (sibling number and gender). His father was a (vocation, rank); the relationship with him was described as (good/distant/conflictual, etc.). His mother was a (vocation, rank); the relationship with her was described as (specify). Parental modeling (did/did not) involve aggressive behavior (specify if same-sexed parent; specify type of violence modeled). There (was/was not) (praise/reward) for aggression. The (accused/client) (did/did not) have (hostile/assaultive) feelings toward (specify parent), (and/but, etc.) was, by his perception, (emotionally abandoned/emotionally secure). There is evidence of (substance abuse/no substance abuse) by the (specify parent). Child abuse, in the sense of (frequent/frequent and severe, etc.) corporal punishment, occurred. The relationship toward other members of the family was (describe relevant interaction with siblings, significant others).

Medically, the following relevant diseases occurred (list those to accused/to significant others). Traumata experienced by the (accused/client, etc.) included (list, e.g., spontaneous loss of consciousness before age 10/self-mutilation/head injuries).

Socially, relationships toward peers could be described as (specify, especially if violent peers) in a cultural environment consisting of (describe, especially adherence to locals with high subcultural acceptance of violence as a solution to interpersonal problems). In school, relevant problems included (specify, especially assaults on teachers, temper tantrums, threats, fights, vandalism) within an overall school social adjustment described as (specify) and an academic performance evaluated as (specify, add corroborating evidence if available). Other developmental events associated with violence include (specify, e.g., pathological triad of pyromania, cruelty to animals, and enuresis/preference for violent TV shows/juvenile record for any crime, especially felony arrest before 15th birthday).

Developmental conditions associated with less likelihood of dangerousness include (e.g., nonviolent parental models/stable home environment/running away from past aggressive encounters, etc.).

Past dangerousness behaviors for this person included (single/multiple, etc.) acts of violence, some of which were of (no injury/injurious/potentially fatal) severity, (involving/not involving) use of weapons and extending back (N) years. Historically, these include (specify violence type, victim injuries, legal and social outcome, weapon use, location sites, his age at the time, other relevant factors). Examination of contextual and social-interactional stimuli that set off or were associated with violence, include (specify, e.g., pain cues from the violence/status threats and insults/institution versus open community/dyadic or two-person contexts/rewarding or nonpunitive consequences for aggression). Signs associated with serious basal violence include (specify potential lethal weapon used/arrests or convictions for violent crimes). His most violent act was (specify). A list of documented violence from police reports is as follows:

6/5/75	Battery on police officer	Case dropped	San Francisco, CA
4/7/76	Battery on police officer	Placed on probation one year	Riverside, CA
1/4/78	Attacked stranger with fists; No arrest made Threw brick in stranger's back		

All the following occurred in Honolulu, Hawaii:

9/5/78	Struck stranger in back of head from behind with fist; chased victim with group	No arrest made	Joined ongoing fight
9/10/78	Robbery with a firearm	Plea bargained for one year jail	Procured $1,500 from victim
2/18/79	Struck HPD officer in face	Placed on five-year probation	Associated with theft: after discovery of "white powder" in vial on accused
3/12/79	Robbery with a knife	Charges dropped due to insufficient evidence	Procured $920 from victim

| 7/9/79 | Lunged at police officer | Accused escaped and was later misidentified | Associated with theft; followed threat to victim |

| 6/9/80 | Multiple fist strikes to stranger | Victim refused to cooperate | Associated with theft; discovered by victim |

| 5/11/80 | Struck boss in face with fist | No charges filed | Lost job |

| 4/13/86 | Struck girlfriend's face with fist in public and broke her nose | Victim refused to press charges | Preceded by grabbing throat |

| 8/13/86 | Attempted to force entry into friend's apt. | 30 days in jail | Escorted by police |

| 2/4/87 | Killed victim with firearm during course of a robbery | Guilty of murder | Instant offense |

Historical conditions associated with less likelihood of violence include (see Factor List, e.g., no past serious violence/pain cues from past victims diminished perpetrator's violence/treatment for aggressive tendencies by mental health professionals, etc.). In general, basal violence for this (subject/ client) can be described as (weak/average/prepotent).

PRESENT LONG-TERM OPERATING CONDITIONS: Significant demographic variables associated with a higher incidence of violence toward others include (demographic variables first—e.g., young age/male sex/low SES/separated, divorced marital status/unemployed work status). Significant personality (traits/beliefs/behaviors) that may be reinforcing causes of violence, maintaining behaviors that may lead to characteristic ways of acting out include (e.g., belief that certain classes of violence will go unpunished, such as spouse or child abuse/obsessive thoughts of revenge or violence/low frustration tolerance/"external" versus "internal" locus of control/high suspiciousness/high hostility/high blame projection/deficits in verbal skills and expression/substance abuse or dependence). Significant long-term environmental events that are reinforcing causes of violence include (e.g., violent friends/chronic work relationship problems with authority figures or colleages/a weak community support base/prolonged conflict in central love relationships).

For demographic, personality, and behavioral features of the (client/subject), suppressing events include (e.g., old age/infirm status/high education/high guilt).

TRIGGERING STIMULI ASSOCIATED WITH REPERTOIRE: Triggering stimuli, short term in duration and intense in impact, and which tend to set violence into motion for this individual include (e.g., internal triggers such as alcohol and/or drug intoxication/command auditory hallucinations/threatening visual hallucinations/high perceived stress; external triggers, e.g., breakup of central love relationship/body space invasion/status threat especially in group context/placement in legal confinement/sudden worsening of financial state/fired from work/peer pressure to join violence as in gang rapes or fights/instructions to aggress).

OPPORTUNITY VARIABLES: Conditions that tended to raise the opportunity for dangerousness to occcur, or that expanded the possible varieties of violence exhibited, included for the defendant (e.g., recent purchase of a firearm with ammunition, access to a vehicle, recent parole, release from the hospital into the comunity).

Conditions that tended to lower the opportunity for dangerous behavior for the defendant included (e.g., legal incarceration and placement in confinement two weeks ago/physical or chemical castration/physical sickness, hospitalization/phobias such as fear of crowds/children removed from home).

DEFENDANT'S RECONSTRUCTION OF INSTANT OFFENSE(S): (If available, a detailed account of the alleged crime is presented by the accused, e.g., see police investigation report/JAG files).

Generally,the accused stated, during the present assessment, that the killing was (in self-defense/accidental/deliberate, etc.) after the victim (struck him/threatened him, etc.). After the killing, (witnesses stated/the accused self-described) his behavior as (describe), his affect as (describe), his cognitive functioning as (describe), his verbal remarks in substance as (paraphrase or quote).

The accused stated that the robbery was (repeat sequence for all charged crimes).

(If amnesia claimed) Of particular interest is the claimed loss of memory (following onset of strangulation of the victim/after the second gunshot, etc.). This amnesia, if genuine, could be caused by an elevated emotional state such as intense anger or fear, or other conditions such as (head trauma/an alcoholic blackout/psychosis/dissociative reaction/substance intoxication/ epileptic seizure/other organic states) at the time of the crime. For the instant offense, the claimed amnesia is most compatible with the occurrence of (type or combination, include malingering as a possibility; refer reader back to section on the distortion analysis).

(If auditory hallucinations claimed) The accused also stated that he heard a "voice" to the effect that (the victim was trying to kill him, etc.). Four points are relevant here. First, volunteering that the voice was experienced at the time of the crime (e.g., did not take place until long after the accused rendered previous statements on the crime that did not include auditory hallucinations/took place at the crime scene to investigating officers, etc.). Second, if instant offense events were as the accused describes, his acts (may have been in self-defense and therefore the voice is of little relevance/may have indeed been promoted by the auditory hallucinations). Recall that the victim had (describe relevant behaviors) and the context was (describe relevant contextual stimuli). Third, hearing the "voice" (is/is not) tantamount to obeying it, as the accused (related a number of instances, when the voice's command was disregarded; give examples/has acquiesced to it in all reported instances). Fourth, the "voice" is described as (ego syntonic/ego dystonic). Given the chance to rid himself of the "voice," he (would/would not) because of its (describe positive or negative properties). This means that (describe implications of ego-syntonic/dystonic experience).

(Describe and evaluate if other unusual features of defendant's instant offense experience claimed.)

MENTAL CONDITION DIAGNOSIS: The diagnoses representing a reconstructed mental condition for the time of the alleged crime is the same as for the time of the evaluation and is as follows:

Axis I: R/O Schizophrenia, Paranoid Type, Alcohol Abuse (presently in remission due to incarceration)

Axis II: Particular attention is paid to the personality disorders, which may include chronic violence as part of the diagnostic picture (e.g., antisocial personality disorder)

Axis III: Cite physical conditions that may be related to Axis I or II (e.g., neuropsychological disinhibition associated with 1985 anoxic encephalopathy)

Axis IV: Severity and type of stressors; cite which stressors appear to trigger violence

Axis V: Assessment of Global Functioning (GAF); include GAFs for the time of evaluation and highest point within last year

(If two diagnoses are identical) The diagnosis of (specify) for the time of the alleged crime (is temporally linked to the same diagnosis at the time of the evaluation in the sense that both mental conditions have been continually operative during the two time points/even though identical to the diagnosis at the time of the evaluation, represents the mental condition occurring episodically with no implication of continued operation between the two temporal points).

An assault cycle reveals itself as follows. The period of previous adjustment (Phase I) applies to general traits and characteristics for an individual in addition to past violence. For the accused, this includes character features such as a spotty work history, disrupted central love relationships, much involvement with the law, and substance-abuse tendencies. As listed, there is a previous history of violence toward others.

Phase II of the typical assault cycle of the accused consists of alcohol intoxication, which may be a partial trigger to the instant offense. The associated mood is most likely anger, with few suggestions of anxiety or depression behaviors until after the violence is consummated. Victim patterning shows that the most -likely targets have been nonlocal male or those in authority (e.g., police officers, work supervisors). Preassault behavior during the triggering phase almost always consists of aggressive behavior toward the victim to include yelling, cursing, rapid motor movement, and/or grabbing/striking.

Phase III of the assault cycle consists of the actual violence and, for the accused, is characterized by high self-control and low behavioral disorganization (see next section). The focus of attack is likely to be a specific person under a special set of circumstances, rather than toward himself or property. Perseveration of assaultive response is not likely once the violence starts.

Phase IV of the assault cycle consists of the time period up to several hours after the violence. For the accused, this consists of usual attempts to distort data in the direction of attempting to escape the negative consequences of the aggression. His history is replete with instances of distortion by omission or comission exhibited after antisocial behavior.

The last phase consists of a return to baseline.

CONCLUSIONS:
1. Violence-related themes for defendant are as follows:

- Violence is multiple and chronic.

- Recent severe violence is suggested.

- Victim injury has resulted from some violence.

- Direction of violence is toward others (primarily strangers) and toward property, but not toward self.

  – Violence to others is associated with presence of peers; bystanders have no suppressing effect on violence.

  – Violence to property is associated with theft.

- Victim patterning shows racial/ethnic differentiation.

- Focus of attack is specific.

- Assaults on others are more likely associated with substance intoxication.

- Sudden violence is more likely than long period of deliberation.

- Mode of attack is more likely to involve fist strikes to head/face region; weapons are used for crimes of profit and self-gain.

- Attacks are preceded by verbal abuse or attempts to control the victim.

- Aggressive behavior continues despite pain cues or distress of victim.

- Assaultive behavior is followed by attempts to avoid/escape aversive stimuli.

2. Based on the foregoing analysis, it is my opinion that the defendant is imminently dangerous (specify direction, i.e., to others, to property, to self) to a (specify degree, i.e., negligible, minimal, mild, moderate, substantial). (Explain term chosen both in words and percentage range.) This is based on the assumption that the following factors in particular remain constant; (specify, e.g., possession of his loaded firearm/continued substance intoxication/continued high state of stress and disorganization/continued command hallucinations to kill).

(If requested) Given the risk of imminent dangerousness, suggestions for intervention are (specify).

Based on the foregoing conditions or events, it is my opinion that Mr. Doe is dangerous (specify direction) on a short-term basis (up to twelve months after evaluation) to a (specify degree). This is assuming the following factors in particular remain constant (specify, e.g., continued substance dependence/living with current wife for spouse-abuse cases).

(If requested) Given such risk of short-term dangerousness, recommendations for intervention include (specify).

3. The feedback mechanism to reassess these opinions includes a (specify method, e.g., a hospital staff review, case conference) for the imminent dangerousness prediction, within (specify time, e.g., 48, 72 hours). A reevaluation for the short-term dangerousness prediction should include (specify method, e.g., a forensic clinical examination/complete neuropsychological testing/interdisciplinary case conference) within (specify time, e.g., one, two, three months). The predictive value of this report is limited to the above time frames.

Thank you for this referral and the trust that it implies,
Sincerely,

HAROLD V. HALL, Ph. D., ABPP
Diplomate, Clinical Psychology, Forensic Psychology
American Board of Professional Psychology

Appendix D

THE HONORABLE JOHN SMITH

[Date]
The Honorable John Smith
[Address]

RE: State of Hawaii v. [Defendant]
       CR. NO.
       Counts 1–111: Sexual Assault in the Third Degree

Dear Judge Smith:

Pursuant to your (Date) order granting the state's attorney for assessment of dangerousness of (Defendant), DOB_____, POB_____, SSN _____, this report is presented. The defendant is a __-year-old, single man who is currently being detained at the _____ jail. No empirically based risk assessments were found in his records.

This same report has been submitted to the Honorable Jane White in the sentencing for the kidnapping offense in Criminal Number _____. The sole difference is that the index offense used as a basis for prediction corresponds to the separate charges for which the defendant was found guilty. The change in index offenses did not alter the risk probability as discussed in this report.

Forensic Database: Records supplied by the Department of the Prosecuting Attorney included police and Grand Jury audio and video tapes relevant to Criminal Numbers _____ and _____ (original arrests for kidnapping, sexual assault in the third degree and failure to register as a sex offender; convicted of kidnapping and sexual assault in the third degree). Police report _____ for sexual assault and kidnaping was reviewed. An Adult Protection Division criminal history list and background information as well as a Hawaii OBTS/CCH form were also reviewed.

Measures administered to the defendant at _____ High Security Facility or later scored from data obtained fro the defendant or from the _____ medical and the above records included the following:

1. Clinical interview and mental status evaluation
2. Shipley Institute of Living Scale (estimated WAIS–R Full Scale IQ = 64–71
3. Wechsler Memory Scale–Revised (Mental Control, 6/6 correct)
4. Wechsler Adult Intelligence Scale (Digit Span, Digits Forward = 6; Digits Backward = 4)
5. Violence Risk Appraisal Guide (VRAG): 82% (probability of violent recidivism over 10-year period)
6. Hare Psychopathy Checklist–Revised: 36 (severe psychopath)
7. Predictors of Violent Recidivism (meta-analysis): Positive for violent recidivism (see below)
8. HCR–20 (Historical, Clinical, Risk Management Items: 28 (high risk for violent recidivism)
9. SVR–20 (Sexual, Violence, Risk): 13 indicators, high risk
10. Rapid Risk Assessment for Sexual Offense Recidivism: 4; 48.6 percent risk of sexual recidivism over 10-year period
11. Static Risk Assessment: 9; high-risk classification for recidivism
12. Minnesota Sex Offender Screening Tool–Revised (MnSORT–R): 8; percent correct high risk (70 percent)
13. National Severity Scoring System (increasing degrees of violence from 1970s, 1980s to 1990s)
14. Problem Identification Checklist (6-month period): Negative for violence
15. Dangerousness Prediction Decision Tree (3-month period): Negative for violence based on history, opportunity, and triggering stimuli
16. Dynamic Antisociality (1-month period): Negative for violence based on traits and relevant behavior

1. The forensic database is sufficiently diverse and comprehensive to arrive at conclusions beyond a reasonable degree of psychological probability. Deception analysis revealed that for the defendant's history and most recent convictions he minimized and denied past violence and events/behaviors associated with violence.

2. The Violence Risk Appraisal Guide (VRAG) is considered the best validated extant measure of violence risk and generates a 10-year probability of recidivism as a function of risk scores (Quinsey, Harris, Rice, and Cormier, 1998). The percent probability for the defendant for the 10-year period was 82 percent (96th percentile, category 8). Predictive items typically considered but not weighted into the VRAG included the following:
   a. Results of IQ testing

Results: <90 = high risk

Results of Shipley testing yielded a WAIS–R Estimated Full Scale IQ of 67 with impaired vocabulary (T = 22; <1st percentile) and abstraction skills IT = 36; <10th percentile). The Standard Error of Measurement (SEM) for the Shipley is 8.6, which suggested that the defendant's true IQ ranges from defective to borderline. All test data considered, border-line intelligence is indicated.

Attentional skills were overall low average to average (DF = 6; 24.6.th percentile; Mental Control = 6/6); his ability to concentrate was low average (Digits Backward = 4; 17.6.th percentile)

Ability to abstract was poor (e.g., he said the "Strike while the iron is hot" means "iron clothes, cause it is hot"; he defined a "green thumb" as "your hand").

Judgement was poor (e.g., he would "run" if he were the first person in a movie theater to see smoke and fire, then return and make sure everyone was out of the theater).

Possible brain damage from years of sniffing paint thinner (see arrest history), which then, as with the above items, may increase his danger-ousness beyond the obtained risk probability.

b. Attitudes supportive of crime:

Yes = high risk

Includes for the defendant a criminal history from an early age with incarceration at the Hawaii Youth Correctional Facility, denial of respon-sibility for many offenses and/or projection of blame to others, and being critical of his victims.

c. Attitudes toward convention:

Yes = high risk

Poor work history, chronic polysubstance abuse, limited responsibility for maintaining continual employment, poor attachment and bonding with others.

Since 1989, the defendant has been free in the community for only one year (1997 to 1998); he was imprisoned for the remainder of the time. His response to treatment has been poor.

3. The Hare Psychopathy Check List–Revised is considered an excellent measure of violence by itself and is included in the VRAG of Quinsey et al. (1998) as well as in some other tests discussed below. The defendant's score of 36 out of a possible 40 reflects a severe psychopath with behav-iors and attitudes in the two main factors: (1) selfish, callous, and remorseless use of others and (2) chronically unstable antisocial and socially deviant lifestyle.

4. Positive predictors of violent recidivism from a meta-analysis involving 52 studies and 16,191 persons by Bonta, Law, and Hanson (1998) includ-

ed adult criminal history, juvenile delinquency, antisocial personality, nonviolent criminal history, family problems, and violent history. Only one negative predictor was found (age).

5. The HCR–20, Version II (Webster et al., 1997) (History, Clinical and Risk Management items) score of 28 is considered high risk. Although the HCR–20 was designed as a guide to risk assessment and not a formal psychological test, empirical studies from a variety of settings and countries have validated the concept that increased risk occurs with increased scores. On this measure, the defendant revealed his problem with alcohol consumption (drinking cheap wine) despite attendance at Alcoholics Anonymous. After the undersigned proceeded through the defendant's rap sheet, the defendant reluctantly admitted to an 8-year history of arrests for inhaling paint thinner with a rage (first arrest for promoting intoxication compound on November 5, 1980, and last on September 3, 1988, with a total of seven arrests). He minimized his abuse of paint thinner by stating that it was infrequent and that paint thinner is not really a drug since it was inhaled and only resulted in dizziness.

6. The SVR–20 (Boer et al., 1997), much as the HCR–20, is a guide to sexual-risk evaluation. The defendant's sexual violence was rated high based on his scores. Relevant items that applied to the defendant included, but were not limited to high-density offenses (particularly with multiple victims in 1998); multiple sex offense types (i.e., forced sex with adults to sexual overtures to children); escalation in frequency/severity; extreme minimization/denial of offenses; attitudes that support or condone violence (e.g., he alleged that the 1989 victim was a prostitute, which in part justified his behavior).

7. The Rapid Risk Assessment for Sexual Offense Recidivism (RRASOR) yielded a 48.6 chance of sexual violence over a 10-year period. The relatively low 48.6% change occurred because the measure loads heavily on male-on-male victims and only sexual violence. Nevertheless, the base rate for sexual offenses in the normal population is <1 percent and about 30 percent over ten years among sexual offenders. Hence, the defendant's score is significantly higher than the base-rate group to which he belongs (sexual offenders).

8. The Static Risk Assessment indicated a high recidivism risk classification for the defendant. The static as opposed to dynamic items means that the high-risk classification will unlikely change in the future.

9. The Minnesota Sex Offender Screening Tool–Revised (MnSORT–R) score of 8 yields a percent correct high risk of 70 percent. This means that evaluators would be correct 70 percent of the time if they predicted a high risk of sexual violence for an individual such as the defendant over a six-year follow-up period.

10. The National Severity Scoring System, based on the survey of over 60,000 Americans by the National Institute of Justice (1985), allows for comparison and possible escalation of violence over time. Multiplying the scaled weights for the defendant shows an acceleration of violence for the 1970s to the 1990s, even though he spent much of the 1990s in prison. The resumption of sexual violence not long after he was released from prison is a very poor prognostic sign.

11. The Problem Identification Checklist, Dangerousness Prediction Decision Tree, and Dynamic Antisociality predict violence for periods of one month, three months, and six months, respectively.

    Together they show that the defendant is not an imminent danger to others and comports with his overall good institutional adjustment. Further, risk is low because the defendant does not have the opportunity to aggress against others in the community. Overall, these low rates represent fine tuning for short periods of time within an overall high risk (84 percent on the VRAG over the one-year period).

    The above represent results from quantitatively derived, empirically based systems of prediction. Qualitatively, violence has been shown over the last century to fall into two types: affective (impulsive) and predatory (self-controlled aggression). A number of the defendant's violent acts and behaviors clearly fit the predatory type. For example, the 1998 kidnapping and sexual assault in the first degree yielded a statement from him that he was going to pay the victim ($100) for the sex but did not particularly enjoy the act itself. He neglected to discuss the proactive nature of the crime, the force that was employed, the threats to the victim, and the assault on the male party. He later admitted to assaulting the male party. For the 1998 offenses, he neglected to mention the planned, purposeful acts and denied that he sexually abused, molested, or raped anyone in his life.

    When asked to state what he would say to the victims of the offenses if he had an opportunity, he disparaged and blamed the victims as well as their significant others (e.g., "Why do you do this to me?"; "I screw your mother every day; she is a dope addict").

Summary: Testing on multiple scales of violence prediction revealed a 41-year-old sexual psychopath who has a high risk of violent recidivism for the next decade. Many strong signs of violent recidivism were apparent on these empirically derived scales. The defendant does not appear to be "burning out" in terms of his aggression toward others, a particularly disturbing finding. He is a low risk of violence while incarcerated because, among other factors, he does not have ad lib access to the victim pool in the community. The defendant has a significant history of dangerousness to others resulting in criminally violent conduct, and such a history makes him a serious danger to others.

APB
Dangerousness Assessment Worksheet

Associated Features of Previous Violence		Individual Acts of Violence						
Use the last six most recent acts of violence. There does not have to have been an arrest or conviction for a particular act to be included in this assessment.		1 Most recent act	2	3	4	5	6 Least recent act	Row Totals
Type	H = History; O = Opportunity; T = Triggers							
1)	Source of data (check all that apply for each act)							
a.	Police report (put report number in blank)							
b.	Defendant							
c.	Victim							
d.	Court records (put case number in blank)							
e.	Neighbor							
f.	Family member							
g.	Acquaintance/friend							
h.	Other							
2) H	Type of violence:							
a. H	Domestic/Spouse/Elder/Child abuse							
b. H	Institutional (police, guard, hospital, etc.)							
c. H	Other							
		Number of Victims	Number of Victims	Number of Victims	Number of Victims	Number of Victims	Number of Victims	
3) H	Date of violence or serious threat (put month/year in blank).							
4) H	Injury to the victim:	----	----	----	----	----	----	----
a. H	Verbal or physical intimidation of victim (threats only, no aggressive physical contact)							
b. H	Intimidation by weapon							
c. H	Minor harm (not resulting in medical treatment)							
d. H	Treated and discharged (e.g., ambulance or emergency room treatment only)							
e. H	Hospitalized (spent at least one night)							
f. H	Killed							
5) H	Forced sex act							
	Total number of victims for each act							

APB

Violence Potential Summary Table

		Total number of victims	Scale weight	Total score for each category
	If you are using this table from the WordPerfect file, the number of victims in the appropriate blank and the program will enter the scores for you. If you are doing this by hand, multiply number of victims in (#V) by the weight (the number in parentheses following the injury description) to obtain score for each act's injury category. Total columns for both number of victims and score for each act.			
I.	Degree of Harm			
	a. Verbal or physical threats		X (4.9)	
	b. Intimidation by weapon		X (5.6)	
	c. Minor harm		X (1.47)	
	d. Treated & discharged		X (8.53)	
	e. Hospitalized		X (11.98)	
	f. Killed		X (35.67)	
	g. Forcible sex acts		X (25.92)	
	Grand total (victims / score) for all acts			
II.	Were there at least two acts of violence during the past two years, one occurring during past 12 months? Do not count time spent in an institution (i.e., hospital, jail, residential program, etc. as part of the two years. Acts occurring within the two-year period prior to completing this assessment are more valid in predicting violence potential than older incidents. YES NO			
	Other history factors? NO YES (Specify which ones):			
III.	Opportunity:			
	Past opportunity factors:			
	Current presence of above opportunities NO YES (Specify which ones):			
IV.	Triggers:			
	Past triggers (Specify):			
	Current presence of above triggers NO YES (Specify which ones):			
V.	Conclusion: Dangerous? NO YES			
	Additional Comments:			

APB 2 / DSW 2

6)	H	Did violent act occur in the last 2 years	YES NO	YES NO	YES NO	YES NO	YES NO	YES NO
7)	H	Relationship of defendant to victim follows:	-------	-------	-------	-------	-------	-------
a.	H	Stranger	YES NO	YES NO	YES NO	YES NO	YES NO	YES NO
b.	H	Acquaintance	YES NO	YES NO	YES NO	YES NO	YES NO	YES NO
c.	H	Family	YES NO	YES NO	YES NO	YES NO	YES NO	YES NO
d.	H	Institutional (e.g., police, military)	YES NO	YES NO	YES NO	YES NO	YES NO	YES NO
8)	H	Positive consequences to "justify" the violence (e.g., money, praise, peer approval)						
9)	H	Work-related violence	YES NO	YES NO	YES NO	YES NO	YES NO	YES NO
10)	H	Characteristics of victim:	-------	-------	-------	-------	-------	-------
a.	H	Gender	YES NO	YES NO	YES NO	YES NO	YES NO	YES NO
b.	H	Weighs less than accused	YES NO	YES NO	YES NO	YES NO	YES NO	YES NO
c.	H	Shorter than accused	YES NO	YES NO	YES NO	YES NO	YES NO	YES NO
d.	H	Alone before violence	YES NO	YES NO	YES NO	YES NO	YES NO	YES NO
e.	H	Victim displayed weapon	YES NO	YES NO	YES NO	YES NO	YES NO	YES NO
f.	H	Physical or mental disability/infirmity in the victim	YES NO	YES NO	YES NO	YES NO	YES NO	YES NO
11)	H	Acknowledgment of violence (e.g., spontaneous statements, written confession)	YES NO	YES NO	YES NO	YES NO	YES NO	YES NO
12)	H	Apologizes for violence to victim or law enforcement right after the violent act	YES NO	YES NO	YES NO	YES NO	YES NO	YES NO
13)	H	Suicidal/self-mutilative gestures by defendant in response to violence	YES NO	YES NO	YES NO	YES NO	YES NO	YES NO
14)	H	Accomplice present (whether the accomplice participated or merely observed)	YES NO	YES NO	YES NO	YES NO	YES NO	YES NO
15)	H	Weapons (one or more of the following):	-------	-------	-------	-------	-------	-------
a.	H	Firearm	YES NO	YES NO	YES NO	YES NO	YES NO	YES NO
b.	H	Knife	YES NO	YES NO	YES NO	YES NO	YES NO	YES NO
c.	H	Other weapon (e.g., hammer, rope)	YES NO	YES NO	YES NO	YES NO	YES NO	YES NO
d.	H	Weapon found at scene	YES NO	YES NO	YES NO	YES NO	YES NO	YES NO
e.	H	Use of protected body part (e.g., victim kicked with boot)	YES NO	YES NO	YES NO	YES NO	YES NO	YES NO
f.	H	Use of unprotected body part (e.g., hands)	YES NO	YES NO	YES NO	YES NO	YES NO	YES NO
g.	H	Use of primitive weapons (e.g., bites, clubs victim with head)	YES NO	YES NO	YES NO	YES NO	YES NO	YES NO

DSW 3

16)	0	Cessation of prescribed medication	YES NO	YES NO	YES NO	YES NO	YES NO	YES NO	YES NO	------
17)		Violence context characteristics:	------	------	------	------	------	------	------	------
a.		Nighttime occurrence	YES NO	YES NO	YES NO	YES NO	YES NO	YES NO	YES NO	
b.		Weekend occurrence	YES NO	YES NO	YES NO	YES NO	YES NO	YES NO	YES NO	
c.		Private residence	YES NO	YES NO	YES NO	YES NO	YES NO	YES NO	YES NO	
d.		Public building	YES NO	YES NO	YES NO	YES NO	YES NO	YES NO	YES NO	
e.		Roadway or transportation system	YES NO	YES NO	YES NO	YES NO	YES NO	YES NO	YES NO	
f.		Property destruction	YES NO	YES NO	YES NO	YES NO	YES NO	YES NO	YES NO	
18)	T	Substance abuse:	------	------	------	------	------	------	------	
a.	T	Alcohol intoxication	YES NO	YES NO	YES NO	YES NO	YES NO	YES NO	YES NO	
b.	T	Other drug intoxication	YES NO	YES NO	YES NO	YES NO	YES NO	YES NO	YES NO	
c.	T	Pathological intoxication (e.g., addiction)	YES NO	YES NO	YES NO	YES NO	YES NO	YES NO	YES NO	
19)	T	Increased signs of distress from victim caused the defendant to increase violence	YES NO	YES NO	YES NO	YES NO	YES NO	YES NO	YES NO	
20)	T	Disrupted central love relationship (e.g., anything from an argument to divorce between the defendant and a significant other)	YES NO	YES NO	YES NO	YES NO	YES NO	YES NO	YES NO	

Appendix E

DANGEROUSNESS PREDICTION TASK #2: JOHN BROWN

Previous Criminality and Current Hospital Progress

Hospital ward notes in recent years contain examples of serious prevarication by Mr. Brown to include recent lying to get off a particular ward after permission had been denied by staff of an earlier work shift. Significant distortion of facts by Mr. Brown appears to have occurred since at least 1978. When questioned in 1979 about previous suicide gestures, be stated that the only instance occurred while he was incarcerated in 1978 as a ruse to change cells. During that year, a social worker, during a social intake noted, ". . . he has been observed in animated interaction and activity with other patients but when speaking to staff assumes a "depressive" attitude" (1978). Assuming the role of a depressed individual had spanned at least one-half year.

During that year, a doctor observed that "the MMPI findings would strongly indicate that the patient is faking the symptoms of isolation and impoverishment of emotional experience" (1978).

Other suggestions of faking bad from psychological, neuropsychological, and achievement testing existed: (1) He obtained better scores on some intellectual subtests when allegedly mentally retarded than when "normal." His Wechsler Adult Intelligence test IQ rose from 57 to 116 over three separate administrations; from mentally defective to bright normal in 35 months. (2) During administration of different tests in the same general temporal period, he showed the ability to perform multiplication and other complex mathematical manipulations on one test, while exhibiting the inability to correctly do simple addition problems on another test. (3) He correctly identified words such as "kayak," "descend," "bereavement," "appraising," "amphibian," while showing the inability to define simpler words such as "winter," "slice," conceal," "enormous." (4) He exhibited inconsistent memory skills

224

(digits forward, digits backward) over time instead of a general suppressed performance. (5) He reversed performance and verbal IQs as the superior mode of functioning over time, instead of relative improvement within the dominant modes upon retesting. (6) MMPI profile results are grossly inconsistent with ward behavior.

During the forensic examinations by the undersigned in 1979 and 1981, other instances of distortion were observed to include outright prevarication and minimizing past behavior. Three superimposed MMPI profiles obtained over the years revealed little personality change had occurred, with the diagnosis of Antisocial Personality Disorder (DSM–IV Code 301.7) the most compatible condition given test results and chronicity of historical violence included in this report. Coupled with serious distortion during recent years, Mr. Brown can be considered an unreliable source of information; psychometric tests or instruments used in the future to assess Mr. Brown's condition should include built-in devices to detect misrepresentation. Finally, these results suggest that Mr. Brown pretended to be insane and retarded during his incarceration in 1977 and 1978 and the early portion of his stay at the state hospital in 1978; he then shifted to a strategy of minimization and denial in order to obtain conditional release.

Relevant Historical Violence: The arrest history for Mr. Brown includes the following:

Juvenile Record:
1965	Robbery in the second degree
1965	Robbery in the second degree
1967	Larceny
1967	Larceny
1967	Larceny
1969	Unlawful inhalation
1970	Paint sniffing
1970	Unlawful inhalation
1970	Burglary in the second degree
1970	Burglary in the second degree
1971	Assault in the second degree

Adult Record:
1972	Drunk and disorderly
1973	Assault in the third degree
1974	Terroristic threatening
1975	Attempted homicide
1975	Possession of prohibited firearm
1976	Attempted murder

1976   Terroristic threatening
1976   Assault in the third degree
1976   Carrying firearm without permit
1976   Robbery in the first degree
1977   Attempted rape in the first degree; attempted murder; kidnapping;
        attempted sodomy in the first degree; sexual abuse in the first degree
        (three counts)

Mr. Brown did not volunteer information to the undersigned on the above arrests except for the instant offenses. Instead, the information was presented to him and he confirmed or denied memory of the arrest and surrounding circumstances. He recalled about half of the arrests; several robbery, firearm, and burglary charges were not recalled. Explanations for the violence-related offenses appeared self-serving, for example, shooting a "lesbian" in the leg for her alleged inappropriate behavior, and harassing police officers because of their attempts to overcontrol Mr. Brown.

Since commitment to the state hospital, a number of violent or potentially violent behaviors have occurred to include fistfights, instigating others to fight and then standing back to watch the results, discussing on the telephone plans to bring in firearms in order to break out, and throwing objects at other patients. While expressing little remorse for the victim or the magnitude of his offenses, Mr. Brown has over the years become a dominant figure at the hospital, as one staff stated, "A big fish in a little pond," a status that may have been achieved by his ability to manipulate others, frequent intimidation and actual aggression that have a decided instrumental quality, and a higher-than-average intelligence.

Since 1983, Mr. Brown has displayed bursts of temper at both staff and other patients (September 1983, October 1983 (twice), April 1985) and has received insults and aggression from others (September 1983 (twice), March 1985). Again, one is struck with the high degree of self-control shown by Mr. Brown. In 1984, he was confined to the seclusion room for 24 hours for physical aggression toward a patient (June 1984; aggression unspecified). In 1985, he was observed by staff to push another patient forcefully and then call for staff as the irate patient was about to deliver a physical blow to Mr. Brown. As of February 1985, the hospital team noted that Mr. Brown does not feel aggression is one of his problems, stating at a team meeting (January 1985), "1 feel I have no problems. Everyone else is idiots."

Triggering Stimuli Associated with Repertoire: Substance intoxication, particularly that due to drugs alone or in combination with alcohol, appears to trigger violent behavior in Mr. Brown. Many of his arrests involve substance intoxication, to include the instant offenses themselves.

Parenthetically, a March 1978 EEG examination involved the use of sleep, photic stimulation, hyperventilation, and alcohol. Mr. Brown displayed lip smacking, hyperventilation, screaming, and combative behavior following ingestion of eight ounces of alcohol. These were not accompanied by seizure bursts or other electrographic disturbances, however. During that year, he was punished for having marijuana in the living area of the hospital forensic ward (December 1978). Since 1978, Mr. Brown has attended a number of Alcoholics Anonymous (AA) and other substance-control interventions, for example group therapy on the ward. The team plan for release of Mr. Brown into the community also involved a mental health/substance abuse component (May 1985). Yet it is this same team that approved many dozens of doses of Tylenol® with codeine at Mr. Brown's request, a most peculiar intervention considering the chronic substance abuse history of the patient and the unverifiable nature of his distress (e.g., headaches, sometimes for pain).

Other triggers associated with violent behavior appear to be the opportunity to cause distress in others, to create excitement, or to establish social dominance. These triggers appear well under Mr. Brown's self-control and can be turned on and off at will.

Opportunity Variables: Conditions that would tend to raise the opportunity for dangerousness to occur would include outright release into the community and the availability of firearms. Presently, opportunity factors cannot be properly assessed due to the controlled nature of his current environment.

Inhibitions to Aggress: Despite the multiple, severe, and chronic nature of past exhibited violence, the critical question becomes one of temporal recency. A completely violence-free year at the state hospital would be strong evidence that Mr. Brown had at least decided not to agitate others or play dominance and intimidation games with both patients and staff—this has not been the case to date. Until that occurs, less-than-severe forms of exhibited violence by Mr. Brown must be taken seriously by evaluation personnel because of the repressive and watchful institutional context in which they occur and because their appearance connotes that little real internalization of violence-free, prosocial attitudes has taken place. The most recent act of unprovoked violence, moreover, can be taken as a temporal landmark in that it clearly says the inhibitions to aggress created by the hospital as a function of their interventions (e.g., work experiences, education, psychotherapy) were not sufficient to prevent the occurrence of violence. The use of Mr. Brown's last actual exhibited violence to evaluate his dangerousness becomes even more relevant when one considers the chronic argumentativeness, hostility, manipulation, and superficial relationships with others. These behaviors are extremely difficult to treat despite their long-term maladaptive outcome.

Case Outcome: Based on almost a decade of data, the distortion style used by Mr. Brown was faking bad (to avoid prison incarceration) followed by faking good (to obtain release). He should have been predicted to be dangerous to others but not to self if released, based upon history, triggers, and opportunity factors. He remains forensically hospitalized as of 2001.

Appendix F

DANGEROUSNESS PREDICTION CASE #3: ENSLEY TAKAMURA

The Instant Offenses: On November 24, 1975, at 8:30 p.m., Doris Tanaka walked into the Criminal Investigation Unit of the Honolulu Police Department (HPD) and reported that she had been raped and sodomized by an individual, later identified as Ensley Hiroshi Takamura.

Ms. Tanaka provided a statement in which she related the following: Early in the afternoon she had left her home in the Palama section of Honolulu to catch a bus to the University of Hawaii where she was a first-year undergraduate student. As she waited at the bus stop, a yellow late-model Mercury Cougar pulled up alongside her, and the perpetrator, who was holding an unfolded map, called to her, asking for directions to a street in the area.

The perpetrator, feigning confusion as she explained the proper route, asked her to accompany him to show him the way. Inasmuch as he present-ed a clean-cut, young, perplexed appearance and it was broad daylight, she agreed to do so. The perpetrator had also told her that he would drop her off at school, thus actually saving her time. She then directed the perpetrator to the location he had asked about, which was an unpaved road leading to the rear of Koko Head Park.

The perpetrator stopped the car after it was hidden from view, reached down near his seat, and pulled out a large kitchen knife. He pointed it at her and in a soft voice said, "All right, take off your clothes." She initially refused, but removed her clothing when he brandished the knife viciously. The per-petrator ordered her into the back seat. While she was obeying, he removed his pants and shorts, leaving his shirt on.

He then said to her, "I want you to suck me first." At that point, he had an erection. She lay on the back seat and the perpetrator leaned over her, thrust his penis into her mouth, and again told her to perform oral sex. After a few minutes, he turned her over onto her stomach and attempted to enter her anus. Upon finding it difficult, he called her a "bitch." He persisted and managed to enter her anus, which was painful to her. They had intercourse in this manner for about one minute; then the perpetrator told her to turn over onto her back, whereupon he had vaginal intercourse with her to ejaculation.

Following the culmination of the acts, the perpetrator pulled out a second knife and stared at her as if debating some course of action. A car passed and the perpetrator seemed to snap out of it." Doris then asked him to take her to school and he replied, "I don't know, I don't have gas." He subsequently dropped her off on a main street a few blocks away. He was quiet and did not volunteer any information.

A vaginal examination conducted on Doris following her report was positive for the presence of spermatozoa.

On January 25, 1976, police were dispatched to the Red Hill area of Diamond Head Park, where they found a group of people gathered around the body of a young Asian female, later identified as 14-year-old Linda Asari, who showed no signs of life. A witness related that while riding his bicycle up the road, he had observed the female lying face down on the road in a puddle of blood. He related that she had displayed a weak pulse, and he reportedly attempted to render aid. She had tried to speak but had only coughed blood. Another witness reported hearing the voice of an angry male, followed by "what sounded like a loud shriek" shortly before observing a yellow sedan speeding away from the area.

An examination of the deceased revealed the presence of spermatozoa in her vagina. An autopsy revealed that the victim had sustained five deep stab wounds anterior, three of which had passed completely through the heart, and one stab wound, posterior, in the upper back. Her bloodstream was negative for alcohol and barbiturates.

During the ensuing investigation, a bloodstained knife with a five-inch blade was found near the scene of the crime. It was presented to Doris Tanaka, the previous rape and sodomy victim, who positively identified it as the one that had been used against her.

Defendant's Statement: Primarily through the tracking efforts of the first victim, the defendant was arrested and formally charged with murder, two counts each of rape and sodomy. (During the sexual assault, Doris Tanaka noticed the number of a parking sticker of a local high school. Searching through the yearbooks, Doris identified the perpetrator. For several months, HPD refused to act on this information, claiming that since they had contacted the school and the administration refused to reveal the student/owner of the sticker, the information might not be allowed in court. Only after noticing similarities between the rape/sodomy incident and the subsequent murder, did they pursue the investigation.)

When arrested, Ensley Takamura declined to make a statement, and he was subsequently placed in a youth detention home. In a written statement, the perpetrator later addressed the question of his motive for the multiple acts of violence. He said he had no insight in to his reasons for the crimes and added that he was sorry. He claimed no unusual stresses or state of mind due to ingestion of chemicals or alcohol on the days of the offenses. Indeed, later questioning of acquaintances and family revealed that no one had noticed Takamura acting in an atypical fashion. He had no history of significant violence before these facts.

Referring to the rape of Doris Tanaka, he wrote, "All I know is before all this started I would read the newspapers and read about sex. All my classmates were always talking about sex. It seemed like the magazines were filled with sex. I was a virgin before the [Tanaka] rape. I felt a lot of pressure to have sex with someone, but I did not know how to do it. I was afraid and embarrassed to ask anybody."

Referring to the murder of Linda Asari, he offered the following, "I never meant to kill the [Asari] girl. I freaked out when she jumped out of my car and started running down the road screaming because she knew me and could tell somebody what I had done. I panicked, lost control. I didn't mean to do it. It just happened like an accident. I was so scared."

Takamura further added that he had told Linda not to tell anyone of the rape. When she allegedly jumped out of his car, he knew that she had "bullshitted" him. Recall was affirmed for the murder up to the second knife thrust. The subject claimed that at that point, everything went blank, and he did not remember anything until he drove away from the murder site. At that time, he was not even sure he had killed anyone, as he reported seeing Linda sitting up on the road when he looked in the rear view mirror. Behavior at the detention home was uneventful except for one event, which will be presented later. After several months, Takamura was allowed to return home and attend a new high school under an assumed name to finish out his senior year. Shortly after he had resumed school, an attractive coed of Japanese descent from that high school was found raped and murdered in the English department building. The victim was strangled with a yellow scarf. The only other party present at the high school that evening, a groundskeeper, observed a light-colored vehicle speeding out of the school parking lot. Although Ensley Takamura was a prime suspect, this murder was never solved.

Subject's Background: What historical influences would shape a man to commit multiple sexual assaults, a murder, and possibly other crimes as well? Born and raised in Honolulu, this full-blooded Japanese youth ostensibly came from traditional middle-class circumstances. The probation officer who conducted the presentence report stated, "The defendant is the oldest of three children in the family. He has two sisters, two years and five years younger than he. He described his family as close knit and reported no other members of his family have been in trouble with the law. His relationship with his parents is "better than satisfactory," although he did feel that the rules they imposed upon him as a youth were strict; however, he did not view this as a problem. He indicated that his parents were not particularly approving of any sexual interests he showed when he was younger. Generally, he described his childhood as no different or unusual from other children.

"The defendant's father is the youngest of five boys and four girls and was reared in the Waianae area of Oahu. Economically, the family was not particularly well, off but his childhood was considered by him to be a normal and stable one. Relationships with his siblings were good and he was especially close to his older sister, Sumi, who has been described as the "backbone" of the family. During World War II, Mr. Takamura's father's business as a small-scale general contractor was confiscated and he was nearly interned. Later, he suffered a stroke, which resulted in his mother working long hours to support the family. He attended Waianae Elementary School and Kapiolani Intermediate and High School. Following his graduation from high school, he worked as a radio repairman and was drafted into the U.S. Army where he served from 1952 to 1955. Following his discharge from the service, he resumed his employment as a radio repairman until October 1957, when he began working with the Alexander and Baldwin Company repairing business machines.

"Mrs. Takamura was born and raised on Oahu in a lower-middle-class family. Her father was a construction laborer and in later years, worked as a janitor and did yard work. Her own mother intermittently worked at a pineapple company and was also a housemaid. She has four brothers and two sisters and is the fifth-oldest child. Reportedly, her home life was for the most part a harmonious one, and she attended Waipahu Elementary School, Kalakaua Intermediate School, and Waipahu High School She has done clerical work at Downtown Market and at the Tanaka Market from 1952 to 1956. For a short period, she worked at a library, finally transferring to the State Tax Office for about five years. Since 1964, she has been with the Hawaii State Department of Social Services and Housing. The marriage has reportedly been a stable one with home life and activities centering around the children.

"The defendant was described as a full-term baby with normal delivery. Development was described as normal as well as his health. His peer group was described as middle class, socially and economically, and predominantly of Oriental backgrounds. He was active in Little League baseball for five years. In intermediate school, he and several other boys formed a social club which had parties with other female club groups and raised funds through car washes and other means. An incentive system was worked out by his father and the defendant during his school years to improve his grades; however, the defendant took himself out of the system during the first quarter of his tenth-grade year.

"His parents described the defendant as never presenting any major disciplinary problems and felt he was "generally orderly, neat, even tempered, and keeps his cool." The defendant did not yell or swear because he knew he was not supposed to behave in such a manner. He was a willing worker, considerate, and at times, went out of his way to help others. From all indications the parents gave the Family Court intake worker, the defendant was as close as possible to being a "perfect son." Other individuals who had contact with the defendant while he was in detention reported him to be cooperative, a good worker and able to relate well with peers and staff. On April 3, 1976, following a period of socialization with others, a teacher found the defendant sitting alone, withdrawn and depressed, with the splintered remnants of a piece of his wood work, which he had smashed with his fist, next to him."

Psychological Evaluation: Senior probation officer Roland Wo referred the subject for psychological examination relevant to a presentence evaluation. The referral questions were several: compared to the time the instant offenses were committed, did the defendant significantly improve his psychological functioning and ability to control unacceptable impulses? Related to this, was the defendant dangerous in the sense of representing a menace to self or others? About four years had passed since the murder. Delays were caused by a number of factors, the primary one being stalling tactics by the retained defense counsel. Although the subject was a minor when he committed the offenses at age 17, he was eventually waived over to the adult criminal court for prosecution due to the seriousness of the crimes. During this time the subject had lived at home and volunteered work in a radio repair shop. He had also attended biweekly outpatient therapy sessions, primarily of a supportive and insight-directed type, with a local psychiatrist.

Psychological testing was conducted on the subject by a Family Court psychologist several months after arrest, and will be discussed shortly. Just prior to the arraignment, Takamura was seen for neurpsychological testing and by a three-person sanity commission. Concerning the former assessment, which employed an expanded Halstead-Reitan battery, the subject obtained a full scale Wechsler Adult Intelligence Scale (WAIS) I.Q. of 104 (Verbal I.Q. 99; Performance I.Q. 108), a Peabody Picture Vocabulary Test score of 109, and a Wechsler Memory Test M.Q. of 110. On the Wide Range Achievement Test, he attained a reading score equivalent to a 15.8 grade level, with spelling and arithmetic at a 12.2 grade level and 10.0 grade level, respectively. There was noticeable difficulty in those tasks designed to measure his ability to comprehend logical sequencing and to evaluate and reconstruct situations (e.g., Visual Recognition Test, Picture Arrangement on WAIS).

The neuropsychologist summarized his findings as follows: "[Ensley] is seen to have average mental ability and good brain function, but attention is called to some difficulty with tests which would appear to indicate some possible dysfunction within the right temporal lobe of the cortex. It would be possible for epileptic-type behavior to result if there is a dysfunction in this area, and a suspicion of such a possibility is suggested by responses on the Rorschach Test. It should be stressed, however, that our tests indicate very good brain function in general and only a hint of possible malfunction in the right temporal lobe."

Notwithstanding a possible organic involvement, the three sanity commissioners unanimously agreed on their findings. This "unanimous" agreement took place after conferring with one another, contrary to the spirit of the Hawaii Penal Code, which requires independent evaluations. They found that the subject had no apparent mental disease or disorder at the time of the examination or when the offenses occurred, was fit to proceed, did have the cognitive capacity at the time of the crimes to know that what he was doing was wrong and to appreciate the wrongfulness of his conduct, and did have at the time of the instant offenses the volitional capacity to control himself from committing the crimes.

An adjudication of guilt was plea bargained by the prosecutor's office for reduced charges. The charge of murder was reduced to manslaughter, and the two counts each of first-degree rape and sodomy were reduced to second-degree offenses. Because sentences in Hawaii may be concurrent rather than consecutive, this effectively reduced the maximum prison sentence to 10 years with parole possible after a minimum of about 5 years (mean 6.4 years on manslaughter charges in Hawaii). The present evaluation addressed the referral questions as listed earlier. Multiple assessment procedures were used. Testing involved the Minnesota Multiphasic Personality Inventory (MMPI, form R, Hathaway and McKinley, 1948), Mooney Problem Check List (Gordon and Mooney, 1950), Social Readjustment Rating Scale (Holmes and Rahe, 1967), Incomplete Sentences Blank (Rotter, 1950), MMPI Critical Items Scale (Grayson, 1951), Auditory Discrimination Test (Wepman, 1958), and a nonstandardized memory test of 15 simple shapes and numbers clustered for easy recall. Family Court and Adult Probation Division records were reviewed, and interviews were conducted with the defendant, a forensic psychologist on the sanity commission, the neuropsychologist, and a clinical psychologist who conducted a (blind) analysis of the subject's MMPI profiles.

Appearance and Test Behavior: Cooperative and presenting a logical and coherent stream of thought, this oriented, single, normal-appearing 21-year-old Japanese male was seen twice for testing and interviewing for a total of approximately six hours. Verbal and articulate, he clinically presented normal intelligence and no overt psychopathy. He stated that assessment was not influenced by ingestion of chemicals or alcohol, or modified by any unusual state of mind. The only stress reported was related to fear of outcome of the legal proceedings. Responses from a standardized stress test indicated that he was under moderate stress as of the dates of the testing. Item analysis revealed the most potent stressors, besides fear of incarceration, were related to his girlfriend recently terminating their relationship, sex difficulties due to an unsatisfied sexual appetite, and the deaths of close family members. These were two uncles who reportedly kept in close contact with the Takamura family.

Pretending false psychopathology (faking bad) or denying true psychological problems with or without exaggeration of positive traits (faking good) were not suggested from the interview or measures specifically included to detect test-taking bias (Auditory Discrimination Test, MMPI Validity Scales, the memory test of simple recall items). In general, results were considered valid.

Test Results: Did the subject significantly change in his coping style and personality since 1976? Review of the mental-status examinations conducted several years ago revealed then, as now, that Takamura was never considered mentally ill but did have a number of psychological problems. The most comprehensive of these evaluations was based on a five-and-a-half hour examination by Dr. Thomas of the Family Court. Relevant to a trait description, the following statement was proffered: "In essence, the combination of (1) compulsive attention to being in control and being "good"; (2) sensitivity toward the "bad" areas of anger and sexuality; (3) strong concern over his self-image; (4) attention to a network of numerous daily concerns; (5) obsession over all of these concerns; and (6) strong suppression and denial of negative or inappropriate behaviors, feelings, and ideas—all of these combined to make [Ensley] particularly vulnerable to occasionally becoming "overloaded" and, under such anxiety and pressure, to "blowing" or to losing control."

Employing several of the same measures (e.g., MMPI, clinical interview), the present examination also revealed these traits. Takamura himself acknowledged many of the suggested psychological difficulties on the problem checklist, where more than 100 personal problems were affirmed. In general, he described himself as an unhappy, conflicted individual who interpersonally could be described as dependent and lonely. Low self worth was marked with the subject affirming dozens of traits or behaviors that were negative in quality, ranging from a bad temper to a reported short-term memory deficit. As on previous testing, there was a paranoid flavor to the subject's responses manifested in projecting blame to others for his short-comings and feeling that others are unjustly persecuting him. (His paranoid ideation had a partial basis in reality, however, in that the office of the prosecution was out to convict him.)

A blatant example of Takamura's lack of moral acceptance for the murder was reflected in his interview remark that the killing would not have taken place had the victim not lied to him after the rape by attempting to run. Therefore, according to Takamura, she was partially to blame for her death. Also, he stated that both rape victims, upon observation prior to the rapes, had acted in a "sexy" manner, in dress and nonverbal behavior. They looked like they were ". . . just asking for it."

In general, the clinical scales from both testing periods revealed the same general personality configuration and showed little difference in clinical sub-scales (corrected–K) as well. The change in the F–K ratio suggested either a change in test-taking attitude from one of less seriously paying attention to questions to an attitude of more attentiveness or to one of less confusion. Both profiles appeared valid.

The initial profile appeared indicative of a rather severe schizoid character disorder. The HS elevation could have been indicative of either an organic involvement or possibly a somatic delusional component of a schizophrenic psychosis. In light of data from other mental health evaluations, organicity seems the more likely explanation. In addition, the profiles do not reflect the severe depression of many schizophrenics; they both have the minimal depression characteristics of many character disorders. A third hypothesis is that the elevated HS reflected a noticeable trait among Oriental subjects in Hawaii to somaticize stress. Norms for this population subgroup are not available.

The 1980 profile is qualitatively similar to the initial profile except that the suggested pathology may reflect itself in a more subdued form. Except for the high HS, the latest profile describes an 8-4 personality. Lachar (1974) sees subjects who display this profile as angry and rebellious individuals who exhibit a psychopathic-psychotic personality combination. Alienation from others is marked but may be disguised by superficially appropriate behavior. Gilberstadt and Duker (1965) affirm this interpretation and further state that other than being diagnosed as schizoid, subjects who exhibit this profile are often labeled pseudopsychopathic schizophrenics. Within the offender population, the 8-4 profile describes the violent personality (Lothstein and Jones, 1978). This may not apply to minority cultural groups, however.

A blind analysis of the MMPI results by a local clinical psychologist who specializes in this personality test confirmed the writer's opinion that little significant personality change had taken place over the intervening years. He further confirmed the writer's impression that a schizoid disorder was the most probable diagnosis.

MMPI test-retest comparisons suggested that despite potential change variables (e.g., late adolescent maturation, counseling, various life experiences), the subject had not significantly changed his basically schizoid personality and coping styles. The profiles also suggested criminality and some traits traditionally associated with dangerousness. These included an amoral stance in perceiving the world, the tendency to use others as objects and not to invest much energy into meaningful relationships, hypersensitivity towards anger stimuli combined with low frustration tolerance, hostility, and impulsivity. These traits appear to be chronic.

Case Outcome: Is Takamura dangerous to self or others? Relative to inflicting harm upon himself or leading a self-injurious lifestyle, testing suggested a self-destructive bent to his behavior in terms of social consequences. Although depression was not noticed, there were two alleged suicide attempts. The first attempt was by ingestion of an unknown quantity of over-the-counter sleeping medication, type and dosage unknown. The subject stated that he merely slept the effects off with no one knowing of his behavior, although his parents had been in the living room of the house at the time. The other reported attempt was by breath holding. Because of the presumably nonlethal and unrealistic methods of self-destruction, the high chances of rescue, and no hospitalization, the lack of present suicide ideation, an the subject stating that he is "... too afraid of pain" to actually kill himself, it was this writer's opinion that he was a low suicide risk.

Concerning dangerousness to others, the subject admitted committing the crimes and had recall for both sexual assaults and the killing up until the time of the second knife thrust into Ms. Asari. He stated that his motivation for both crimes could "... be summed up in one word *"inexperience"* (writer's emphasis). Reportedly, he had been unsuccessful in his prior efforts to have intercourse with occasional dates, and he stated that sex was the primary motivating force behind both sexual assaults. He stated he was not angry at either victim but believed then, as now, that they must accept partial responsibility for the instant offenses.

In this writer's opinion, the defendant was a significant danger to the community for at least an intermediate term period of several years. Direction of dangerousness was seen as being toward others, with a minimal risk toward self or property. The decision of dangerousness towards others was based on the (1) multiple frequency and lethal nature of past offenses, (2) use of weapons in committing the crimes, (3) attribution of partial blame for the assaults on the victims along with a denial of obvious anger towards both girls, (4) test-retest data that suggested only minimal personality change had taken place between the time of the crimes and the retest, (5) suggestion from test responses of chronic traits that tend to lower the threshold for violence to occur, and (6) present disruptions in interpersonal relationships with a relatively weak support system. In this writer's opinion, traditional outpatient treatment would be of little long-term benefit.

Ensley Hiroshi Takamura was sentenced to the maximum sentence of ten years in the Hawaii State Prison. Several months after incarceration, due to frequent clashes with fellow inmates, he was transferred for his own protection to a federal prison on the mainland. Violence can be considered to be established due to several attacks on weaker fellow prisoners after which they obtained medical treatment.

Appendix G

DANGEROUSNESS PREDICTION TASK OUTCOME: POLICE OFFICER LEED

Outcome for Case #3: Police Sergeant Leed

Follow-up data for six months revealed no exhibited violence to others, self, or property. The sergeant eventually received his desired transfer and planned to finish his police career. The individual who urinated on his duffle bag was never discovered. No violence was reported after two more years of duty.

Note: There is an absence of historical violence towards self and therefore, it should not have been predicted. Violence toward others was remote with the future chances of its occurrence reduced further by the predictee's supervisor sitting in on the therapy sessions.

Appendix H

DANGEROUSNESS PREDICTION TRAINING: QUESTIONS FOR PARTICIPANTS DANGEROUSNESS PREDICTION SAMPLE QUESTIONS FOR EXPERT WITNESSES

Basic: Have you traced the decision-making process of the evaluator who has proffered a dangerousness prediction (e.g., from an adequate forensic database to distortion analysis to examination of triggering variables, etc.– see dangerousness prediction decision tree). Has the examiner present their decision-making process to the court.

Relevant Questions:

1. Forensic Database

   a. Does the dangerousness prediction rely on conclusions offered by an examiner who is professionally competent to render such prognostications? What is his/her "batting average" in dangerousness prediction? How can this be verified? Probe using Ziskin-type questions.

   b. Are the assessment methods used adequate to examine violence potential of the predictee? What are the validity and reliability coefficients of the measures used? What sources for that information are cited?

   c. Could an adequate database be gathered given the state or condition of the predictee? What is the predictee's level of cooperation in the dangerousness prediction evaluation?

2. Distortion Analysis

   a. Has the client distorted the forensic database?

   b. If so, what is the direction of the distortion?

   c. What is the magnitude of the distortion?

   d. Are a, b, and c different for data offered by the predictee relevant to the past and data offered relevant to his/her current condition?

   e. How are a, b, c, and d quantitatively measured by the examiner?

3. History

   a. Is there a significant history of serious violence for this individual? How does the examiner operationally define "significant"? Does the proffered decision conform to those used in successful dangerousness prediction studies?

   b. Concerning the predictee's history of violence, what was the topography of the violence shown? What was the context of the violence that occurred in each case?

   c. What events precipitated and followed the violence? Was the violence "rewarded" by no aversive consequences or other reinforcing factors?

   d. What is the base rate of violent behavior for the predictee of this background? What is the source of that information?

   e. How similar are the contexts in which the predictee has used violence in the past to contexts he/she will likely encounter in the future?

4. Opportunity and Triggering Variables

   a. Who are the most likely victims?

   b. What means will most likely be used to commit violence? Are weapons available?

   c. What stresses are currently operative in the predictee's life?

d. What are the predictee's relevant demographics that affect the dangerousness prediction?

e. What cognitive (thinking) or affective (emotional) factors indicate violence may occur?

f. What are the inhibitions to violence in this case? Probe current and historical inhibitions. How do you know these inhibitions will be operative for the future? Where does it say so in the empirical literature?

5. Conclusions

a. What is the degree of dangerousness, on a scale from negligible, minimal, mild, moderate, substantial? Are these terms tied to the empirical literature? Where?

b. What is the direction of dangerousness–to self, others, or property? Is a specific type of violence (e.g., spouse abuse) predicted within the category of dangerousness to others?

c. What are the factors or events associated with violence, that formed your conclusion?

d. What factors or events, associated with violence, must stay constant in order for your prediction to remain valid for the relevant time span (e.g., continued substance dependence)?

e. What factors or events, associated with reduced violence, are anticipated or recommended which would change your prediction (e.g., psychotherapy)?

f. What are some suggestions for interventions designed to lower the propensity to aggress or to prevent its occurrence entirely?

g. What feedback mechanism can be used to reevaluate your prediction (e.g., case conference in one month)?

OTHER RELEVANT QUESTIONS:

1. What is the current status of dangerousness prediction as a scientific field?

a. Review for the court the approximately one-half dozen major prospective studies on dangerousness prediction.

b. What is a false negative in regard to dangerousness prediction? What are the inaccuracy rates for false negatives?

c. Does level of training affect accuracy of dangerousness prediction?

d. What is meant by a functional statement of violence prediction factors? What is your functional statement of violence prediction factors? What weight do you assign to each factor? Are those weights statistically derived? What are your sources in the empirical literature?

2. Haven't explicit disclaimers been issued by both the American Psychological Association and the American Psychiatric Association to the effect that no one can predict dangerousness to an acceptable degree of accuracy?

a. Are you a member of one of these organizations?

b. Do you subscribe to those views?

c. Then why are you offering a dangerousness prediction?

3. What is your theory regarding how and why violent behavior occurs?

a. Does that affect your dangerousness prediction and if so, how?

b. Would another examiner with a different theory of violence arrive at a similar dangerousness prediction? How do you know that?

4. Does DSM–IVR have a decision tree for violent, aggressive, or oppositional behavior?

a. If you offered a diagnosis in this case from DSM–IVR, why did you not also use the decision tree for violence?

b. Are you aware that the decision tree in DSM–IVR cannot in fact predict dangerousness? What other decision trees for dangerousness prediction are available in the empirical literature?

Appendix I

DANGEROUSNESS PREDICTION TRAINING:
PROGRAM EVALUATION FORMAT
PSYCHOLOGICAL CONSULTANTS
DANGEROUSNESS PREDICTION WORKSHOP
PRETEST/POSTTEST #1

1. List six characteristics of previous violence associated with an increased likelihood of future violence.
   a.
   b.
   c.
   d.
   e.
   f.

2. List three opportunity variables associated with increased violence.
   a.
   b.
   c.

3. List three triggering stimuli associated with dangerousness when super-imposed on a history of violence.
   a.
   b.
   c.

4. List six inhibitions to aggress according to the empirical literature.
   a.
   b.
   c.
   d.

e.

f.

5. How common is unreported violence to others?
   a. —— About 3/4 of violence is unreported.
   b. —— About 1/2 of violence is unreported.
   c. —— About 1/4 of violence is unreported.

6. Once reported to police authorities, how much violence is cleared, where the probably perpetrator is identified and brought into custody?
   a. —— Overall, about 3/4 of reported violence is cleared.
   b. —— Overall, about 1/3 of reported violence is cleared.
   c. —— Overall, about 1/8 of reported violence is cleared.

7. Previous research on dangerousness prediction indicates:
   a. False-negative rates exceed true-positive rates.
   b. True-negative rates are less than true-positive rates.
   c. False-positive rates equal false-negative rates.
   d. False-negative and true-positive rates combined are actually less than true-negative rates

8. "Anchoring" refers to a prediction strategy in which
   a. The vocational status of the predictee is the basis of prediction.
   b. Statistical deviations from an extension of the ideosyncratic functions of the predictee are deemed not important.
   c. The base rate of violence to which the predictee holds membership is the first estimate of individual dangerousness probability.
   d. Case-specific information is the basis for prediction.

9. Discuss the assaultive risk screening sheet (Michigan Department of Corrections) by the decision-tree path used to predict high risk of dangerousness.

   _____

   _____

10. Discuss the three main types of violence, according to the motivation of the perpetrator, that have been revealed in the behavioral science literature.

   _____

   _____

   _____

   Pretest_____Posttest_____   Signature

PSYCHOLOGICAL CONSULTANTS
DANGEROUSNESS PREDICTION WORKSHOP
PRETEST/POSTTEST #2

1. Trace the decision-making process used in this text to predict violence.

_____

_____

_____

2. What are several distortion styles that could be employed by the predictee when assessed for violence potential?_____

_____

_____

3. List six methods to detect "faking good" and/or "faking bad" presented in the behavioral science literature.

    a. _____

    b. _____

    c. _____

    d. _____

    e. _____

    f. _____

4. What is false positive?

_____

_____

5. What is true negative?

_____

_____

6. Dangerousness can be predicted with accuracy from certain psychiatric diagnoses.

True _____ False_____

7. Dangerousness generally can be predicted with accuracy in the absence of past dangerous behavior.

True _____ False_____

8. Certain personality traits, such as high hostility and low frustration tolerance, are good predictors of dangerousness.
   True _____ False_____

9. The base rate for aggravated assault, robbery, and rape within four years after conviction and release for a violent crime is actually quite low.
   True _____ False_____

10. Opportunity factors in the open community account for a major portion of exhibited dangerous behavior.
    True _____ False_____

11. Those of older age, female sex, and lower educational level tend to perceive more behaviors as dangerous.
    True _____ False_____

12. Level of training in predicting dangerousness influences accuracy of those predictions.
    True _____ False_____

13. In their acceptance by judges, dangerousness prediction does not depend on how prediction conclusions were gathered (e.g., through psychological testing, recidivism statistics).
    True _____ False_____

14. Violence perpetrators represent a large majority of criminal offenders.
    True _____ False_____

15. Association with violence peers (friends, relatives) does not increase your chances of a violent encounter.
    True _____ False_____

Pretest_____Posttest_____   Signature

Date

Appendix J

DANGEROUSNESS PREDICTION TRAINING:
NEEDS ASSESSMENT INVENTORY

This survey has been sent to you as a prior participant in the forensic workshop of Psychological Consultants. The purpose of this survey is to find out if the specific forensic programs offered in the workshop are meeting your needs and those of your professional peers. Answer the questions as truthfully as possible, keeping in mind that your responses will be used to help design future training efforts.

I. Indicate the areas of your forensic work in which you want or need the most help. First, prioritize the top five items from one to five on the left margin. Then indicate the extent of the priority of those five items on the accompanying scale on the right.

Priority

Forensic professionals in child
custody cases   ___ ___ ___ ___ ___

Forensic professionals in wrongful-
death and personal-injury suits   ___ ___ ___ ___ ___

Eyewitness identification   ___ ___ ___ ___ ___

Victim behavior   ___ ___ ___ ___ ___

Police selection and training   ___ ___ ___ ___ ___

Right to receive/refuse treatment   ___ ___ ___ ___ ___

Training in forensics   ——   ——   ——   ——   ——

Legal tests of insanity   ——   ——   ——   ——   ——

Current tests of insanity   ——   ——   ——   ——   ——

Forensic case study   ——   ——   ——   ——   ——

Crime and substance abuse   ——   ——   ——   ——   ——

Use of instrumentation in
forensic cases   ——   ——   ——   ——   ——

Forensic hypnosis   ——   ——   ——   ——   ——

Parole and probation considerations   ——   ——   ——   ——   ——

Racial factors in crime   ——   ——   ——   ——   ——

Rape   ——   ——   ——   ——   ——

Current forensic research models   ——   ——   ——   ——   ——

Duty to warn of possible violence   ——   ——   ——   ——   ——

Informed consent issues in
forensic assessment   ——   ——   ——   ——   ——

Countermeasures to client violence   ——   ——   ——   ——   ——

Therapeutic considerations with
violence problems   ——   ——   ——   ——   ——

Current and future roles of the
forensic mental health professional   ——   ——   ——   ——   ——

Jury selection   ——   ——   ——   ——   ——

Expert testimony in forensic cases   ——   ——   ——   ——   ——

Increasing dangerousness prediction
through statistical methods and
decision trees   ____   ____   ____   ____   ____

Increasing validity of mental-capacity
report conclusions through statistical
methods and decision trees   ____   ____   ____   ____   ____

Forensic mental health professional
state and national certification   ____   ____   ____   ____   ____

Forensic malpractice issues   ____   ____   ____   ____   ____

Competency to proceed examination   ____   ____   ____   ____   ____

Assessment of short-term
violence potential   ____   ____   ____   ____   ____

Client distortion analysis   ____   ____   ____   ____   ____

Examination of volitional capacity   ____   ____   ____   ____   ____

Examination of cognitive capacity   ____   ____   ____   ____   ____

II. Please list below the patient/client populations and/or presenting problems that you and your colleagues feel are a priority now in terms of future forensic research and training (e.g., the antisocial personality, factitious disorders).
   a.
   b.
   c.
   d.
   e.
   f.
   g.

III. What training programs do you specifically recommend to fit your needs and goals?

Program topic(s)_____

Suggested length _____

Contact frequency_____

Remarks _____

IV. Please add any other ideas or suggestions you have for future forensic programs.

Name (Optional)

THANK YOU.

REFERENCES

Abel, G., Blanchard, E., Becker, J., & Djenderedjian, A. (1978). Differentiating sexual aggressiveness with penile measures. *Criminal Justice and Behavior, 5,* 315–332.

Adams, S. (1974). Measures of effectiveness and efficiency in corrections. In Glaser, D. (Ed.), Handbook of Criminology. Chicago, Rand McNally College Publishing.

Adelman, R. & Howard J. (1984). Expert testimony on malingering: The admissibility of clinical procedures for the detection of deception. *Behavioral Science and the Law, 2,* 5–19.

Allyon, T. & Azrin, N. (1964). Reinforcement and instructions with mental patients. Journal of *Experimental Analysis of Behavior, 7,* 327–331.

American Psychiatric Association. (1974). *Clinical Aspects of the Violent Individual.* Washington, D.C.: American Psychiatric Association Task Force Report.

American Psychiatric Association. (1980). *Diagnostic and Statistical Manual of Mental Disorders* (3rd ed.). Washington, D.C.: American Psychiatric Association.

American Psychiatric Association. (1994). *Diagnostic and Statistical Manual of Mental Disorders* (4th ed.). Washington, D.C.: American Psychiatric Association.

American Psychological Association. (1992). Ethical principles of psychologists and code of conduct. *American Psychologist, 47,* 1597–1611.

American Psychological Association. (1978). Report of the task force on the role of psychology in the criminal justice system. *American Psychologist, 33,* 1099–1113.

Andrews, D. & Bonta, J. (1995). *The Level of Service Inventory–Revised–User's Manual.* Toronto, Ontario: Multi-Health Systems, Inc.

Andrews, D., Kiessling, J., Mickus, S., & Robinson, D. (1982). *The Level of Supervision Inventory: Interview and Scoring Guide.* Toronto: Ontario Ministry of Correctional Services.

Appelbaum, P. (1994). *Almost a Revolution: Mental Health Law and the Limits of Change.* New York: Oxford University Press.

Applebaum, P. (1997). A theory of ethics for forensic psychiatry. *Journal of the American Academy of Psychiatry & the Law. 25*(3), 233–247.

Atlas, R. (1982). Crime site selection for assaults in four Florida prisons. *Man-Environment Systems, 12,* 59–66.

Avanesov, G. (1982). *The Principles of Criminology.* Moscow. Progress Publishers.

Azrin, N. (1967). Pain and aggression. *Psychology Today,* 27–33.

Bach-Y-Rita, G., Lion, F., Clement, C., & Ervin, F. (1971). Episodic dyscontrol: A study of 130 violent patients. *American Journal of Psychiatry, 127,* 49–54.

Bach-Y-Rita, G. & Veno, A. (1974). Habitual violence: A profile of 62 men. *American Journal of Psychiatry, 131,* 154–217.

Bandura, A. & Walters, R.H. (1959). *Adolescent Aggression.* New York, Ronald Press.

Bandura, A. (1969). *Principles of Behavior Modification.* New York: Holt, Rinehart, & Winston.

Bandura, A. (1971). Vicarious and self-reinforcement processes. In R. Glasser (Ed.), *The Nature of Reinforcement.* New York: Academic Press, 2228–2278.

Bandura, A. (1973). *Aggression: A Social Learning Analysis.* Englewood Cliffs, New Jersey: Prentice-Hall.

Barbaree, H. (1991). Denial and minimization among sex offenders: Assessment and treatment outcomes. *Forum on Corrections Research 3*(4), 30–33.

Barbaree, H., & Seto, M. (1998). Empirical evaluation of the WSBC Multifactorial Assessment of Sex Offender Risk for Reoffense. 2nd Annual Research Day, Forensic Psychiatry Program, Department of Psychiatry, University of Toronto.

Barefoot v. Estelle, 103 S.Ct. 3383, 1983.

Barratt, E. (1994). Impulsiveness and aggression. In J. Monahan & H. J. Steadman (Eds.), *Violence and Mental Disorder: Developments in Risk Assessment.* (61–79) Chicago: University of Chicago Press.

Bazelon, D. (1982). Veils, values and social responsibility. *American Psychologist, 37,* 115–121.

Beck, J. (1985). *The Potentially Violent Patient and the Tarasoff Decision in Psychiatric Practice.* Washington, American Psychiatric Press.

Becker, J., & Coleman, E. (1988). Incest. V. B. Van Hasselt, R. Morrison, A. Bellack, & M. Hersen (Eds.) In *Handbook of Family Violence.* New York: Plenum.

Belanger, N. & Earls, C. An actuarial model for the prediction of recidivism among sexual offenders. *The Journal of Interpersonal Violence,* In press.

Belanger, N. & Earls, C. Prediction of recidivism. *The Journal of Interpersonal Violence,* In press.

Bem, D. & Allen A. (1974). On predicting some of the people some of the time: The search for cross-situational consistencies in behavior. *Psychological Review, 81,* 506–520.

Berkowitz, L. & LePage, A. (1967). Weapons as aggression-eliciting stimuli. *Journal of Personality and Social Psychology,* 202–207.

Berkowitz, L. (1983). Aversively stimulated aggression: Some parallels and differences in research with animals and humans. *American Psychologist, 38,* 1135–1144.

Bernstein, H. (1981). Survey of threats and assaults directed toward psychotherapists. *American Journal of Psychotherapy, 35,* 542–549.

Block, R. (1981). Victim-offender dynamics in violent crime. In *Victims of Crime, A Review of Research Issues and Methods.* Washington, D.C.: National Institute of Justice.

Blumenthal, M. (1976). Violence in America: Still viewed bv manv as a necessary tool for social order, social change. *Institute for Social Research Newsletter, 4,* 2–23.

Bobbitt, J. M. & Hock, E. L. (1968). Order- and psychologist-in the court. *American Psychologist, 16,* 152.

Boer, D., Hart, S., Kropp, P., & Webster, C. (1997). *Manual for Sexual Risk-20.* Burnaby, British Columbia: Mental Health, Law & Policy Institute, Simon Frazier University.

Bonnie, R., & Monahan, J. (Eds.). (1997). *Mental Disorder, Work Disability, and the Law.* Chicago: University of Chicago Press.

Bonta, J., & Hanson, R.: (1994). *Gauging the Risk for Violence: Measurements, Impact and Strategies for Change.* Ottawa: Ministry Secretariat, Solicitor General Canada.

Bonta, J., Law, M., & Hanson, K. (1998). The prediction of criminal and violent recidivism among mentally disordered offenders: A meta-analysis. *Psychological Bulletin, 123,* 123–142.

Boroson, W. & Snyder, D. (1980). The First Nuclear War. *NEXT Magazine,* 29–37, Oct.

Boston Globe, US crime rate dips to 25-year low, December 28, 1998, A3.

Borum, R. (1996). Improving the clinical practice of violence risk assessment: Technology, guidelines, and training. *American Psychologist, 51,* 945–956.

Borum, R., & Grisso, T. (1995). Psychological test use in criminal forensic evaluations. *Professional Psychology: Research and Practice, 26*(5), 465–473.

Borum, R., & Otto, R. (2000). Advances in forensic assessment and treatment: An overview and introduction to the special issue. *Law and Human Behavior, 24* (1), 1–7.

Borum, R., Swartz, M., & Swanson, J. (1996). Assessing and managing violent risk in clinical practice. *Journal of the Practice of Psychiatry and Behavioral Health, 4,* 205–215.

Boyanowky, E. & Griffith, C. (1982). Weapons and eye contact as instigators or inhibitors of aggressive arousal in police-citizen interaction. *Journal of Applied Social Contact, 12,* 398–407.

Bradley, V. & Clarke, G. (Eds.). (1975). *Paper Victories and Hard Realities.* Washington, Health Policy Center, Georgetown University.

Breiman, L., Friedman, J., Olshen, R., & Stone, C. (1984). *Classification and Regression Trees.* Pacific Grove, Wadsworth and Brooks/Cole.

Brenner, M. (1997). Does employment cause crime? *Criminal Justice Newsletter, 5,* 5.

Briere, J. (1993). *Child Abuse Trauma: Theory and Treatment of the Lasting Effects.* Newbury Park, Sage.

Brittain, R. (1970). The sadistic murderer. *Medicine, Science and the Law, 10,* 198–207.

Brown, F. (1965). The Bender gestalt and acting out. In L. Abt & S. Weissman (Eds.): *Acting Out: Theoretical and Clinical Aspects.* New York: Grune and Stratton.

Brown, M. R. (1926). *Legal Psychology.* Indianapolis: Bobbs-Merrill.

Buckhout, R. (1980). Eyewitness identification and psychology in the courtroom. In G. Cooke (Ed.): *The Role of the Forensic Psychologist.* Springfield, Charles C Thomas.

Bureau of Justice Statistics Crime Data Brief. (1998). U.S. Department of Justice, Office of Justice Programs, Washington.

Bureau of Justice Statistics Crime Data Brief. (1999). U.S. Department of Justice, Office of Justice Programs, Washington.

Busch, K. & Cavanaugh, J. (1986). The study of multiple murder. *Journal of Interpersonal Violence 1*(1), 5–23.

Buss, A. H. (1961). *The Psychology of Aggression.* New York: John Wiley and Sons.

Buss, A. H. (1963). Physical aggression in relation to different frustrations. *Journal of Abnormal and Social Psychology, 67,* 1–7.

Campbell, J. (1995). Prediction of homicide of and by battered women. In J. Campbell (Ed.): *Assessing Dangerousness: Violence by Sexual Offenders, Batterers, and Child Abusers.* Thousand Oaks, Sage.

Carp, A. & Shavzin, A. (1950). The susceptibility of falsification of the Rorschach psychodiagnostic technique. *Journal of Consulting Psychology, 14,* 230–233.

Carter, R. M. (1978). *Presentence Report Handbook* (Law Enforcement Assistance Administration, U.S. Department of justice Publication No. 027-000-00577-2). Washington, D.C.: U.S. Government Printing Office.

Cavanaugh, J. & Rogers, R. (1984). Malingering and deception. *Behavioral Sciences and the Law, 2,* 1–3.

Chapman, L. & Chapman, J. (1967). Genesis of popular but erroneous psychodiagnostic observations. *Journal of Abnormal Psychology, 72,* 193–204.

Chapman, L. & Chapman, J. (1969). Illusory correlations as an obstacle to the use of valid psychodiagnostic signs. *Journal of Abnormal Psychology, 74,* 271–280,

Cocozza, J., Melick, M., & Steadman, H. (1978). Trends in violent crime among ex-mental patients. *Criminology, 16,* 317–334.

Cocozza, J. & Steadman, H. (1968). Prediction in psychiatry: An example of misplaced confidence in experts. *Social Problems, 25,* 265–276.

Cocozza, J. & Steadman, H. (1976). The failure of psychiatric predictions of dangerousness: Clear and convincing evidence. *Rutgers Law Review, 29,* 1084–1101.

Cohen, R. L. & Harnick, M.A. (1980). The susceptibility of child witnesses to suggestion. *Law and Human Behavior, 4*, 201–210.

Coleman, J., Butcher, J., & Carson, R. (1980). *Abnormal Psychology and Modern Life* (6th. ed.). Glenview, IL: Scott, Foresman and Company.

Cook, P. (1975). The correctional carrot: better jobs for parolees. *Policy Analysis, 1*, 11–54.

Cooke, G. (1980). *The Role of the Forensic Psychologist.* Springfield, Charles C Thomas.

Curnutt, R. & Corozzo, L. (1960). The use of the Bender Gestalt cutoff scores in identifying juvenile delinquents. *Journal of Projective Techniques, 24*, 353–354.

Daley, M. & Piliavin, I. (1982). "Violence against children" revisited: some necessary clarification of findings from a major national study. *Journal of Social Service Research, 5*, 61–81.

Danton, D. (1986). Violence Management. Presented at Veterans Administration, Honolulu.

Davies, J. (1955). *Phrenology, Fad and Science.* New Haven, Yale University Press.

Davis v. Lihm, Mich. Wayne County Circuit Court, No. 77-726989 NM (June 11,1981).

Davis, F. B. (1966). *Standards for Educational and Psychological Tests.* Washington, D.C.: American Psychological Association.

Dent, H. R. (1982). The effects of interviewing strategies on the results of interviews with child witnesses. In A. Trankell (Ed.), *Reconstructing the Past.* Deventer, the Netherlands, Kluver.

Department of Justice. (1978). *Criminal Victimization in the United States.* Washington, D.C., Superintendent of Documents, U.S. Government Printing Office

Depaulo, B. & Rosenthal, R. (1979). Telling lies. *Journal of Personal and Social Psychology, 17*, 1713–1721.

Dietz, P. (1986). Mass, serial and sensational homicides. *Bulletin of the New York Academy of Medicine, 62*(5), 477–491.

Dix, G. (1975). Determining the continued dangerousness of psychologically abnormal sex offenders. *Journal of Psychiatry and the Law, 3*, 327–344.

Dix, G. E. (1976). "Civil" commitment of the mentally ill and the need for data on the prediction of dangerousness. *American Behavioral Scientist; 19* (3), 318–334.

Donaldson v. O'Connor, 422 U.S. 563 (1975).

Donnerstein, E. cited in *Monitor* (June 1998), American Psychological Association,

Doren, D. (1999). The accuracy of sex offender recidivism risk assessments. Presented at the XXIV International Congress on Law and Mental Health, Toronto.

Douglas, J. (1995). *Mind Hunter.* New York, Scribner.

Douglas, K. & Webster, C. (1999). The HCR-20 violence risk assessment scheme: concurrent validity in a sample of incarcerated offenders. *Criminal Justice and Behavior, 26*, 3–19.

Dubonowsky, W. (1980). Pain cues as maintainers of human violence. Presented at *Symposium on Dangerousness Prediction.* Honolulu.

Duncan, E., Whitney, P., & Kunen, S. (1982). Integration of visual and verbal information on children's memories. *Child Development, 53*, 1215–1223

Dutton, D., Bodnarchuk, M., Kropp, R., Hart, S., & Ogloff, J. (1997). Wife assault treatment and criminal recidivism: an 11-year follow-up. *International Journal of Offender Therapy and Comparative Criminology, 41*, 9–23.

Dutton, D. & Hart, S. (1992). Risk markers for family violence in a federally incarcerated population. *International Journal of Law and Psychiatry, 15*, 101–112.

Ebert, R. (1987). Avoiding murder by a violent patient. *The Psychiatric Times, 12*, 4–30,1987.

Ekman, P. (1992). *Telling Lies.* New York: Norton.

Ekman, P. & Friesen, W. (1969). Nonverbal leakage and clues to deception. *Psychiatry, 32*, 88–106.

Ekman, P. & Friesen, W. (1972). Hand movements. *Journal of Communication, 22*, 353–374.

Ekman, P., Friesen, W., & Scherer, K. (1976). Body movements and voice pitch in deceptive interaction. *Semiotica, 16,* 23–27.

Ekman, P. & O'Sullivan, M. (1991). Who can catch a liar? *American Psychologist, 46,* 913–920.

Ennis, B. & Emery, R. (1978). *The Rights of Mental Patients.* New York: Avon.

Epperson, D., Kaul, J., & Hesselton, D. (1998). Final report of the development of the Minnesota Sex Offender Screening Tool–Revised (MnSOST-R). Presentation at the 17th Annual Research and Treatment Conference of the Association for the Treatment of Sexual Abusers, Vancouver.

Epperson, D., Kaul, J., & Huot, S. (1995). *Predicting risk for recidivism for incarcerated sex offenders: Updated development on the Sex Offender Screening Tool (SOST).* Poster session presented at the Annual Conference of the Association for the Treatment of Sexual Offenders, New Orleans.

Eriksen, C. W. & Collins, J. F. (1968). Sensory traces versus the psychological moment in the temporal organization of form. *Journal of Experimental Psychology, 77,* 376–382.

Faulkner, L. (1990). Threats and assaults against psychiatrists. *Bulletin of the American Academy of Psychiatry and the Law, 18,* 37–46.

Faust, D. & Hart, K. (1988). Pediatric malingering: the capacity of children to fake believable deficits on neuropsychological testing. *Journal of Consulting and Clinical Psychology, 56,* 578–582.

Feldmann, T. B. & Johnson, P. W. (1996). Workplace violence: A new form of lethal aggression. *Lethal violence 2000: A sourcebook on fatal domestic, acquaintance and stranger aggression.* Kamuela, HI: The Pacific Institute for the Study of Conflict and Aggression.

Fersch, E. (1980). Ethical Issues for psychologists. In J. Monahan (Ed.), *Who is the Client? Ethics of Psychological Intervention in the Criminal Justice System.* American Psychological Association.

Firestone, P., Bradford, J., Greenberg, D. Nunes, K., & Broom, A. (1999). A comparison of the Sex Offender Risk Appraisal Guide (SORAG) and the Static-99. Paper presented at the Association for the Treatment of Sexual Abusers Annual Convention, Orlando.

Fischer, M. (1997). The psychologist as a "hired gun." *American Journal of Forensic Psychology, 15*(2), 25–30.

Ford, C. & Beach, F. (1951). *Patterns of Sexual Behavior.* New York: Harper & Row.

Forst, B., Rhodes, W., Dimm, J., Gelman, A., & Mullin, B. (1983). Targeting federal research on recidivists: an empirical view. *Federal Probation, 10.*

Frederick, C. (1978a). *Dangerous Behavior: A Problem in Law and Mental Health.* NIMH, DHEW Publication No. (ADM) 78–563. Washington, D.C.: Superintendent of Documents, U.S. Government Printing Office, 153–191.

Frederick, C. (1978b). An overview of dangerousness: Its complexities and consequences. In *Dangerous Behavior: A Problem in Law and Mental Health,* NIMH, DHEW Publication No. (ADM) 78–563. Washington, D.C.: Superintendent of Documents, U.S. Government Printing Office.

Frederick, C. (1975). Determining dangerousness. In V. Bradley & G. Clark (Eds.): *Paper Victories and Hard Realities: The Implementation of the Legal and Constitutional Rights of the Mentally Disabled.* Washington D.C., Georgetown University.

Frederick, R. & Crosby, R. (2000). Development and validation of validity indicator profile. *Law and Human Behavior, 24*(1), 59–82.

Freud, S. (1959). Fragment of an analysis of a case of hysteria (1905). *Collected Papers, 3,* New York: Basic Books.

Freund, K. & Watson, R. (1991). Assessment of the sensitivity and specificity of a phallometric test: An update of phallometric diagnosis of pedophilia. *Psychological Assessment, 3,* 254–260.

Fromm, E. (1973). *The Anatomy of Human Destructiveness.* New York: Holt, Rineholt, and Winston.

Fujioka, N., Iha, D. Wong, S., & Wong, W. (1978). *What determines a sentence? Factors used by probation officers and judges.* Unpublished thesis, University of Hawaii, Honolulu.

Furby, L., Weinrott, M. & Blackshaw, L. (1989). Sex offender recidivism: a review. *Psychological Bulletin, 105,* 3–30.

Gandreau, P., Little, T., & Goggin, C. (1996). A meta-analysis of the predictors of adult offender recidivism: What works! *Criminology, 34,* 575–607.

Gardner, W., Lidz, C., Mulvey, E., & Shaw, E. (1996). A comparison of actuarial methods for identifying repetitively violent patients with mental illness. *Law and Human Behavior, 20,* 35–48.

Geen, R. & Berkowitz, L. (1967). Some conditions facilitating the occurrence of aggression after the observation of violence. *Journal of Personality, 35,* 666–676.

Geis, G. & Meier, R. (1978). Looking backward and forward: Criminologists on criminology and career. *Criminology, 16,* 273–288.

Gilberstadt, H. & Duker, J. (1965). *A Handbook for Clinical and Actuarial MMPI Interpretation.* Philadelphia: Saunders.

Glezor, D. (1981). Current contributions for psychiatry in rape cases. *Psycholgie Medicate, 13,* 1583–1585.

Goldstein, R. (1975). Brain research and violent behavior. *Archives of Neurology, 30,* 1–18.

Goodman, J. (1994). Credibility problems in sadistic abuse. *Journal of Psychohistory, 21*(4), 479–496.

Gordon, L. & Mooney, R. (1950). *Mooney Problem Check List.* New York, Psychological Corporation.

Goring, C. (1913). *The English Convict.* London, His Majesty's Stationary Office.

Goshen, C. (1967). *Documentary History of Psychiatry.* New York, Philosophical Library.

Gottfredson, M. & Gottfredson, D. (1988). *Decision-making in Criminal Justice: Toward the Rational Exercise of Discretion* (2nd. ed.). New York, Plenum.

Grann, M., Belfrage, H., & Tengstrom, A. (2000). Actuarial assessment of risk for violence: predictive validity of the VRAG and historical part of the HCR-20. *Criminal Justice and Behavior, 27,* 97–114.

Grann, M., Langstrom, N., Tengstrom, A., & Kullgren, G. (1999). Psychopathy (PCL-R) predicts violent recidivism among criminal offenders with personality disorders in Sweden. *Law and Human Behavior, 23,* 205–17.

Gratzer, T., & Bradford, J. (1995). Offender and offense characteristics of sexual sadists: a comparative study. *Journal of Forensic Sciences, 40*(3), 450–455.

Grayson, H. (1951). *A Psychological Admissions Testing Program and Manual.* Los Angeles, Veterans Administration Center, Neuropsychiatric Hospital.

Greenberg, S. & Shuman, D. (1997). Irreconcilable conflict between therapeutic and forensic roles. *Profesional Psychology: Research and Practice, 28*(1), 50–57.

Grisso, T. (1986). *Evaluating Competencies: Forensic Assessments and Instruments.* New York, Plenum.

Grisso, T. (1998). *Forensic Evaluation of Juveniles.* Sarasota, Professional Resource Press.

Grisso, T. (1999). Presentation on Risk Assessment to Massachusetts Designated Forensic Clinicians, Worcester.

Grisso, T. & Applebaum, P. (1992). Is it unethical to offer predictions of future violence? *Law and Human Behavior, 16,* 621–633.

Grossman, J. (1980). The forensic psychologist and the rapist: disposition and treatment. In G. Cooke (Ed.): *The Role of the Forensic Psychologist.* Springfield, Charles C Thomas .

Groth, N., Longo, R. & McFadin, J. (1982). Undetected recidivism among rapists and child molesters. *Crime and Delinquency*, 102–106.

Grove, W. & Meehl, P. (1996). Comparative efficiency of informal (subjective, impressionistic) and formal (mechanical, algorithmic) prediction procedures: the clinical-statistical controversy. *Psychology, Public Policy, and Law*, *2*, 293–323.

Groth, A. N. & Burgess, A.W. (1977). Rape: a sexual deviation. *American Journal of Orthropsychiatry*, *47*, 400–406.

Grubin, D. (1998). Sex offending against children: understanding the risk. *Police Research Series Paper 99*. London, Home Office.

Guze, S. (1976). *Criminality and Psychiatric Disorders*. London, Oxford University Press.

Hall, H. V. (1982). Dangerousness predictions and the maligned forensic professional: suggestions for detecting distortion of true basal violence. *Criminal Justice and Behavior*, *9*, 3–12.

Hall, H. V. (1983). Guilty but mentally ill: feedback from state attorney general offices. *Bulletin of the American Academy of Forensic Psychologists*, *4*, 2–7, 1983.

Hall, H. V. (1984). Predicting dangerousness for the courts. *American Journal of Forensic Psychology*, *4*, 5–25.

Hall, H. V. (1985). Cognitive and volitional capacity assessment: a proposed decision tree. *American Journal of Forensic Psychology*, *111*, 3–17.

Hall, H. V. (1986). The forensic distortion analysis: a proposed decision tree. *American Journal of Forensic Psychology*, *4*, 31–59.

Hall, H. V. (1987). *Violence Prediction: Guidelines for the Forensic Practitioner*. Springfield, Charles C Thomas.

Hall, H. V. (1994). Deception. In *Encyclopedia of Psychology*. New York, Macmillan.

Hall, H. V. (1994). Malingering. In *Encyclopedia of Psychology*. New York, Macmillan.

Hall, H. V. (Ed.). (1996) *Lethal violence 2000: A Sourcebook on Fatal Domestic, Acquaintance and Stranger Aggression*. Kamuela, Pacific Institute for the Study of Conflict and Aggression.

Hall, H. V.: (2001). *Manual for the Workplace Violence Risk Assessment Checklist (WVRA)*. Kamuela, HI: Pacific Institute for the Study of Conflict and Aggression.

Hall, H. V.: *Workplace Violence: Effective Prediction and Intervention Strategies*. Kamuela, Pacific Institute for the Study of Conflict and Aggression, In press.

Hall, H. V., Catlin, E., Boissevain, A., & Westgate, J. (1984). Dangerous myths about predicting dangerousness. *American Journal of Forensic Psychology*, *2*, 173–193.

Hall, H. V. & McLaughlin, D. (1981). *Impact of psychologists' dangerousness predictions in the courtroom*. Honolulu, Hawaii Psychological Association.

Hall, H. V., Price, A. B., Shinedling, M., Peizer, S. B., & Massey, R. H. (1973). Control of aggressive behavior in a group of retardates using positive and negative reinforcement procedures. *Training School Bulletin*, *70*, 179–186.

Hall, H. V. & Pritchard, D. (1996). *Detecting malingering and deception: Forensic Distortion Analysis (FDA)*. Winter Park, PMD Publishers Group, Inc.

Hall, H. V. & Pritchard, D. (2001). *Workplace Violence Risk Analysis: Effective Prediction and Intervention Strategies*. Kamuela, HI: The Pacific Institute for the Study of Conflict and Aggression.

Hall, H. V. & Poirier, J. (2001). *Detecting Malingering and Deception: Forensic Distortion Analysis* (2nd ed.). Boca Raton, FL: CRC Press.

Hall, H. V. & Sbordone, R. (1993). *Disorders of Executive Functioning: Civil and Criminal Law Applications*. Winter Park, FL: PMD Publishers Group, Inc.

Hall, H. V., Shinedling, M. A., & Thorne, D. E. (1973). Overcoming situation-specific problems associated with typical institutional attempts to suppress self-mutilative behavior.

Training School Bulletin, 70, 111–114.

Hall, H. V. & Whitaker, L. (Eds.) (1999). *Collective Violence: Effective Strategies for Assessing and Interviewing in Fatal Group and Institutional Aggression.* Boca Raton, CRC Press.

Hanson, R. (1997). Development of a Brief Actuarial Risk Scale for Sexual Offense Recidivism. Department of the Solicitor General of Canada. Public Works and Government Services Canada. Cat. No. J54-1/1997-E; ISBN: 0-662-26207-7.

Hanson, R. (1998). What do we know about sex offender risk assessment? *Psychology, Public Policy and Law, 4,* 50–72.

Hanson, R. & Bussiere, M. (1998). Predicting relapse: a meta-analysis of sexual offender recidivism studies. *Journal of Consulting and Clinical Psychology, 66*(2), 348–362.

Hanson, R. & Harris, A. (1998). *Dynamic predictors of sexual recidivism* (User Report 1998–01). Ottawa, Department of the Solicitor General of Canada.

Hanson, R. & Harris, A. (1999). Where should we intervene?: dynamic predictors of sexual assault recidivism. *Criminal Justice and Behavior, 27*(1), 6–35,

Hanson, R., Scott, H., & Steffy, R. (1995). A comparison of child molesters and nonsexual criminals: Risk predictors and long-term recidivism. *Journal of Research in Crime and Delinquency, 32*(3), 325–337.

Hanson, R., Steffy, R., & Gauthier, R. (1992). *Long-term follow-up of child molesters: Risk predictors and treatment outcomes.* User Report No. 1992-02. Ottawa, Corrections Branch, Ministry of the Solicitor General of Canada.

Hanson, R., Steffy, R., & Gauthier, R. (1993). Long-term recidivism of child molesters. *Journal of Consulting and Clinical Psychology, 61,* 646–652.

Hanson, R. & Thornton, D. (2000). Improving risk assessments for sex offenders: A comparison of three actuarial scales. *Law and Human Behavior, 24*(1), 119–136.

Hare, R. (1980). A research scale for the assessment of psychopathy in criminal populations. *Personality and Individual Differences, 1,* 111–119.

Hare, R. (1991). *The Hare Psychopathy Checklist–Revised.* Toronto: Multi-Health Systems.

Hare, R. (1996). Psychopathy: A clinical construct whose time has come. *Criminal Justice and Behavior, 23*(1), 25–54.

Harlow, C. (1985). *Reporting Crimes to the Police.* U.S. Department of Justice, Bureau of Justice, NCJ-99643, Rockville.

Hart, S. (1998). The role of psychopathy in assessing risk for violence: Conceptual and methodological issues. *Legal and Criminological Psychology, 3,* 123–140.

Hart, S., Cox, D., & Hare, R. (1995). *The Hare Psychopathy Checklist. Screening Version (PCL-SV).* North Tonowanda, Multi-Health Systems, Inc.

Hart, S., Hare, R., & Forth, A. (1994). Psychopathy as a risk marker for violence: development and validation of a screening version of the Revised Psychopathy Checklist. In J. Monahan & H. Steadman (Eds.): *Violence and Mental Disorder: Developments in Risk Assessment.* Chicago, University of Chicago Press, pp. 81–98.

Hart, S., Kropp, P., Roesch, R., Ogloff, J., & Whittemore, K. (1994). Wife assault in community resident offenders. *Canadian Journal of Criminology, 36,* 435–446.

Hartogs, R. (1970). Who will act violently: the predictive criteria. In R. Hartogs & T. Artz (Eds.): *Violence: The Causes and Solution.* New York, Dell.

Hathaway, S. & McKinley, C. (1948). *The Minnesota Multiphasic Personality Inventory.* New York, The Psychological Corporation.

Hawkins, J., Herrenkhol, T., Farrington, D., Brewer, D., Catalona, R., & Harachi, T. (1998). A review of predictors of youth violence. In R. Loeber & D. Farrington (Eds.): *Serious and Violent Juvenile Offenders: Risk Factors and Successful Interventions.* Thousand Oaks, Sage,106–146.

Hazelwood, R. & Burgess, A. (1995). (Eds.) *Practical Aspects of Rape Investigation.* New York, CRC Press.

Healey, K. & Smith, C. (1998). *Batterer Intervention: Program Approaches and Criminal Justice Strategies.* NCJ Publication No. 168638. Washington, DC, National Institute of Justice.

Heaton, R., Smith, H., Lehman, R., & Vogt, A. (1978). Prospects for faking believable deficits on neuropsychological testing. *Journal of Consulting and Clinical Psychology, 46*, 892–900.

Hedlund v. Orange County, 669 P.2d 41 (Cal. 1983).

Heilbrun, K., O'Neill, M., Strohman, L., Bowman, Q., & Philipson, J. (2000). Expert approaches to communicating violence risk. *Law and Human Behavior, 24*(1), 137–148.

Heller, K. & Monahan, J. (1977). *Psychology and Community Change.* Homewood, Dorsey.

Hellman, D. & Blackman, N. (1966). Enuresis, firesetting, and cruelty to animals: A triad predictive of adult crime. *American Journal of Psychiatry, 122*, 1431–1435.

Hemphill, J., Hare, R., & Wong, S. (1988). Psychopathy and recidivism: a review. *Legal and Criminological Psychology, 3*, 139–170.

Herman, J. (1992). *Trauma and Recovery.* New York, Basic Books.

Hirschi, T. & Hindelang, M. (1977). Intelligence and delinquency: a revisionist review. *American Sociological Review, 42*, 571–587.

Hoffman, M. (1960). Power assertion by the parent and its impact on the child. *Child Development, 31*, 129–143.

Hoffman, P. J. (1960). The paramorphic representation of clinical judgment. *Psychological Bulletin, 57*(2), 116–131.

Holland, T., Holt, N., & Beckett, G. (1982). Prediction of violent versus nonviolent recidivism from prior violent and nonviolent criminality. *Journal of Abnormal Psychology, 3*, 178–182.

Holmes, R., & De Burger, J. (1988). *Serial Murder.* Newbury Park, Sage.

Holmes, T. & Rahe, R. (1967). The social readjustment rating scale. *Journal of Psychosomatic Research, 11*, 213–218.

Hooton, E. (1955). *Crime and the Man.* Cambridge, Harvard University Press.

Honolulu Police Department. (1979). *Annual Statistical Report.* City and County of Honolulu.

Horowitz, I. & Willging, T. (1984). *The Psychology of Law.* Boston, Little, Brown, and Company.

Hotchkiss, S. (1978). The realities of rape. *Human Behavior, 7*, 18–23.

Howell, J., Krisberg, B., Hawkins, J. & Wilson, J. (1995). (Eds.) *Serious, Violent and Chronic Juvenile Offenders: A Sourcebook.* Beverly Hills, Sage.

Hunter, R. & Macalpine, I. (1963). *Three Hundred Years of Psychiatry.* London, Oxford University Press.

Huot, S. (1997). *Sex Offender Treatment and Recidivism.* Minnesota Community Services Division, Department of Corrections.

International Reference Organization in *Forensic Medicine and Science,* (1981). 227–230.

Irvine, M. & Gendreu, P. (1974). Detection of the "good" and "bad" responses on the 16 personality factor inventory in prisoners and college students. *Journal of Consulting and Clinical Psychology, 42*, 465–466.

Jablonski v. U. S., 712 F.2d 391 (9th Cir. 1983).

James, E. & Meehl, P. (1997). Assessing the legal standard for predictions of dangerousness in sex offender commitment proceedings. *Psychology, Public Policy and Law, 3*, 33–64.

Janoff-Bulman, R. (1992). *Shattered assumptions: Towards a New Psychology of Trauma.* New York, The Free Press.

Janus, E. & Meehl, P. (1997). Assessing the legal standard for the prediction of dangerousness in sex offender commitment proceedings. *Psychology, Public Policy and Law, 3*, 33–64.

Jenkins v. U. S., 307 F. 2d 637 (1962)

Jurek v. Texas, 96, CT 2950, (1976).

Justice, B. & Justice, R. (1982). Clinical approaches to family violence: I. Etiology of physical abuse of children and dynamics of coercive treatment. *Family Therapy Collections, 3,* 1–20.

Justice, B., Justice, R., & Kraft, J. (1974). Early warning signs of violence: is a triad enough? *American Journal of Psychiatry, 131,* 457–459.

Juvenile Justice Bulletin. (1998). U.S. Department of Justice, Office of Justice Programs, Rockville.

Kahle, L. & Sales, D. (1980). Due process of law and the attitudes of professionals toward involuntary civil commitment. In P. Lipsett and B. Sales (Eds.): *New Directions in Psychological Research.* New York: Van Nostrand Reinhold.

Kahneman, D. & Tversky, A. (1973). On the psychology of prediction. *Psychological Review, 80,* 237–251.

Kalogerakis, M. (1971). The assaultive psychiatric patient. *Psychiatric Quarterly, 45,* 372–381.

Kanfer, F. (1965). Vicarious human reinforcement: a glimpse into the black box. In L. Krasner & L. Ullman (Eds.): *Research and Behavior Modification.* New York, Holt, Rinehart and Winston, 244–267.

Kastermeier, R. & Eglit, H. (1973). Parole release decision-making: rehabilitation, expertise, and the demise of mythology. *American University Law Review, 22,* 477–1137.

Katz, L. (1975). Presentation of a confidence interval estimate as evidence in a legal proceeding. *The American Statistician, 29*(4), 138–142.

Kelly, C. (1976). *Crime in the United States: Uniform Crime Reports.* Washington, D.C., Superintendent of Documents, U.S. Government Printing Office.

Kinzel, A. (1970). Body-buffer zones in violent prisoners. *American Journal of Psychiatry, 127,* 59–64.

Kirby, M. P. (1977). The effectiveness of the point scale. Washington, DC: Pretrial Services Resource Center.

Klassen, D. & O'Connor, W. (1989). Assessing the risk of violence in released mental patients: a cross-validation study. *Psychological Assessment, 1,* 75–81.

Knapp, M. (1978). *Nonverbal Communication in Human Interaction* (2nd ed.). New York, Holt, Rinehart and Winston.

Korn, R. & McCorkle, L. (1961). *Criminology and Penology.* New York, Holt, Rinehart and Winston.

Koss, M., Goodman, L., Brown, A., Fitzgerald, L., Keita, G., & Russo, N. (1994). *No Safe Haven: Male Violence Against Women at Home, at Work, and in the Community.* Washington, DC, American Psychological Association.

Kozol, H. (1975). The diagnosis of dangerousness. In S. Pasternack (Ed.): *Violence and Victims.* New York: Spectrum, 3–13.

Kozol, H., Boucher, R., & Garofalo, R. (1972). The diagnosis and treatment of dangerousness. *Crime and Delinquency, 18,* 371–391.

Kraemer, H., Kazdin, A., Offord, D., Kessler, R., Jensen, P., & Kupfer, D. (1997). Coming to terms with the terms of risk. *Archives of General Psychiatry, 54,* 337–343.

Kramer, G. & Heilbrun, K. (2000). Decade of advances in risk assessment: implications for corrections. *Correctional Mental Health Report, 2,* 17–32.

Kraut, R. (1978). Verbal and nonverbal cues in the perception of lying. *Journal of Personality and Social Psychology, 36,* 380–391.

Kroner, D. & Mills, J. (1997). *The VRA G: Predicting institutional misconduct in violent offenders.* Paper presented at the Annual Convention of the Ontario Psychological Association, Toronto.

Kropp, P. & Hart, S. (2000).The spousal assault risk assessment (SARA) guide: reliability and validity in adult male offenders. *Law and Human Behavior, 24*(1), 101–118.

Kropp, P., Hart, S., Webster, C., & Eaves, D. (1994). *Manual for the Spousal Assault Risk Assessment Guide.* Vancouver, British Columbia Institute on Family Violence.

Kropp, P., Hart, S., Webster, C., & Eaves, D. (1995). *Manual for the Spousal Assault Risk Assessment Guide* (2nd ed.). Vancouver, British Columbia Institute on Family Violence.

Kropp, P., Hart, S., Webster, C., & Eaves, D. (1999). *Spousal Assault Risk Assessment Guide User's Manual.* Toronto, Multi-Health Systems, Inc. and B.C. Institute Against Family Violence.

Krug, S. (1978). Further evidence on sixteen PF distortion scales. *Journal of Personality Assessment, 42,* 513–517.

Lachar, D. (1974). *The MMPI. Clinical Assessment and Automated Interpretation.* Los Angeles, California, Western Psychological Services.

Lefkowitz, M., Eron, L., Walder, L., & Heusmann, L. (1977). *Growing Up to be Violent.* New York: Pergamon.

Lessard v. Schmidt, 349 F. Supp. 1078 (E.D. Wis.1972).

Levinson, R. & Ramsay, G. (1969). Dangerousness, stress and mental health evaluations. *Journal of Health and Social Behavior, 20,* 178–187.

Leyton, E. (1986). *Hunting humans: Inside the minds of mass murderers.* New York, Pocket Books.

Lidz, C., Mulvey, E., & Gardner, W. (1993). The accuracy of predictions of violence to others. *Journal of the American Medical Association, 269,* 1007–1111.

Lightcap, J., Kurland, J., & Burgess, R. (1982). Child abuse. *Ethnology and Sociobiology, 3,* 61–67.

Link, B. & Stueve, A. (1994). Psychotic symptoms and the violent/illegal behavior of mental patients compared to community controls. In J. Monahan & H. Steadman (Eds.), *Violence and Mental Disorder. Developments in Risk Assessment.* Chicago: University of Chicago Press, 137–159.

Lipsett, P., Lelos, D. & McGarry, A. (1971). Competency for trial: a screening instrument. *American Journal of Psychiatry, 128,* 105–109.

Loew, C. A. (1967). Acquisition of a hostile attitude and its relationship to aggressive behavior. *Journal of Personality and Social Psychology, 5,* 335–341.

Loftus, E. F. (1983). Misfortunes of memory. *Philosophical Transactions of the Royal Society.* London, B302, 413–421.

Loftus, E. F. & Davis, G. (1984). Distortions in the memory of children. *Journal of Social Science, 40,* 51–67.

Loftus, E. & Monahan, J. (1980). Trial by data: psychological research as legal evidence. *American Psychologist, 35*(3), 270–283.

Lorei, T. (1970). Staff ratings of the consequences of release from or retention in a psychiatric hospital. *Journal of Consulting and Clinical Psychology, 34,* 46–55.

Lothstein, I. & Jones, P. (1978). Discriminating violent individuals by means of various psychological tests. *Journal of Personality Assessment, 42,* 237–242.

Lovaas, O. (1961). Effective exposure to symbolic aggression on aggressive behavior. *Child Development, 32,* 37–44.

Madden, D., Lion, J. & Penna, M. (1976). Assaults on psychiatrists by patients. *American Journal of Psychiatry, 133,* 422–425.

Maletzky, B. (1991). *Treating the sexual offender.* Newbury Park, Sage.

Marin, B. V., Holmes, D. L., Guth, M., & Kovac, P. (1979). The potential of children as eyewitnesses. *Law and Human Behavior, 3,* 295–305.

McClain, P. (1982). Black female homicide offenders and victims: are they from the same population? *Death Education, 6,* 265–278.

McIntosh v. Milano, 403 A. 2d 500 (1979).

McNiel, D., Sandberg, D., & Binder, R. (1998). The relationship between confidence and accuracy in clinical assessment of psychiatric patients' potential for violence. *Law and*

Human Behavior, 22, 655–669.

Meehl, P. (1954). *Clinical Versus Statistical Prediction. A Theoretical Analysis and a Review of the Evidence.* Minneapolis, University of Minneapolis Press.

Meehl, P. (1965). Seer over sign. The first sound example. *Journal of Experimental Research in Personality, 27,* 32.

Megargee, E. (1970). The prediction of violence with psychological tests. In C. Spielberger (Ed.): *Current Topics in Clinical and Community Psychology.* New York, Academic Press.

Megargee, E. (1976). The prediction of dangerousness. *Criminal Justice and Behavior, 3,* 1–21.

Meloy, J. (1988). *The Psychopathic Mind: Origins, Dynamics, and Treatment.* Northvale, Jason Aronson.

Meloy, J. (1992). *Violent attachments.* Northvale, Jason Aronson.

Meloy, J. (2000). *Violence Risk Analysis.* Workshop in Honolulu.

Melton, G. (1983). Training in psychology and law. A directory. Newsletter, Division 41, *American Psychological Association, 3,* 1-3.

Melton, G., Petrila, J., Poythress, N., & Slobogin, C. (1997). *Psychological   Evaluations for the Courts: A Handbook for Mental Health Professionals and Lawyers* (2nd. ed.). New York: Guilford.

Menzies, R., Webster, S., McMain, S., Stanley, S., & Scaglione, R. (1994). The dimensions of dangerousness revisited. *Law and Human Behavior, 18,* 1-28.

Menzies, R., Webster, C., & Sepejak, D. (1985). The dimensions of dangerousness: evaluating the accuracy of psychometric predictions of violence among forensic patients. *Law and Human Behavior, 9,* 49-70.

Michigan Corrections Department, 1978. Reported in Monahan, J. (1981). *The Clinical Prediction of Violent Behavior.* National Institute of Mental Health, DHHS Publication Number (ADM) 81-92, Superintendent of Documents, Washington, D.C.

Milgram, S. (1963). Behavioral study of obedience. *Journal of Abnormal and Social Psychology, 67,* 371-378.

Milgram, S. (1965). Some conditions of obedience to authority. *Human Relations, 18,* 57-76.

Miller, W. (1958). A lower class culture as a generating milieu of gang delinquency. *Journal of Social Issues, 14,* 5-19.

Milner, J. & Campbell, J. (1995). Prediction issues for practitioners. J. In Campbell (Ed.): *Assessing Dangerousness: Violence by Sexual Offenders, Batterers, and Child Abusers.* Thousand Oaks, Sage, 20-40.

Mischel, W. (1968). *Personality and Assessment.* New York, Wiley.

Monahan, J. (1977). Empirical analyses of civil commitment: critique and context. *Law and Society Review, 11,* 619-628.

Monahan, J. (1978). Prediction research and the emergency commitment of dangerous mentally ill persons: a reconsideration. *American Journal of Psychiatry, 135,* 198-201.

Monahan, J. (1978). The prediction of violent criminal behavior: a methodological critique and prospectus in deterrence and incapacitation: Estimating the effects of criminal sanctions on crime rates. *National Academy of Sciences,* 244-269.

Monahan, J. (1981a). *The Clinical Prediction of Violent Behavior.* National Institute of Mental Health, DHHS Publication Number (ADM) 81-92. Superintendent of Documents, Washington, D.C.

Monahan, J. (1981b). *Predicting Violent Behavior.* An Assessment of Clinical Techniques. Beverly Hills, Sage.

Monahan, J. (1984). The prediction of violent behavior: toward a second generation of theory and policy. *American Journal of Psychiatry, 141,* 10-15.

Monahan, J. (1986). Personal communication. Richmond.

Monahan, J. & Hood, G. (1978). Ascriptions of dangerousness: The eye (and age, sex, education, location, and politics) of the beholder. In R. Simon (Ed.), *Research in Law and Sociology*. Greenwich, Johnson, 143-151.

Monahan, J., & Steadman, H. (1994). (Eds.) *Violence and Mental Disorder*. Developments in Risk Assessment. Chicago, University of Chicago Press.

Monahan, J., Steadman, H., Appelbaum, P., Robbins, P., Mulvey, E., Silver, E., Roth, L., & Grisso, T.: Developing a clinically useful actuarial tool for assessing violence risk. *British Journal of Psychiatry*. In press.

Morse, S. (1978). Law and mental health professionals: the limits of expertise. *Professional Psychology, 9*, 389-399.

Mosher, D. L. (1965). Interaction of fear and guilt in inhibiting unacceptable behavior. *Journal of Consulting Psychology, 29*, 161-167.

Mossman, D. (1994). Assessing predictions of violence: being accurate about accuracy. *Journal of Consulting and Clinical Psychology, 62*, 783-792.

Nadeau, J., Nadeau, B., Smiley, W., & McHattie, L. (1999). The PCL-R and VRAG as predictors of institutional behaviour. Paper presented at conference on "Risk assessment & risk management: Implications for the prevention of violence." Vancouver.

National Crime Victimization Surveys. (1997). Bureau of Justice Statistics, U.S. Department of Justice, Washington.

National Institute of Justice (1989, January). Stranger abductive homicides of children. Washington, DC: Office of Juvenile Justice and Delinquency Prevention.

New York Times, Crime drops in '97; murders are at 30-year low, November 23,1998

Newman, J. (1985). *Differential Diagnosis in PTSD*. Readjustment Counseling Services Region V1 Annual Training Conference, San Diego.

News and Notes. (1990). American Association on Mental Retardation, Washington.

Nichols, T., Vincent, G., Whittemore, K., & Ogloff, J. (1999). Assessing risk of inpatient violence in a sample of forensic psychiatric patients: Comparing the PCL:SV, HCR-20, and VRAG. Paper presented at the conference on "Risk assessment and risk management: Implications for the prevention of violence." Vancouver.

Nicholson, R. & Norwood, S. (2000). The quality of forensic psychological assessments, reports, and testimony: Acknowledging the gap between promise and practice. *Law and Human Behavior, 24*(1), 9-44.

Norris, J. (1988). *Serial Killers*. New York, Doubleday.

Novaco, R. (1994). Anger as a risk factor for violence among the mentally disordered. In J. Monahan & H. Steadman (Eds.): *Violence and Mental Disorder*. Chicago, University of Chicago, 269-295.

Nuttfield, J. (1982). *Parole Decision-Making in Canada: Research Towards Decision Guidelines*. Ottawa, Ministry of Supplies and Services.

Otto, R. (1992). Prediction of dangerous behavior: A review and analysis of "second generation" research. *Forensic Reports, 5*, 103-133.

Overall, J. & Gorham, D. (1962). The brief psychiatric rating scale. *Psychological Reports, 10*, 799-812.

Pankratz, L. (1981). A review of the Munchausen syndrome. *Clinical Psychological Review, 1*, 65-78.

Patterson, G., Cobb, J., & Ray, R. (1972). A social engineering technology for retraining the families of aggressive boys. In H. Adams & I. Unikel (Eds.): *Issues in Transient Behavior Therapy*. Springfield, Charles C Thomas.

Peck v. Counseling Services of Addison County, Inc., 449 A. 2d, (1985).

Perkins, K. (1980). Multivariate prediction of institutional dangerousness using life history characteristics. Presented at American Psychological Association Conference.

Perlin, M. (1977). The legal status of the psychologist in the courtroom. *Journal of Psychiatry and Law, 5*, 41-54.

Petersilia, J., Greenwood, P., & Lavin, M. (1977). *Criminal Careers of Habitual Felons.* Santa Monica, Rand.

Petersen v. Washington, 671 P.2d 230 (Wash.1980).

Poythress, N. (1992). Expert testimony on violence and dangerousness: roles for mental health professionals. *Forensic Reports, 5*, 135-150.

Prentky, R., & Knight, R. (1991). Identifying critical dimensions for discriminating among rapists. *Journal of Consulting and Clinical Psychology, 59*(5), 643-66.

Pritchard, D. (1977). Stable predictors of recidivism. *Journal Supplement Abstract Service, 7*, 72.

PROMIS Research Project. (1977). *Highlights of Interim Findings and Implications.* Washington, D.C., Institute for Law and Social Research.

Prouix, J., Pellerin, B., McKibben, A., Aubut, J., & Quimet, M. (1995). Static and dynamic predictors of recidivism in sexual aggression. Unpublished raw data.

Proulx, J., Pellerin, B., McKibben, A., Aubut, J., & Ouimet, M. (1997). Static and dynamic predictors of recidivism in sexual offenders. *Sexual Abuse, 9*, 7-28.

Quinsey, V. (2000). Personal communication.

Quinsey, V., Harris, G., Rice, M., & Cormier, C. (1998). *Violent Offenders: Appraising and Managing Risk.* Washington, DC, American Psychological Association.

Quinsey, V., Rice, M., & Harris, G. (1995). Actuarial prediction of sexual recidivism. *Journal of Interpersonal Violence, 10*(1), 85-105.

Rector, M. (1973). Who are the dangerous? *Bulletin of the American Academy of Psychiatry and the Law, 1*, 186-188.

Resnick, P. (1984). The detection of malingered mental illness. *Behavioral Sciences and the Law, 2*, 21-38.

Rice, M., & Harris, G. (1995). Violent recidivism: Assessing predictive validity. *Journal of Consulting and Clinical Psychology, 63*, 737-748.

Rice, M., & Harris, G. (1997). Cross-validation and extension of the Violence Risk Appraisal Guide for child molesters and rapists. *Law and Human Behavior, 21*, 231-241.

Rice, M., Harris, G., & Quinsey, V. (1990). A follow-up of rapists assessed in a maximum security psychiatric facility. *Journal of Interpersonal Violence, 5*(4), 435-448.

Rice, M., Harris, G., & Quinsey, V. (1991). Sexual recidivism among child molesters released from a maximum security institution. *Journal of Consulting and Clinical Psychology, 59*, 381-386.

Robinson, D. (1995). Federal offender family violence: estimates from a national file review study. *Forum on Corrections Research, 7*(2), 15-18.

Rofman, E., Askinazi, C., & Fant, E. (1980). The prediction of dangerous behavior in emergency civil commitment. *American Journal of Psychiatry, 137*, 1061-1064.

Rogers, R. (1988). (Ed.) *Clinical Assessment of Malingering and Deception.* New York, Guilford.

Rogers, R. (1997). (Ed.) *Clinical Assessment of Malingering and Deception* (2nd ed.). New York, Guilford.

Rogers, R. (1984). Towards an empirical model of malingering and deception. *Behavioral Sciences and the Law, 2*, 93-111.

Rogers, R. (1992). *Structured Interview of Reported Symptoms.* Odessa, FL, Psychological Assessment Resources.

Romans, J., Hays, J. & White, T. (1996). Stalking and related behaviors experienced by counseling center staff members from current or former clients. *Professional Psychology: Research and Practice, 27*, 595-599.

Rosenhan, D. (1973). On being sane in insane places. *Science, 179*, 250-258.

Rotter, F. (1950). *Incomplete Sentences Blank.* New York, The Psychological Corporation.

Rubin, D. (1972). Prediction of dangerousness in mentally ill criminals. *Archives of General Psychiatry, 72*, 397-407.

Rudacille, W. (1994). *Identifying Lies in Disguise.* Dubuque, Kendall/Hunt.

Rule, B. & Nesdale, A. (1976). Emotional arousal and aggressive behavior. *Psychological Bulletin, 83*, 851-863.

Salter, A. (1988). *Treating Child Sex Offenders and Victims: A Practical Guide.* Newbury Park, Sage.

Scheibe, K. (1978). The psychologists' advantage and its nullification. *American Psychologist, 33*, 869-880.

Schiller, G. & Marques, J. (1999). *California Actuarial Risk Assessment Tables (CARAT).* Presented at A. Salter Predicting Sexual Recidivism Conference. Honolulu. Available from Gary Schiller, Program Development and Evaluation, 1600 Ninth Street, Sacramento, California 95814.

Schretlen, D. (1988). The use of psychological tests to identify malingered symptoms of mental disorder. *Clinical Psychology Review, 8*, 451-476.

Schwitzegebel, R. L. & Schwitzegebel, R. K. (1980). *Law and Psychological Practice.* New York, Wiley.

Seidman, B., Marshall, W., Hudson, S., & Robertson, P. (1994). An examination of intimacy and loneliness in sex offenders. *Journal of Interpersonal Violence, 9*, 518-534.

Shah, S. (1978). Dangerousness and mental illness: some conceptual, prediction and policy dilemmas. In C. Frederick (Ed.): *Dangerous Behavior: A Problem in Law and Mental Health.* NIMH, DHEW Publication Number (ADM), 78-563, Washington, D.C., Superintendent of Documents, U.S. Government Printing Office, 153-191.

Shapiro, A. (1977). The evaluation of clinical prediction: a method and initial application. *New England Journal of Medicine, 296*, 1509-1514.

Shaw, H.S. (1978). A paradigm for exploring some issues on law and psychology. *American Psychologist, 33*, 224-238.

Shinnar, S. & Shinnar, R. (1975). The effects of the criminal justice system on the control of crime: A quantitative approach. *Law and Society Review, 9*, 581-611.

Short, J. F. (1968). (Ed.) *Gang Delinquency and Delinquent Subcultures.* New York, Harper & Row.

Sierles, F. (1984). Correlates of malingering. *Behavioral Sciences and the Law, 2*, 113-118.

Silver, E. & Banks, S. (1998). *Calibrating the potency of violence risk classification models: The Dispersion Index for Risk (DIFR).* Paper presented at the American Society of Criminology Conference, Washington, DC.

Soothill, K. & Gibbens, T. (1978). Recidivism of sexual offenders. *British Journal of Criminology, 18*, 267-276.

Spurzheim, J. (1826). *Phrenology, Study of Physiognomy.* London, Treuttel, Wurtz and Richter.

Steadman, H. (1981). A situational approach to violence. *International Journal of Law and Psychiatry, 5*, 171-186.

Steadman, H. (1977). A new look at recidivism among Patuxent inmates. *The Bulletin of the American Academy of Psychiatry and the Law, 5*, 200-109.

Steadman, H. (1980). The right not to be a false positive: problems in the application of the dangerousness standard. *Psychiatric Quarterly, 52*, 84-99.

Steadman, H. (1975). Employing psychiatric predictions of dangerous behavior: policy vs. fact. In C. Frederick (Ed.): *Dangerous Behavior: A Problem in Law and Mental Health.* NIMH, DHEW Publication Number (ADM) 78-563, Washington, D.C., Superintendent of Documents, U.S. Government Printing Office.

Steadman, H. & Cocozza, J. (1974). *Careers of the Criminal Insane.* Lexington, Lexington Books.

Steadman, H. & Cocozza, J. (1980). Prediction of violent behavior in the role of the forensic psychologist. In G. Cooke (Ed.): *The Role of the Forensic Psychologist.* Springfield, Charles C Thomas.

Steadman, H., Cocozza, J., & Melick, M. (1978). Explaining the increased crime rate of mental patients: the changing clientele of State hospitals. *American Journal of Psychiatry, 135,* 816-820.

Steadman, H. & Halton, A. (1971). The Baxstrom patients: backgrounds and outcome. *Seminars in Psychiatry, 3,* 376-386.

Steadman, H. & Keveles, C. (1972). The community adjustment and criminal activity of the Baxstrom patients. *American Journal of Psychiatry, 129,* 304-310.

Steadman, H., Monahan, J., Appelbaum, P., Grisso, T., Mulvey, E., Roth, L., Robbins, P., & Klassen, D. (1994). Designing a new generation of risk assessment research. In J. Monahan & H. Steadman (Eds.): *Violence and Mental Disorder. Developments in Risk Assessment.* Chicago, University of Chicago Press, 297-318.

Steadman, H., Mulvey, E., Monahan, J., Robbins, P., Appelbaum, P., Grisso, T., Roth, L., & Silver, E. (1998). Violence by people discharged from acute psychiatric inpatient facilities and by others in the same neighborhoods. *Archives of General Psychiatry, 55,* 393-401.

Steadman, H., Silver, E., Monahan, J., Appelbaum, P., Robbins, P., Mulvey, E., Grisso, T., Roth, L., & Banks, S. (2000). A classification tree approach to the development of actuarial violence risk assessment tools. *Law and Human Behavior, 24*(1), 83-100.

Steadman, H., Vanderwyst, D., & Ribner, S. (1978). Comparing arrest rates of mental patients and criminal offenders. *American Journal of Psychiatry, 135,* 1218-1220.

Stone, A. (1975). *Mental Health and the Law: A System in Transition.* National Institute of Mental Health, DHEW Publication Number (ADM) 76-176. Washington, D.C.: Superintendent of Documents, U.S. Government Printing Office.

Stone, A. (1984). The ethical boundaries of forensic psychiatry: a view from the ivory tower. *Bulletin of the American Academy of Psychiatry and the Law, 12*(3), 209-219.

Strasburger, L., Gutheil, T., & Brodsky, A. (1997). On wearing two hats: role conflict in serving as both psychotherapist and expert witness. *American Journal of Psychiatry, 154*(4), 448-456.

Stromberg, C., Lindberg, D. & Schneider, J. (1995). A legal update on forensic psychology. *The Psychologist's Legal Update,* National Register of Health Service Providers in Psychology, 6, 3-16.

Sutker, P., Winstead, D., Galina, H. & Allain, A. (1991). Cognitive defects and psychopathology among former prisoners of war and combat veterans of the Korean conflict. *American Journal of Psychiatry, 148,* 67-72.

Suzuki et al. v. Yuen, G. et al, Civil 73-3854, Hawaii, (1977).

Swanson, J., Borum, R., Swartz, M., & Monahan, J. (1996). Psychotic symptoms and disorders and the risk of violent behaviour in the community. *Criminal Behavior and Mental Health, 6,* 317-338.

Swanson, J., Holzer, C., Ganju, V., & Jono, R. (1990). Violence and psychiatric disorder in the community: Evidence from the Epidemiologic Catchment Area surveys. *Hospitals and Community Psychiatry, 41,* 761-770.

Sweetland, J. (1972). "Illusory correlations" and the estimation of dangerous behavior. Unpublished doctoral dissertation, Department of Psychology, Indiana University.

Tarasoff v. Regents of the University of California, 131 Cal. Rptr. 14 (1976).

Tengstrom, A., Grann, M., Langstrom, N., & Kullgren, G. (2000). Psychopathy (PCL-R) as a predictor of violent recidivism among criminal offenders with schizophrenia. *Law and Human Behavior, 24*(1), 45-58.

Terr, L. (1983). Chowchilla revisited: The effects of psychic trauma four years after a school-bus kidnapping. *American Journal of Psychiatry, 140,* 1543-1550.

Terr, L. (1991). Childhood traumas: an outline and overview. *American Journal of Psychiatry, 148,* 10-20.

Thornberry, T. & Jacoby, J. (1979). *The Criminally Insane: A Community Follow-up of Mentally Ill Offenders.* Chicago, University of Chicago Press.

Toch, H. (1969). *Violent Men.* Chicago, Aldine.

Underwood, B. (1979). Law and the crystal ball: predicting behavior with statistical inference and individualized judgment. *Yale Law Review, 88,* 1409-1448.

Undeutsch, U. (1989). Statement reality analysis. In A. Trankell (Ed.): *Reconstructing the Past.* Deventer, the Netherlands, Kluver, Law and Taxation Publishers.

Undeutsch, U. (1984). Methods in detecting assessee misrepresentation. European Military Psychologists Conference, Nurenberg.

Uniform Crime Reports for the United States, 1993. Federal Bureau of Investigation, U.S. Department of Justice, Washington, D.C.: U.S. Government Printing Office.

U.S. Department of Justice. (1985). *National Survey of Crime Severity.* NCJ-96017, Washington, DC: Superintendent of Documents.

Vanden Bos, G. R. & Bulatao, E. (Eds.) (1996). *Violence on the Job: Identifying Risks and Developing Solutions.* Washington, DC. American Psychological Association.

Warren, J., Hazelwood, R., & Dietz, P. (1996). The sexually sadistic serial killer. *Journal of Forensic Sciences, 41,* 970-974.

Warren, J., Reboussin, R., Hazelwood, R. & Wright, J. (1991). Prediction of rapist type and violence from verbal, physical, and sexual scales. *Journal of Interpersonal Violence, 6*(l), 55-67.

Webster, C., Douglas, K., Eaves, D., & Hart, S. (1997). *HCR-20: Assessing risk of violence.* Burnaby, Mental Health, Law, and Policy Institute of Simon Fraser University.

Webster, C., Harris, G., Rice., M., Cormier, C., & Quinsey, V. (1994). *The violence prediction scheme: Assessing dangerousness in high risk men.* Toronto, Centre of Criminology, University of Toronto.

Webster, C., Slomen, D., Sepejak, D., Butler, B., Jensen, F., & Turral, G. (1979). Dangerous Behavior Rating Scheme (DBRS): Construction and Inter-Rater Reliability. Unpublished manuscript, Toronto.

Webster, W. (1982). *Uniform Crime Reports. Crime in the United States.* Washington, D.C.: Superintendent of Documents, U.S. Government Printing Office.

Wenk, E., Robinson, J., & Smith, G. (1972). Can violence be predicted? *Crime and Delinquency, 18,* 393-402.

Wepman, Jr. (1958). *Auditory Discrimination Test.* Chicago, Language Research Associates.

Werner, P., Rose, T., & Yesavage, J. (1984). Psychiatrists' judgements of dangerousness in patients on an acute care unit. *American Journal of Psychiatry, 1411,* 263-266.

Wetzel, L. & Ross, N. (1983). Psychological and social ramifications of battering: observations leading to a counseling methodology for victims of domestic violence. *Personnel and Guidance Journal, 61,* 423-428.

Wiebush, R., Baird, C., Krisberg, B., & Onek, D. (1995). Risk assessment and classification for serious, violent, and chronic juvenile offenders. In J. Howell, B. Krisberg, J. Hawkins & J. Wilson (Eds.), *A Sourcebook: Serious, Violent, and Chronic Juvenile Offenders.* Thousand Oaks, Sage, 171-212.

Williams, W. & Miller, K. (1977). The role of personal characteristics in perceptions of dangerousness. *Criminal Justice and Behavior, 4,* 421.

Wilson, C. & Seaman, D. (1992). *The Serial Killers.* London, Virgin Books.

Wilson, J. (1977). The political feasibility of punishment. In J. Cederblom & W. Blizek (Eds.): *Justice and Punishment.* Cambridge, Ballinger, ,107-123.

Wilson, R. (1999). Emotional congruence in sexual offenders against children. *Sexual Abuse: A Journal of Research and Treatment, 11*, 33-47.

Wolfgang, M. (1977). From boy to man–from delinquency to crime. National Symposium on the Serious Juvenile Offender. Minneapolis.

Wolfgang, M. (1978). An overview of research into violent behavior. Testimony before the U.S. House of Representatives Committee on Science and Technology.

Wolfgang, M., Figlio, R., & Sellin, T. (1972). *Delinquency in a Birth Cohort.* Chicago, University of Chicago Press.

Wolfgang, M., Figlio, R., Tracy, P., & Singer, S. (1985). *The National Survey of Crime Severity.* Superintendent of Documents, U.S. Government Printing Office, Washington, D.C. (NCJ-96017).

Wyatt v. Stickney, 325 F. Supp. 781 (M.D.Ala. 1971).

Yochelson, S. & Samenow, S. (1976). *The Criminal Personality* (Volumes I, II, & III). New York, Jason Aronson.

Zinger, I. & Furth, A. (1998). Psychopathology and Canadian criminal proceedings: the potential for human rights abuse. *Canadian Journal of Criminology,* 237-276.

Ziskin, J. (1981). *Coping with Psychiatric and Psychological Testimony* (2nd ed., Volumes I & II). Beverly Hills, Law and Psychology Press.

Ziskin, J, & Faust, D. (1988). *Coping with Psychiatric and Psychological Testimony* (4th ed.). Marina del Rey, Law and Psychology Press.

AUTHOR INDEX

271

SUBJECT INDEX

DATE DUE

GAYLORD			PRINTED IN U.S.A.